THE GREATEST FISHING
STORIES EVER TOLD

THE GREATEST FISHING STORIES EVER TOLD

Twenty-Eight Unforgettable Fishing Tales

EDITED BY LAMAR UNDERWOOD

Guilford, Connecticut

To Ted Kesting,
one of the most avid anglers I have ever known, and the man
whose editorship and influence at Sports Afield *magazine*
raised the bar of reader reward in outdoor magazines
to levels never known before his time

An imprint of The Rowman & Littlefield Publishing Group, Inc.
4501 Forbes Blvd., Ste. 200
Lanham, MD 20706
www.rowman.com

Distributed by NATIONAL BOOK NETWORK

Copyright © 2000 by The Rowman & Littlefield Publishing Group, Inc.

British Library Cataloguing in Publication Information available

Library of Congress Cataloging-in-Publication Data available

ISBN 978-1-4930-3958-6 (paper : alk. paper)

∞™ The paper used in this publication meets the minimum requirements of American National Standard for Information Sciences—Permanence of Paper for Printed Library Materials, ANSI/ NISO Z39.48-1992.

Contents

PREFACE

"Fishing should be the exercise of your skills—and its rewards the places it brings you to."

—Negley Farson
Going Fishing

The other day, while wandering through some of the lesser-known regions of angling literature, I stumbled across the following little gem by John M. Dickie in the Preface of his anthology *Great Angling Stories*, published in England and Scotland [the edition I have in hand is 1953, but the book obviously was first published much earlier]:

"Against books on sport," writes John Dickie, "the charge may often be laid that they depend too little on merit, too much on a bond of sympathy between author and reader."

Hello! Mr. Dickie hasn't merely thrown down the gauntlet: He has smacked me across the face with it.

Now, my experiences in both books and magazines have taught me that the editor's chair is often an uneasy one, but Dickie's observation is so much on the mark that he positively has me squirming. How many times, I must ask myself, have I rushed some work into print, in fact heralded its coming with gushes of praise, simply because it was authored by "one of the boys"? Or because the subject matter struck a warm and familiar chord? What's the harm of a little lame and undistinguished prose between friends?

Further words by John Dickie provide a positive answer to this dilemma. Of the anthology he has edited, he notes: "But angling is a fair literature and no stories have here been included which do not possess, quite apart from their subject, intrinsic literary worth."

Let's hear that again: "Intrinsic literary worth." Now there's a benchmark to live up to, and I am going to attempt to do exactly that in this volume of stories, just as John Dickie did in his superb book.

While poking through the works of a lifetime of reading about fishing in preparation for this book, I was struck more than once by a trend that emerged in the eighties and nineties of angling stories, mostly fly fishing, that linked the sport to self-discovery. Words like "saving the soul," "inner peace," "inner compass"—expressions of gooey sentimentality of that sort—begin to appear in dust-jacket and magazine cover blurb copy.

Perhaps I am weird, or just plain lucky, but I am quite sure I began to love fishing, and reading about fishing, when I was so young that I had not yet blundered, fumbled, and in general screwed up enough to need spiritual cleansing. The reason I sometimes had trouble sleeping the night before a big fishing trip was the sheer excitement of anticipating catching fish and seeing the places where fish lived. Both prospects aroused (and still do!) in me a yearning so deep and part of my psyche that quite honestly I have little desire to trace its origins to its sources. Perhaps, as the scientific-minded might point out, the trigger that says "Let's Go Fishing" might be traced to some distant hunter-gatherer ancestor who stood at the mouth of the cave every day and wondered where he was going to find something to eat. Perhaps thousands of years have left that spark alive in only a few of us, people like you and me, and not the guy down the street. But for me there is no mystery in the fact that the fish I buy at the market can never replace the fish that I pulled from the edge of the sea and now lies on the cutting board, ready for broiling. Were the reverse true, that because I can buy fish I will cease all fishing myself, I would become an emotional basket case, asking myself, "What happened to you, boy?"

Of course, fishing for food is only part of the story. The freezer will only hold so much; there are only so many fish dinners one can eat. Still, we press on, eager as ever, armed with new tactics and equipment to meet any angling challenge. Because it's fun, damn it!

This is the point in the story where "catch-and-release" comes on stage. Either because the freezer is stuffed, or because of dwindling numbers that need protection in certain places, "catch-and-release" fishing becomes as natural to many sensible anglers as yelling, "Got one!" And it works. We are seeing many cases—in trout fishing especially—where resources would be dwindling or wiped out completely were it not for catch-and-release.

One type of angler I do not want in the boat with me or at the fishing camp where I'm staying is the emotional idiot who fishes to prove something. He's got to catch the most and the biggest. Always! The successes or disappointments of others mean nothing to him. Scratch this guy deep enough and you'll find a miserable bastard who isn't fishing for food or pleasure, but for some weird and dark obsession to excel.

Now don't think I'm saying there's something wrong with catching big fish, or a lot of fish. No sir! I'm right in there pitching to do both, but there are boundaries and limits I respect. And I will always hope I'm the kind of good buddy whose eyes and ears are open to seeing *your* big one, hearing about your twenty-fish day and the story about the lunker that wrapped *you* around a limb and broke off.

The time I have spent reading about fishing has always been as important a part of my fishing enjoyment as the time spent with a rod in my hand. But I do not pretend to have unearthed and read every single gem of angling literature. As much as I yearn to live up to the promise of making this a volume of "The Greatest Fishing Stories Ever Told," I am quite certain my selections will not always be the ones the reader would have chosen, given the opportunity. My decisions were guided by several considerations beyond sheer literary merit. One of the most important was to not stumble blindly into focusing on one type of fishing at the expense of others. Obviously, fishing is so diverse that its literature can never be captured in a single book, no matter how ambitious. Entire libraries are needed, and indeed have been built and stocked for just such a project. The astute reader will no doubt have titles in mind that he or she feels should have been included here. And if you are keenly disappointed by the absence of one of your personal favorites, then I regret not serving you better.

It is my hope that the pages ahead will take you fishing in two kinds of places: Those like the ones you have never fished but would like to try, and those like the ones you have fished and enjoy remembering. Places like cold rivers where you will start out by looking for trout but will also truly lift up your eyes unto the hills and remember how fortunate you are to be there; dark pockets under old oaks where bigmouth bass lurk; estuaries where iron-muscled steelhead and salmon are fresh from the throbbing ocean currents; on some sandy beach where the green waves are slashed by slashes of striped bass and bluefish; out on the blue water of the Gulf Stream where your trolled baits barely scratch the surface of the domain roamed by marlin and tuna; and on the tidal flats where the thin clear pushes of water give the fishing for tarpon, bonefish and permit the visual drama of hunting.

You'll find all kinds of fishing here. And all kinds of fishermen. They have wonderful stories to tell you. You'll especially enjoy them on those long winter evenings when real fishing seems a distant promise. Throw another log on the fire, get your favorite chair and lamp just right, and hope everybody in the house will leave you alone. The fact that the stories have "intrinsic literary worth" won't bother you at all. I guarantee it!

—*Lamar Underwood*

The Song of the Angler

By A. J. McClane

AMONG THE REALLY GREAT FISHING WRITERS WE LOST IN THE FINAL decade of the last century, Al McClane's name leads my list in heartbreak. Not that he was a personal friend (I only met him once), but because he wrote about fishing with such love and feeling and intelligence that every time I saw his byline I knew I was going to be in for tremendous reading reward.

In my teenage years, I worshiped McClane's words so much that I began clipping every *Field & Stream* Angling Editor Column he wrote into notebooks. Today, McClane's best articles are collected in books, and one in particular is an absolute treasure—*Fishing With McClane*, published by Prentice-Hall in 1975, an anthology of McClane pieces edited with great affection by George Reiger, who also includes an excellent biography of McClane, the man, the writer, and the angler. Reiger has wonderful descriptions and interviews describing how McClane emerged from World War Two after being wounded in combat in Europe to land the *Field & Stream* job and go on to angling writing fame.

Back in my introduction to this book, you no doubt noticed that I certainly did not dwell on creating much of an explanation of the reasons we fish. I would have probably bungled the job, and anyway I knew what was coming: My main man, A. J. McClane, on "The Song of the Angler."

———

People often ask me why I enjoy fishing, and I cannot explain it to them because there is no reason in the way they want meanings described. They are asking a man why he enjoys breathing when he really has no choice but to wonder at its truth. Psychologists such as Dr. Ronald Ley have tried to explain its mystique in terms of behavioral conditioning, but this is as oddly misleading as his comparison of angling to golf. There are also pundits who believe that the rod provides an outlet for our hostilities, our frustrated egos, or our competitive instincts, or that it symbolizes the primitive feelings of man in his search for food, ergo the need to kill. To a degree I believe all these qualities exist in every participant in any sport, and if so, healthfully so, as it is far more harmless to vent one's spleen on a trout stream or a golf course than on one's fellow man. However, if this assumption is logical, then the rationale of *angling* is still without explanation.

The chirping plague of analysts who have invaded every chamber of the mind from the bedroom to the tackle room has missed one thing— angling is a robe that a man wears proudly. It is tightly woven in a fabric of moral, social, and philosophical threads which are not easily rent by the violent climate of our times. It is foolish to think, as it has been said, that all men who fish are good men, as evil exists on all of life's paths; but to join Walton's "company of honest men" requires first the ability to accept a natural tempo of misfortune not only in the allegory where failure is represented by the loss of a fish (or success by its capture) but in life itself. In the lockstep slogan of young radicals thumbing their noses at their world, reality is no longer realistic; but I would argue that life is a greater challenge than death, and that reality is as close as the nearest river. Perhaps an exceptional angler doesn't prove the rule, but then anglers are exceptional people.

Lord Fraser of Lonsdale is not only a peer, but he wears the robe of an angler as well. He is a skilled fly-fisherman, and when last we visited together, he caught a 35-pound salmon which was the biggest in the camp for many weeks. What's more, he could charm the socks off Willie Sutton, and I have heard him spellbind a roomful of strangers with tales of his life in South Africa, while sipping rare wines, naming each chateau and its vintage. This introduction would be fatuous were it not for the fact that Lord Fraser is totally blind. Both his eyes were shot out in the First World War. A profoundly intellectual man, Fraser has developed his other senses to a point that most of the people who sat with him that night had no idea that he was unable to see them; yet later he could summarize the physical characteristics of each person as though he was describing a rare burgundy.

I don't know if you have ever tried wading (unaided) and fly-fishing a stream while blindfolded. I cannot do it, and I would probably lack the guts if I *had* to do it. Fraser's explanation for his ability to do this is that he can hear all things around him: the changing tempo of deep and shallow water, the curling smack of a rapid against a boulder, even the roll or rise of a fish. His ear for the music of angling is incredibly keen. Is this Dr. Ley's behavioral conditioning? In terms of a compensatory development of the senses, perhaps, but it does not explain *why* a man, even a blind man, enjoys angling.

The music of angling is more compelling to me than anything contrived in the greatest symphony hall. What could be more thrilling than the ghostly basso note of a channel buoy over a grumbling surf as the herring gulls screech at a school of stripers on a foggy summer morning? Or an organ chorus of red howler monkeys swinging over a jungle stream as the tarpon roll and splash in counterpoint? I have heard them all—the youthful voice of the little Beaverkill, the growling of the Colorado as it leaps from its den, the kettledrum pounding of the Rogue, the hiss of the Yellowstone's riffles, the sad sound of the Orinoco, as mournful as a G chord held on a guitar. These are more familiar to me than Bach, Beethoven, and Brahms, and for my part more beautiful. If there are three "B's" in angling, they are probably the Beaverkill, the Broadhead, and the Big Hole.

Big-game angling has quite another music. The hull creaks and the outriggers clap as the ship comes into the wind while the sea increases the tempo as she turns from stern to bow. Then the frigate birds scream at a ball of bait and you know the marlin are below. As the ship lurches over the chop her screws bite air in a discordant whine and the mullet trails *skitter flap skitter flap* until the pitching hull sounds like the soft rolling of drums.

At last one note assails the ears, the *snap* of white linen pulled from the outrigger. Now the water explodes in a crescendo of hot engines roaring into life before you lean into a quarter ton of shoulder-rocking fury.

And in that ageless walking leap which follows no path in the ocean the angler hears the most exciting sound of all—the wailing of a reel as stark and as lonely as a Basin Street clarinet.

But my protracted maundering leads us away from Dr. Ley's hypothesis which he reinforced with the learned E. L. Thorndike's thesis of punishments and rewards. What *are* the rewards of angling? A dead fish? A trophy? At some point perhaps, but then it takes years to become an angler.

There are tidal marks in our development. In the beginning, when one is very young and inexperienced, fish are measured in quantity. Then, only quality becomes important. Eventually even record fish lose their significance unless they are of a particular species, and ultimately the size doesn't matter provided they are difficult to catch.

The latter condition is fairly easy to find in these days of declining resources. Trout in the upper Beaverkill average about a half pound in weight, but they can be the most demanding kind. The water is diamond clear and at the shadow of a passing bird or the glint of sun against rod they instantly vanish under the nearest boulder. You must work with a leader of cobweb diameter and have enough control to drop your fly in a teacup target through a maze of overhanging limbs. There are large trout in the stream, of course, wise old browns which you might catch a glimpse of once in a while, usually in a pool that everybody believes has been emptied.

Recalling the years when anglers gathered at the old Gould cottage on the Beaverkill—a temple now fallen to death and taxes—which Arnold Gingrich described in his wonderful book, *The Well-Tempered Angler* (you can even smell the waders drying in the rafters)—one man comes to mind who knew perhaps a bit more about the rewards of angling than most of us.

Ellis Newman could cast a fly line to 90 feet with his bare hands. I saw him make three measured casts with tournament tackle, each of which fell short of 200 feet by inches. I doubt if a more polished caster ever lived. He had neither the time nor the inclination to compete in games (except for the pigeon shooting circuit which he did for money). We often fished along opposite banks of the Beaverkill, or alternated pools, just for the pleasure of each other's company.

One day, when the mayflies were on the water, Ellis caught and released several good browns below the dam, one going about three pounds. At the top of the next run we met a young boy who proudly displayed a nine-inch brook trout. Ellis admired it so much that I thought we were looking at the biggest square-tail captured since Cook hit the jackpot on the Nipigon in 1914. When the lad asked Ellis if he had any luck, he looked very serious; "Oh, I caught a few, but none were as *pretty* as yours."

Ellis worked with underprivileged children and handicapped people at his own expense. And the expense was appreciable. He designed Rube Goldberg wheelchairs and tractor-driven bucket seats for fishing and for hunting as well, and he even developed a method of running steel cable through a string of boulders to build "necklace" dams on his eroding Beaverkill. Ellis never waited for the fulmination of a new idea to die down before putting it into practice, and the people who loved him may be consoled with the reflection that angling would have suffered a greater blow had he regarded each new venture carefully.

Arnold Gingrich became, as Charley Ritz once called him, "that terrible fishing machine" in the sense that he was on a first-name basis with every trout in the stream. He would appear with smaller and smaller fly rods, considering any stick over two ounces as heavy tackle, and any leader above 7X suitable only for salmon. But the publisher of *Esquire* magazine is a tremendously energetic individual and the pistonlike style of casting with flea rods was duck soup for him.

Arnold earned his robe in my eyes the first time we angled together; in releasing a tired trout he held the fish underwater gently, almost lovingly, stroking its belly and talking to it. He is a master of conversation and, so help me, at times the fish swim away with an impossible but perceptible grin on their faces. Arnold has that passionate blood fire, typical of anglers, which no psychologist (nor wife who hears her husband stumbling out into an April blizzard at 4 a.m.) has satisfactorily explained.

One morning I was crossing the Swinging Bridge Pool and happened to look down; there stood Arnold in an icy torrent banging away with a little dry fly. Something was protruding from his mouth. I didn't recall that Arnold smoked cigars.

"When did you start smoking cigars?" I called. He pulled the bulbous object from his mouth and examined it as though he didn't know it was there.

"Oh. That's my stream thermometer."

"Your *what?*"

"I'm sick. I have a fever."

"Then what are you doing in the river?"

"Oh hell, it's only 99.8. If I break 100, I'll go to bed."

Whenever somebody asks me why I enjoy fishing another thing that comes to mind is what it means in terms of friendships. General Charles Lindeman was always impeccably dressed, cologne lashed, and wearing his stiff upper lip as Counsel to the British Ambassador in Washington. During the years we fished together he had a running verbal duel with Charles Ritz for reasons which only an Englishman would feel about a Frenchman and vice-versa. There was no evil lurking beneath this play of wit; it had the woolly camaraderie of barracks talk. When Lindeman stepped into the river, Ritz would ask him, "Where is your gaff, old boy? All Englishmen carry gaffs." Although a stranger would think that the General meant to hang Ritz with his old school tie, they were really fond of each other.

This good-natured combativeness continued until we stopped to lunch on the bank of the Stamp River one noon. A sudden change came over the General. For a moment he became misty-eyed. He told us that he had sat in this very spot with his young wife a half-century before and made his life's plans. Now she was buried in France, a geographical anomaly which he made no attempt to explain except to refer to a war-time plane crash. Later that day, while I was beaching a steelhead, I saw Ritz crawling along the bank picking wild flowers. Swearing me to silence he carefully packed a bouquet in his duffle bag. "I know the cemetery outside of Paris. I will take these to her. She would like that."

Lindeman didn't know what he had done, and despite my old friend's deserved reputation as one of the world's great anglers, I would embarrass him now by saying that Charles Ritz wears his robe because he is a truly kind and loving man. The General is gone, and it wasn't until his death a few years ago that a certain irony became apparent in our secret when we learned that General Lindeman had been Chief of the British Secret Service.

The only psychologist I have ever met, who knew anything about anglers, was Dr. J. H. Cooper of Kansas City, Missouri. He made sense because he invented the marabou bonefish jig, which reveals him as a practical man. We met, as anglers so often do, through his giving me a duplicate of his lure at a time when I was having lousy fishing at Andros Island.

Have you ever noticed how often anglers tend to share their good fortune? I have seen this happen many times among perfect strangers who simply meet on a stream. I remember a man, who, after landing a beautiful rainbow trout below the Fair Ground Bridge on the East Branch of the Delaware, turned to a bug-eyed kid holding a 98-cent telescopic fly rod, and snipping the March Brown pattern off his leader gave it to the boy. "See what you can do with it, son." That's all he said. I was that boy and I can't tie a March Brown on my leader today without blessing my Good Samaritan.

Before you conclude that the author has broken loose from his moorings and is bobbing impotently on a sea of virtue, let me reassure you that the world is full of narrowly shrewd self-seeking people, blind to God and goodness, and for all I know, Dame Juliana Berners could have been some piscatorial Mary Poppins or a grosser wart on the face of society than Polly Adler. But I would be untrue to my craft if I did not add that although we live in a curiously touchy age when Mom's apple pie, the flag, and the Boy Scouts oath are losing currency, these still make a better frame of reference than Harvard's pellet fed rats or Pavlov's dogs.

Psychologists tell us that one reason why we enjoy fishing is because it is an escape. This is meaningless. True, a man who works in the city wants to "escape" to the country, but the clinical implication is that (no matter where a man lives), he seeks to avoid reality. This is as obtuse as the philosophical doctrine which holds that no reality exists outside the mind.

Perhaps it's the farm boy in me, but I would apply Aristotelian logic— the chicken came before the egg because it is real and the egg is only potential. By the same reasoning the fluid content of a stream is nothing but water when it erupts from a city faucet but given shores it becomes a river, and as a river it is perfectly capable of creating life, and therefore it is real. It is not a sewer, nor a conveyor of barges and lumber, although it can be pressed to these burdens and, indeed, as a living thing it can also become lost in its responsibilities.

So if escapism is a reason for angling—then the escape is *to* reality. The sense of freedom that we enjoy in the outdoors is, after all, a normal reaction to a more rational environment.

Who but an angler knows that magic hour when the red lamp of summer drops behind blackening hemlocks and the mayflies emerge from the dull folds of their nymphal robes to dance in ritual as old as the river itself? Trout appear one by one and the angler begins his game in movements as stylized as Japanese poetry. Perhaps he will hook that wonder-spotted rogue, or maybe he will remain in silent pantomime long into the night with no visible reward.

And that, Professor, is why anglers *really* angle.

The Return

By Patrick O'Brian

OF THE HUNDREDS OF THOUSANDS OF READERS WHO SNATCH UP EVERY new Aubrey/Maturin novel as fast as Patrick O'Brian finishes them, I doubt that very many O'Brian fans realize that the author of these seagoing epics set in the Napoleonic Wars is also the creator of some of the finest prose ever put on paper regarding fishing, hunting, and nature.

The output of this very talented Irishman, who passed away in the year 2000, is nothing short of prodigious. Besides the numerous Aubrey/Maturin novels for which he is so famous, O'Brian has written twelve other books on a variety of subjects. Some are collections of his short stories, among them one called *The Rendezvous and Other Stories*, published by W.W. Norton in 1994, which includes this story and others originally published back in the 1950s.

I only wish I had become acquainted with Patrick O'Brian's lyrical and eloquent prose in time to present it to my readers back when I was calling the plays at *Sports Afield* and *Outdoor Life*. At least, I'm not making the same mistake three times.

All day the fly had been hatching, and where the stream broadened into a deep pool between two falls the surface was continually broken by the rising of fish, broken with rings spreading perpetually, crossing and countercrossing. It was a perfect day for the hatch, mild, gentle, and full of life. Under the willows on the far side of the pool ephemerids drifted in their thousands, and the trout jostled one another in the shade of the willows, drunk with excitement and greed. Great heavy-headed cannibals with harsh, jutting under-jaws came from their stony fastnesses beneath the fall to rise at the fly; tender young trout rose beside them and took no harm.

All down the length of the stream the trout made holiday: they added a fresh, water-borne note to the incessant, imperceptible noise of the country, a note quite distinct from the purl of the water over the big pebbles above the fall, and from the sharp punctuation of the splash of the diving kingfisher, who flashed up and down his beat, darting ever and again on some minnow or tittlebat, some half-transparent fishlet that strayed up into danger from the green, waving forests in the stream's bed.

The best part of the stream lay between the ruined mill and the bridge: a path, some little way from the water, but roughly parallel with it, ran through the grass from the mill to the bridge. On the other side the woods came down to the water's edge, where huge pollard willows stood knee-deep in the stream, making deep quiet bays for chub and quiet-loving fish. Formerly the underbrush had been cut back for the comfort of fishermen, but now it was overgrown, and the riot of young fresh green was brave in the sun.

Immediately below the pool the stream ran with a deeper note, flowing faster through a more narrow course, being constricted by worn rocks, which it could surmount only when the winter rains came down. Here the bridge spanned it in one leap: an ancient stone bridge it was, exquisitely lichened and its lines all rounded with age. There was an appearance of vast solidity about the bridge; it was massive and immovably firm, but it had a wonderful grace. A few self-sown wallflowers, tawny yellow, grew in its sides, and the sun was upon it now. The road that the bridge carried on its back ran clean a little way into the wood, but after the first bend it was lost and overgrown, for it was quite neglected.

The kingfisher perched on a stump close by the bridge to preen itself in the sunlight. It took no heed of the trout, nor of any of the innumerable sounds that came from hidden places all around it, but all at once it froze motionless on the stump, with its head raised questioningly. Then it sped down the stream in a blur of blue-green light, low over the water.

A little while after a man came down the lost road through the wood. At the bridge-head he paused, blinking in the sudden light. The trout stopped rising; a dabchick dived silently and swam fast away under the water. The pool held still to listen. Treading softly over the encroaching moss, the man came on to the bridge: he leaned over the coping and stared upstream. He was a tall, thick man, with a red face and black hair, quite gross to look at, and urbanized now: on his shoulders he carried a knapsack and a rod. After some minutes he looked down at the stones on which he leaned: initials and dates were scratched and cut into them. He knew almost to an inch where his own should be. They were there, J.S.B. in bold, swaggering letters, deeply carved, with a date of many years ago and a girl's initials in the same hand coming after them. Mary Adams: how very clearly he remembered her. A glaze of sentiment came over his eyes. A pace along the bridge there was J.S.B. and E.R.L., more discreetly this time, and, lower down, J.S.B. and T.M. There was a little cushion of moss spreading over the T.M.: he flicked it off and stood up. She had always called him Jeremy in full.

At the far end of the pool a trout rose, with a clear, round plop. The kingfisher flashed under the bridge and vanished upstream. The man walked on over the bridge to the path that led to the mill. From the path in the meadow he could see the stream, but from far enough away that he would not put the fish down.

He sat down in the sweet, dry grass and threw off his knapsack. He put the joints of his rod together, and it quivered pleasantly in his hand: from the pockets of his knapsack he drew old tobacco tins, a reel with an agate ring, his fly box; his fingers seemed too coarse for the tiny, delicate knots in the translucent cast, but the knots formed and the fly was on—a grannom. At last he stood up and whipped the rod in the air: he worked the line out loop by loop; it whistled and sang. He cast his fly at a dandelion clock, and after a few casts the fly floated down and broke the white ball. Satisfied, he walked gently towards the stream: for some time there had been a recurrent heavy swirl under the alders on the far side. Kneeling down—for the day was bright and the water scarcely ruffled—he worked his line out across the stream and cast a little above the rise. His fly landed clumsily in a coil of the cast; the trout ignored it, but did not take fright. When it had floated down, Jeremy twitched it from the surface and cast again. This time it landed handsomely, well cocked on the surface, and as it came down his hand was tense with anticipation; but the trout took another fly immediately in front of it. The third case was too short, and the next began to drag, and the fly was half-drowned. He switched tiny specks of water from the grannom and cast again: still the trout let the fly go by, and a snag bore it over to a sunken branch. Delicately he tweaked and manœuvred with his outstretched rod, but the barb sank into the wood and held firm.

Will it give? he said, or will I go round and free it? Come now, handsomely does it. He lowered the top of his rod and pulled through the rings. The line stretched and the branch stirred: all around the trout were rising. He gave it a sudden, brutal jerk and the fly shot back across the stream, carrying a white sliver of wood on its point.

I did not deserve that, he said, taking the little piece off; I did not, indeed. He walked some way up the pool, waving his rod as he went. At haphazard, he cast to a small rise by the near bank, hardly pausing in his stride. At once the trout took the fly and went fast away with it in the corner of his mouth. The little fish was game enough, but he was finished in two mad rushes: he played himself, and came rolling in on his side, still defying the hook, but with no more power to fight it. The fisherman took another like the first a little higher up, beyond the pool. They were both about a half a pound—small for that stream—cleanly run and game, but stupid.

After he had put the second fish into his bag, he rested; there was a crick between his shoulders from the unaccustomed exercise. He squatted on his heels, and almost without knowing it he filled his pipe as he gazed over the water: the kingfisher passed again, and in the woods a garrulous jay betrayed a fox.

It was just at this place that he had taken his first trout, tickling under the rill for them with Ralph, who was simple, but who could poach like an otter. The march of the years between those times and now effaced the unhappy days of his boyhood and adolescence, and now that he knew the value of the happiness of the days that remained to him that his former, smaller self had lived in a golden world. He had so little to show for all that he had lost; and sudden, intense regret for it took him by the throat for a moment.

He took off his shoes and socks, laid down his coat, and rolled up his trousers. The water was surprisingly cold as he waded into the stream; he could feel its distinct movement between each toe and the edged stones hurt his feet. He walked on the beds of water plants, sinking his feet to the ankles in the brilliant green: at each step he could feel innumerable tiny hoppings against his soles. The last time he had walked that way the water had been well up his thighs, he remembered, and in the middle the current had sometimes plucked him off his feet. Above him there was a small pool, with a stone rill above and below it. A crayfish exploded before his white toes, shooting through a cloud of silver minnows. Three or four small trout flitted from the weed-beds as he walked, speeding up the open, clean lanes between the orderly weeds; there seemed to be no other fish, but he knew the ways of these trout, and he waded quietly to the bar of stones, where the water came through fast from the pool. The force of the current had washed out a deep hollow here, and the water was too deep to stand in.

The sun had passed well over noon-height, and a deep shadow lay slantwise down the wall of stones beneath the water. Nothing could be seen there, but middle-aged Jeremy, standing thigh-deep at the edge of the scoop, leaned over and passed his hand along the stones, feeling gently into the interstices. Almost at once his fingers touched the firm, living body of a trout: the fish, working in the strong current, moved a little to one side. It was not frightened. He touched it again, drawing one finger up its side, feeling the strong, urgent thrust as the trout pushed continually upstream to hold its position. As his eyes grew used to the deep shadow, he could see the trout's tail, moving steadily to and fro. Carefully he continued to stroke its unresisting body, working the fish into the grip of his fingers: as soon as he could gauge the full length of the fish he knew that it would be too big for one hand, so he brought the other down, changing his foothold as he did so. The trout started and moved restlessly, but the quiet stroking of its belly on each side calmed it. Up and up the fingers stole, now touching the gills for a moment, then lingering. He drew in his breath, made his whole body tense and ready, and then with an instant grasp behind and under the trout's gills he flung it over his back on to the bank, where it sprang and curved in the sun. Grinning like a boy, he waded in a slow hurry back to the edge, killed his fish—a good fish, a very nice fish indeed—and sat down to dry his feet on a handkerchief.

He was hungry now, quite suddenly and unpleasantly hungry. He collected dried grass and twigs: the thin blue smoke of his fire rose straight up high into the air. He fanned it until it had a red heart, and he gutted two fish. He washed them in the stream and cut a green withy: coming back to the fire's black circle, he spitted them and lapped them with a piece of string to keep their bellies in. He twirled the ends and cooked his trout until their skins were wrinkled and golden and their pink flesh showed through the cracks in it. He had a broad leaf for a plate and bread and butter and a screw of salt from his bag. Being rather greedy by nature, he buttered and salted the fish with great care and ate them and the crusty bread in alternate bites, so that the taste came fresh and fresh: and at the end he slit out the little oval pieces from the cheeks of the trout and toasted them on the last piece of crust, so that the morsels spattered for a moment in the heat. After he had wiped his fingers and his mouth, he lay on his back in the soft, cushioning grass with his head under the shade of a bush, and all around him there was a murmur and a drowsy hum, and he slept.

When he woke up the sun had gone down three parts of the way to the horizon. Long shadows stood across the stream, and in the broad motes that came through the trees the spinners still danced in their hosts.

The fisherman raised his head and ran his fingers through his hair: he had not meant to lose his time in sleep, but here he did not mind the loss so much as he might have done on another stream; for he was here on a pilgrimage.

He walked back along the stream so as to fish up the same stretch again, and at the end of the pool by the bridge he saw a big rise—no splash, but the big, swirling ring that it is such a pleasure to see. The trout was on the farther side, well out in the open water, so it was necessary to creep up to an alder and, kneeling precariously on the edge, to cast left-handed from a long way off. Tentatively he worked a long line out, feeling his way across. A capricious little breeze, with no fixed direction, had arisen while he slept: the bushes behind him were a continual anxiety, and his knee kept slipping on the rounded edge of the bank. With his mouth closed tightly, he breathed heavily through his nose and concentrated on the flying line: his fly weaved back and yon, like a detached speck over which he had some occult control. The fly sped out and out, and still further; it was a very long cast. He shot the line, checked its run and bowed his rod; its forward motion stopped and as naturally as a dropping ephemerid the fly touched the surface, precisely where he had wanted it. The trout came straight at it, took it hard and vanished in a series of rings that spread out well across the pool before the fisherman raised his rod in a gentle tightening of the straight line. At once there was a great jar on the line as the trout jerked against the pull and sent the hook right home. The reel screamed, the rod curved, the line raced out. The trout leapt, not once but six times, showing clear a foot above the water at each leap. The man scrambled away from the insecure bank and stood in the water: his rod was thrilling with life under his hands. Three-pounder at least, he said it was, perhaps four, and Aah, would you? he said as the trout turned and dashed for the willow roots. His rod curved almost to a half-circle, checking sideways. The trout leapt again, slapping the water; it changed direction and shot up past him to the other end of the pool, into the deep stones beneath the rill. He could not reel in fast enough, and the line was still slack when the trout reached the stones.

Deep down in the calm water at the side of the rill the fish lay, beneath weeds and a tangle of drifted wood. Anxiously he twitched on the line; it was as dead as if it were tied to a rock. He was almost sure that it must be round the wood if not round the deep weed as well, but with his rod far out on the one side and then on the other he tried to stir the trout. There was no result, no feeling of life. With his rod pointing at the fish, he thrummed on the line, pulled and eased, did everything he knew, but it was entirely of its own foolish will that the trout moved in the end. Moved by some fancy, it turned round from its hole in the rocks and headed downstream with fresh strength. The cast strained shockingly: a green streamer carried away from the weed-bed, the line snaked free through the floating debris, and he was still on to his fish. For a dangerous minute the weed dashed through the water after the trout, but its stems parted before the cast.

Again the reel sang and the line fleeted away in spite of his checking finger and the straining rod: it was a heavy fish and a strong one. When the line was gone to the first knot in the backing, the trout was the whole length of the pool away; he dared not let it run any further, so he stopped the line dead for a second; it stretched and he let it go slack. The trout stopped, leapt twice, but went on under the bridge, down through the dark tunnel of swift water, and the fisherman's heart sank. But he ran down the bank, now in the water, now out of it, stumbling and panting and sweating. The line was fraying against the stone foot of the bridge both this side and that; the strain was unwarrantable, and still the trout was running. He reached the bridge, with a couple of yards of backing on his reel, and the fish curved across to lie under the shade of the far bank, with its gills opening wide and fast.

Jeremy had been under the bridge; he knew its dark-green slipperiness and the almost certainty of a ducking. The rod might break too. However, there was nothing for it: he pushed his rod through, tip foremost, and bowed his head under the arch. The pent-in water took him behind the knees and nearly had him down at once: its note changed as soon as he was under the bridge. Then the trout began to rush across the stream again, and in his flurry of spirit he was through the bridge and on the shingle the other side before he had had time to think about it.

The heavy strain of the angled line had tired the trout, and its rushes were now much shorter, and they lacked the irresistible fire of the first. He made line on it fast, and fought it hard, never giving it a moment to recover. He thought he had it once, and pulled it in towards the bank as it lay inert upon the water, but before he had got it more than halfway it revived with a desperate rush and very nearly broke him against a stone on the bottom.

The trout lay on the bottom and would not move: the fisherman had been so near success and failure that he grew overcautious now. He knew that his cast must be in a bad way, and he dared not pull until a sudden feeling of desperation nerved him to it. The fish had recovered, and it had learnt cunning. It meant to go through the bridge again, and he only stopped it with a strain that came within an ace of snapping the cast at the worst fray. Then he saw the line coming back and he scrabbled his way fast up the bank to keep the strain, reeling in as he went. I know I shall trip, he said, and that will be an end to it: but his good fortune was with him, and he kept his feet among the bushes and lumps. He kept the fish on the top now and bore masterfully on it, because there was no other way. Its strength ebbed in short rushes and a few angry leaps; the continual pressure was breaking its heart, and at the end it lost its head, used up the last of its strength in an unavailing burst and rolled sideways in the water.

He reeled it in very cautiously over the shingle where he stood ankle-deep. He was between the fish and the water as it grounded; there was a wild flurry and he had it out jerking and gasping on the grass in the last golden sunlight of the day.

He took the draggled fly from the corner of its jaw—it had nearly worn free in the fight—and he stood above the fish, gazing at it with satisfied admiration. It was a perfect fish: he looked down on its small, well-formed head, the gleaming pools of its eyes, and the golden yellow under the delicate white of its throat, and it lay there quiet with labouring gills. He must weigh a good four pounds, he said, drawing his finger down the fine, pink-flecked line that divided its belly from its gorgeous spotted sides. The fish bounded at his touch, and lay still again. He saw its strong shoulders, the saffron of its fins and the splendid play of colours over its whole glowing body, and he could not find it in his heart to kill the fish. It was the day and an undefined symbolism that worked upon him too.

Bending to the water, he held the trout upright with its head upstream: it was certainly four pounds. Its gills opened and closed and the cool water laved through them: for minutes he held it so, until fresh life and a little strength flowed into it and it lashed free. The trout almost turned belly-up a little way out, but more strength came to it. It turned into the stronger current and sank down to the waving green. He could see it there plainly, working gently under the soft shelter.

He wound his reel and packed his rod. The first owl cried and he went over the bridge: he went away, through the woods by the lost road, in the dying light.

Jody's Bass

By Marjorie Kinnan Rawlings

WHEN SHE FIRST TOOK UP RESIDENCE AT A PLACE CALLED CROSS CREEK in the Florida pinelands and scrub palmetto country in 1928, Marjorie Kinnan Rawlings had not yet found the inner "voice" of an accomplished novelist. She was willing to work desperately hard for writing success. But her life of reasonable wealth and culture in Washington, D.C., where she was born, and New York state where she worked after going to college in Wisconsin, had created forces which had thrown her creative compass askew. She set out to write the type of romantic fantasies that were popular at that time, and she was not successful.

As her life among the impoverished wilderness residents of the Florida scrub country brought her vision to bear on the realities of life in concert with nature, Marjorie Kinnan Rawlings began to turn her prose toward the material at hand—her neighbors and the wilderness world of black-water swamps and sprawling pinelands where deer, black bear, and panthers roamed and the bird life was simply awesome in its abundance.

Rawlings wrote two novels—*South Moon Under* and *Golden Apples*—set in her new home under the stewardship of the renowned editor Max Perkins at Scribners. The books were critical successes, but far from bestsellers or financially rewarding. Nevertheless, she had found her "voice." Marjorie Kinnan Rawlings had become a writer.

Then lightning struck.

For some time she had been mulling over an incident one of her pinelands neighbors had mentioned in passing. Something about having a pet deer that had become such a pest that his father ("daddy") had made him kill it ... and how bad it all had "hurted" him for the rest of his life.

The Yearling was published in 1939 and won the Pulitzer Prize. Today there is no doubt in my mind that the book ranks among the true American classics. My opinion is not backed up by appropriate degrees in literary academia but only as a voracious, committed reader—one always on the prowl for a good book. Saying *The Yearling* is a novel about a kid and his pet deer is like saying *Les Misérables* is a novel about a Frenchman who steals a loaf of bread and never hears the end of it. This chapter from *The Yearling* captures the very special luminescence of a father-son fishing day in which angling's rewards seem magical and enchanting, almost Eden-like, if you will. Truly, Jody and his father have a great day. So will you!

———

Jody lay comfortably ill, recovering from the fever. His mother called it the fever, so he did not argue. He thought privately that too many half-ripe brierberries might have something to do with his ailment. Treatment for such things was always much more violent than treatment for the fever. His mother had observed his shaking, had laid her big hand on his forehead and said, "Git into the bed. You got chills and fever." He had said nothing.

She came into the room now with a cup of steaming liquid. He eyed it anxiously. For two days she had been giving him lemon-leaf tea. It was aromatic and pleasant. When he had grumbled about its tartness, she had added a teaspoon of jelly to it. He wondered if now, in the mysterious wisdom that sometimes descended on her, she had discovered the truth. If she guessed that his trouble had been the colic, the medicine she held would be either snake-root tonic, or a blood purifier made from Queen's Delight, both of which he abominated.

"If your Pa'd only plant me a root o' fever grass," she said, "I could git both o' you well o' the fever in no time. 'Tain't decent, not havin' fever-grass in the yard."

"What you got in the cup, Ma?"

"None o' your business. Open your mouth."

"I got a right to know. Supposin' you kilt me and I never knowed what medicine you give me."

"Hit's mullein tea, if you got to know. Hit come to me, could be you was comin' down with the measles."

" 'Tain't the measles, Ma."

"How do you know? You ain't never had 'em. Open your mouth. If 'tain't the measles, this here won't hurt you. If 'tis the measles, hit'll bring out the rash."

The thought of bringing out a rash was tempting. He opened his mouth. She grasped him by the hair and poured half the cupful down his throat. He sputtered and fought.

"I won't take no more. 'Tain't the measles."

"Well, you'll die if 'tis, and the rash don't break out."

He opened his mouth again and took the rest of the mullein tea. It was bitter, but not nearly as bad as some of her concoctions. The bitter brew she made from pomegranate peelings, or that from pitcher-plant root, was infinitely worse. He lay back on his moss-stuffed pillow.

"If 'tis the measles, Ma, how soon will the rash come?"

"Soon as you get to sweatin' from the tea. Kiver up."

She left the room and he resigned himself to waiting for the sweat. Being sick was something of a treat. He would not willingly go through the first night again, when cramps had tied him in knots. But the convalescence, the solicitude of his mother and his father, was definitely pleasant. He felt a faint sense of guilt that he had not told about the brierberries. She would have given him a purge, and it would all have been over with by the next morning. Penny had done all the work of the clearing alone for two days. He had hitched old Cæsar to the plow and plowed over the sugar-cane and hilled it up, had worked the corn and the cow-peas and the small patch of tobacco. He had hauled water from the sink-hole, cut wood, fed and watered the stock.

But perhaps, Jody speculated, he did have the fever. Perhaps he was coming down with the measles. He felt his face and stomach. There was no rash yet, no sweat. He flounced back and forth in the bed to hurry the heating. He realized that he felt as well as ever; better, actually, than before the plenitude of meat had tempted him into over-eating. He recalled the quantities of fresh sausage and of venison that he had eaten without his mother's stopping him. Perhaps after all the brierberries had had nothing to do with it. He was sweating at last.

He called, "Hey, Ma, come see! The sweat's done come."

She came to him and examined him.

"You feel as good as I do," she said. "Git outen that bed."

He threw back the covers and stepped out onto the deerskin rug. For a moment he was light-headed.

"You feel all right?" she asked.

"Yessum. Sort o' weakified."

"Well, you ain't et nothin'. Get into your shirt and breeches and come git you some dinner."

He dressed quickly and followed her to the kitchen. The food was still warm. She laid out biscuits for him, and a plate of hash, and poured him a cup of sweet milk. She watched him eat.

"I hoped you'd git up a leetle mite pacified," she said.

"Kin I have some more hash, Ma?"

"I should say not. You've et enough now, to fill a alligator."

"Where's Pa?"

"To the lot, I reckon."

He strolled in search of him. Penny was sitting idly, for once, on the gate.

"Well, son," he said, "you look right peert."

"I feel good."

"You ain't got the measles, or the child-bed fever, or the smallpox?" The blue eyes twinkled.

Jody shook his head.

"Pa—"

"Yes, son."

"I don't figger there was nothin' ailded me but green brierberries."

"That's about what I figgered. I never said nothin' to your Ma, for she's death on a belly-full of green brierberries."

Jody sighed with relief.

Penny said, "I been settin' here studyin'. The moon'll be right in a hour-two. What say you and me git us a couple o' bobs and go fishin'?"

"In the creek?"

"I sort o' crave to fish some o' them saw-grass ponds over where ol' Slewfoot was feedin'."

"I'll bet we kin ketch us a cattywampus in one o' them ponds."

"We kin sure pleasure ourselves tryin'."

They went together to the shed back of the house to gather their paraphernalia. Penny discarded an old hook and rigged two new ones. He cut short hairs from the tail of the deer he had shot and made lures of the gray and white wisps. He tied them invisibly to the fish-hooks.

"If I was a fish, I'd strike at this myself," he said.

He went to the house and spoke briefly with his wife.

"Me and Jody is goin' bobbin' for bass."

"I thought you was give out and Jody was ailin'."

"That's why we're goin' fishin'," he said.

She followed to the door and watched after them.

"If you don't git no bass," she called, "ketch me a leetle bream I kin fry crisp and eat bones and all."

"We'll not come back without somethin'," he promised.

The afternoon was warm but the way seemed short. In a way, Jody thought, fishing was better than hunting. It was not so exciting, but neither was there terror. The heart beat at a reasonable cadence. There was time to look about, and see the increase of green leaves in the live oaks and magnolias. They stopped at a familiar pond. It was shallow from too long dryness. Penny found a grasshopper and threw it into the water. There was no strike; no hungry swirl of waters.

"I'm feered the fish has died outen here," he said. "These leetle ol' ponds in the middle o' no-where has allus been a puzzlement to me. I cain't see how the fish lives here, year on year."

He caught another grasshopper and hurled it without result.

"The pore fish," he said. "Helpless in a world o' their own. 'Stead o' fishin' for 'em, I'd ought to come out here and feed 'em."

He lifted his bamboo rod over his shoulder.

"Mebbe the Lord figgers the same about me," he chuckled. "Mebbe he looks down and says, 'There's Penny Baxter tryin' to make out on that clearin'.'" He added, "But hit's a good clearin'. Likely the fish is as content as me."

Jody said, "Look, Pa, there's people."

Human beings were a strange sight in the lonely place of live oak islands and saw-grass ponds and prairies, than the creatures. Penny shaded his eyes. A file of half a dozen men and women was entering the scrub road they had just left behind.

"Hit's the Minorcans," he said. "Huntin' gophers."

Jody saw now the sacks over their shoulders. The small dusty land-turtles, whose deep burrows were an indication of the poorest soil, were the last food most inhabitants of the scrub considered edible.

"I've allus wondered," Penny said, "didn't they make a medicine mebbe outen the gophers. Don't seem like they'd come here clear from the coast to hunt them things jest to eat."

"Let's slip back clost and look at 'em," Jody said.

"I'd not pry on the pore things," Penny said. "The Minorcans is a people was mighty bad put upon. My father knowed their hull history. A English feller carried 'em to New Smyrna, over by the ocean and the Indian River. He promised 'em a pure Heaven and put 'em to work. And when times got bad and the crops failed, he left 'em to nigh about starve to death. There wasn't many left."

"Is they like gypsies?"

"No, for gypsies is wild. The men is dark, like gypsies, but the women is fair when they're young. They mind their own business and live peaceable."

The procession disappeared into the scrub. Jody tingled, and the hair stirred on the back of his neck. It was like seeing Spaniards. It was as though phantoms, dark and shadowy, and not men and women, had passed before him, weighted with their strange burden of gophers and injustice.

Penny said, "Now the bass had ought to be thick as tadpoles in that pond right over there."

They were in territory a little west of the prairie's rim where old Slew-foot had fed on fire-plant. Dry weather had sucked up much of the water and the marsh had broad areas that were now firm and dry. The ponds showed plainly. They had withdrawn from the saw-grass and only lily pads troubled the water's surface. A Blue Peter ran across them, bright with yellow legs and painted face. A slight breath of air rippled across the marsh and the water rippled under it. The lily pads tipped, an instant, their broad shining leaves to the glint of the sun.

"Jest enough of a riffle," Penny said, "and the moon jest right."

He fastened lengths of line to the two poles and attached the deer-hair bobs.

"Now you work your bob acrost the north end and I'll try the south. Don't make no fuss, walkin'."

Jody stood a moment to watch his father make an expert cast across the pond. He marveled at the skill of the knotted hands. The bob lay at the edge of a cluster of lily pads. Penny began to jerk it slowly across the water. It dipped and bobbed with the irregular rhythm of a live insect. There was no strike and Penny drew in his line and cast again in the same place. He called to invisible fish, lurking near the weedy bottom.

"Now Grandpappy, I kin see you settin' there on your stoop." He jerked the bob more slowly. "You better lay down your pipe and come git your dinner."

Jody tore himself from the fascination of his father's performance and moved to his end of the pond. He cast badly for a time, tangling his line and laying his bob in the most unlikely places; over-reaching the narrow pond and enmeshing the hook in the tough saw-grass. Then something of harmony came to him. He felt his arm swing in a satisfying arc. His wrist flexed at the proper moment. He laid the bob exactly where he had meant to, at the edge of a patch of switch-grass.

Penny called, "Mighty nice, son. Leave it lay jest a minute. Then git ready the first second you jerk it."

He had not known his father was watching. He was tense. He jerked his pole cautiously and the bob flipped across the water. There was a swirl, a silver form shot half clear of the water, an open mouth as big as a cock-pot enveloped the bob. A weight like a millstone dropped at the end of his line, fought like a wild-cat, and pulled him off-balance. He braced himself against the frenzy to which he was irrevocably attached.

Penny called, "Take it easy. Don't let him git under them bonnets. Keep the tip o' your pole up. Don't give him no slack."

Penny left him to the struggle. His arms ached from the strain. He was afraid to tug too hard for fear of breaking the line. He dared not yield an inch for fear a sudden slackness would tell of the loss of the giant. He longed for magic words from his father, indicating some miracle by which he might land his fish and be done with the torment. The bass was sulking. It made a dash for the grasses, where it might tangle the line around their stems and so rip free. It came to Jody that if he walked around the edge of the pond, keeping a taut line, he might lead the bass into shallow water and flounder him at the edge. He worked cautiously. He was tempted to drop the pole and clutch the line itself and come to grips with his adversary. He began to walk away from the pond. He gave his pole a heave and landed the bass, flouncing, in the grass. He dropped the pole and ran, to move the catch to a final safety. The bass would weigh ten pounds. Penny came to him.

"Boy, I'm proud of you. Nobody couldn't of handled him better."

Jody stood panting. Penny thumped him on the back, as excited as he. He looked down, unbelieving, at the stout form and the great maw.

"I feel as good as if 'twas ol' Slewfoot," he said, and they grinned together and pummeled each other's backs.

"Now I got to go beat you," Penny said.

They took separate ponds. Penny called that he was licked and beaten. He began fishing for Ma Baxter's bream with a hand-line and bonnet worms. Jody cast and cast again, but there was never the mad swirl of waters, the great leap, the live and struggling weight. He caught a small bass and held it up to show his father.

"Throw him back," Penny called. "We don't need him for eatin'. Leave him to grow up big as t'other one. Then we'll come back agin and ketch him."

Jody put the small fish back reluctantly and watched it swim away. His father was stern about not taking more of anything, fish or game, then could be eaten or kept. Hope of another monster dwindled as the sun finished its spring arc of the daylight sky. He cast leisurely, taking his pleasure in his increasing dexterity of arm and wrist. The moon was now wrong. It was no longer feed-time. The fish were not striking. Suddenly he heard his father whistle like a quail. It was the signal they used together in squirrel hunting. Jody laid down his pole and looked back to make sure he could identify the tuft of grass where he had covered his bass from the rays of the sun. He walked cautiously to where his father beckoned.

Penny whispered, "Foller me. We'll ease up clost as we dare."

He pointed. "The whoopin' cranes is dancin'."

Jody saw the great white birds in the distance. His father's eye, he thought, was like an eagle's. They crouched on all fours and crept forward slowly. Now and then Penny dropped flat on his stomach and Jody dropped behind him. They reached a clump of high saw-grass and Penny motioned for concealment behind it. The birds were so close that it seemed to Jody he might touch them with his long fishing pole. Penny squatted on his haunches and Jody followed. His eyes were wide. He made a count of the whooping cranes. There were sixteen.

The cranes were dancing a cotillion as surely as it was danced at Volusia. Two stood apart, erect and white, making a strange music that was part cry and part singing. The rhythm was irregular, like the dance. The other birds were in a circle. In the heart of the circle, several moved counter-clock-wise. The musicians made their music. The dancers raised their wings and lifted their feet, first one and then the other. They sank their heads deep in their snowy breasts, lifted them and sank them again. They moved soundlessly, part awkwardness, part grace. The dance was solemn. Wings fluttered, rising and falling like out-stretched arms. The outer circle shuffled around and around. The group in the center attained a slow frenzy.

Suddenly all motion ceased. Jody thought the dance was over, or that the intruders had been discovered. Then the two musicians joined the circle. Two others took their places. There was a pause. The dance was resumed. The birds were reflected in the clear marsh water. Sixteen white shadows reflected the motions. The evening breeze moved across the saw-grass. It bowed and fluttered. The water rippled. The setting sun lay rosy on the white bodies. Magic birds were dancing in a mystic marsh. The grass swayed with them, and the shallow waters, and the earth fluttered under them. The earth was dancing with the cranes, and the low sun, and the wind and sky.

Jody found his own arms lifting and falling with his breath, as the cranes' wings lifted. The sun was sinking into the saw-grass. The marsh was golden. The whooping cranes were washed with gold. The far hammocks were black. Darkness came to the lily pads, and the water blackened. The cranes were whiter than any clouds, or any white bloom of oleander or of lily. Without warning, they took flight. Whether the hour-long dance was, simply, done, or whether the long nose of an alligator had lifted above the water to alarm them, Jody could not tell, but they were gone. They made a great circle against the sunset, whooping their strange rusty cry that sounded only in their flight. Then they flew in a long line into the west, and vanished.

Penny and Jody straightened and stood up. They were cramped from the long crouching. Dusk lay over the sawgrass, so that the ponds were scarcely visible. The world was shadow, melting into shadow. They turned to the north. Jody found his bass. They cut to the east, to leave the marsh behind them, then north again. The trail was dim in the growing darkness. It joined the scrub road and they turned once more east, continuing now in a certainty, for the dense growth of the scrub bordered the road like walls. The scrub was black and the road was a dark gray strip of carpet, sandy and soundless. Small creatures darted across in front of them and scurried in the bushes. In the distance, a panther screamed. Bull-bats shot low over their heads. They walked in silence.

At the house, bread was baked and waiting, and hot fat was in the iron skillet. Penny lighted a fat-wood torch and went to the lot to do his chores. Jody scaled and dressed the fish at the back stoop, where a ray of light glimmered from the fire on the hearth. Ma Baxter dipped the pieces in meal and fried them crisp and golden. The family ate without speaking.

She said, "What ails you fellers?"

They did not answer. They had no thought for what they ate nor for the woman. They were no more than conscious that she spoke to them. They had seen a thing that was unearthly. They were in a trance from the strong spell of its beauty.

Fishing the Run

By John Graves

FROM A YOUNGSTER'S FIRST SHOUT WITH A FISHING POLE IN HIS HANDS, to the wry grin of a senior citizen bank-sitting in a lawn chair, crappie and bluegills leave indelible marks on the fishing scene. However, where fishing literature is concerned, these fish seem to have a problem breaking into print, except in how-to books and articles.

Then, sometimes a writer comes along with the instincts to find a good story in the most common of circumstances. A writer with the talent to hold us in his verbal grasp as he weaves a spell of pure magic, taking us on a journey that leads to a stunning climax.

If the respect of one's peers is the ultimate expression of success, then John Graves is a Texan who has truly made his mark without striking oil, driving cattle, or playing football. With books like *Goodbye to a River*, *The Last Running*, *Hard Scrabble*, *Blue and Some Other Dogs*, and *From a Limestone Ledge*, John Graves has mined pure literary gold from the Texas landscape, capturing all its harshness and beautiful contradictions, its stalwart and hopeful peoples, living and departed. Graves writes with love and care about what he lives and knows. He finds enough subjects close to home to occupy most of his hours at the typewriter, but he certainly is not adverse to dealing with articles which require a plane ticket or to sometimes plumbing the depths of his painful memories of World War Two. You can find examples of both in his collection, *A John Graves Reader*, which also includes this story.

I'd made the mistake, the evening before, of mentioning to my younger daughter that I'd heard the crappie and sand bass were running in the Brazos. Therefore that Saturday morning, a clear and soft and lovely one of the sort our Texas Februaries sometimes offer in promise of coming spring, filled with the tentative piping of wrens and redbirds, I managed to get in only about an hour and a half's work in my office at the rear of the barn before she showed up there, a certain mulish set to her jaw and eyelids indicating she had a goal in mind and expected some opposition.

I said I needed to stay a while longer at the typewriter and afterward had to go patch a piece of net-wire boundary fence in the southeast pasture, shredded by a neighbor's horned bull while wrangling through it with my own Angus herd sire. She reminded me that the winter before we had missed the best crappie day in local memory because I'd had something else to do, one somewhat greedy fellow whom we knew having brought home eighty-three in a tow sack. She was fifteen and it struck me sometimes, though not to the point of neurosis, that maybe she deserved to have been born to a younger, less preoccupied father. In answer to what she said I raised some other negative points but without any great conviction, for I was arguing less against her than against a very strong part of myself that wanted badly to go fishing too.

The trouble was that those two or three weeks of late winter when the crappie and the sandies move up the Brazos out of the Whitney reservoir, in preparation for spawning, can provide some of the most pleasant angling of the year in our region on the fringes of dry West Texas, where creeks and rivers flow trickingly if at all during the warmer parts of a normal year. Even when low, of course, the good ones have holes and pools with fair numbers of black bass and bream and catfish, and I've been fishing them all my life with enjoyment. But it's not the same flavor of enjoyment that a hard-flowing stream can give, and those of us who have acquired—usually elsewhere—a penchant for live waters indulge it, if we've got the time and money, on trips to the mountain states, and look forward with special feeling to those times when our local waters choose to tumble and roll and our fish change their ways in accordance.

The Brazos in this section, my own personal river of rivers if only because I've known it and used it for so long, is a sleepy catfishing stream most of the time, a place to go at night with friends and sit beneath great oaks and pecans, talking and drinking beer or coffee and watching a fire burn low while barred owls and hoot owls brag across the bottomlands, getting up occasionally to go out with a flashlight and check the baited throwlines and trotlines that have been set. Its winter run of sand bass and crappie is dependable only when there's been plenty of rain and the upstream impoundments at Granbury and Possum Kingdom are releasing a good flow of water to make riffles and rapids run full and strong, an avenue up which the fish swim in their hundreds of thousands. To catch them in drouthy winters you have to drive down to Whitney's headwaters above the Kimball Bend, where the Chisholm Trail used to cross the river and the ruins of stone factory buildings recall old Jacob De Cordova's misplaced dream of water-powered empire, back in the 1860s. But that is lake fishing, best done from a boat and short on the concentrated excitement that a strong current full of avid live things can give.

Generally you fish the river run blind, choosing a likely spot where fast water spews into a slow pool, casting across the flow and letting it sweep your lure or fly in a long arc downstream to slack water near shore, working it in with what you hope are enticing twitches and jerks and pauses, then casting again. It is the venerable pattern still most often used with Atlantic salmon and the West Coast's steelheads, though our local quarry is far less impressive than those patrician species, since a pound-and-a-half crappie is a good one and the sandies—more properly known as white bass—only occasionally exceed a couple of pounds or so. There are plenty of them when a good run is on, though, and unless you overmatch them with heavy stiff tackle they can put up a reasonable fight in the strong water. For that matter there's always an outside chance of hooking a big striped bass, a marine cousin of the sandy introduced to the salty Brazos reservoirs in recent years and reaching fifteen or eighteen pounds or more. To have a horse like that on a light rig is quite an emotional experience, at least if you're of the tribe that derives emotion from angling, but the end result is not ordinarily triumphant. The annoyed striper hauls tail swiftly and irresistibly downriver while you hang onto your doubled, bucking rod and listen to the squall of your little reel yielding line, and when all the line has run out it breaks, at the fish's end if you're lucky, at the reel if you're not.

I've never been very happy fishing in crowds, and after word of a run of fish has seeped around our county the accessible areas along the river can be pretty heavily populated, especially on weekends in good weather and even more especially at the exact riverbank locations most worth trying. So that morning when without much resistance I had let Younger Daughter argue me down, I got the canoe out, hosed off its accumulation of old mud-dauber nests and barn dust, and lashed it atop the cattle frame on the pickup. If needed, it would let us cross over to an opposite, unpeopled shore or drop downriver to some other good place with no one at all in sight.

After that had been done and after we had rooted about the house and outbuildings in search of the nooks where bits of requisite tackle had hidden themselves during a winter's disuse, the morning was gone and so was the promise of spring. A plains norther had blown in, in northers' sudden fashion, and the pretty day had turned raw. By the time we'd wolfed down lunch and driven out to the Brazos, heavy clouds were scudding southeastward overhead and there was a thin misty spit of rain. This unpleasantness did have at least one bright side, though. When we'd paid our dollar entrance fee to a farmer and had parked on high firm ground above the river, we looked down at a gravel beach beside some rapids and the head of a deep long pool, a prime spot, and saw only one stocky figure there, casting toward the carved gray limestone cliffs that formed the other bank. There would be no point in using the canoe unless more people showed up, and that seemed unlikely with the grimness of the sky and the cold probing wind, which was shoving upriver in such gusts that, with a twinge of the usual shame, I decided to use a spinning rig.

Like many others who've known stream trout at some time in their lives, I derive about twice as much irrational satisfaction from taking fish on fly tackle as I do from alternative methods. I even keep a few streamers intended for the crappie and white bass run, some of them bead-headed and most a bit gaudy in aspect. One that has served well on occasion, to the point of disgruntling nearby plug and minnow hurlers, is a personal pattern called the Old English Sheep Dog which has a tinsel chenille body, a sparse crimson throat hackle, and a wing formed of long white neck hairs from the amiable friend for whom the concoction is named, who placidly snores and snuffles close by my chair on fly-tying evenings in winter and brooks without demur an occasional snip of the scissors in his coat. Hooks in sizes four and six seem usually to be about right, and I suppose a sinking or sink-tip line would be best for presentation if you keep a full array of such items with you, which I usually don't. . . .

But such is the corruption engendered by dwelling in an area full of worm-stick wielders and trotline types, where fly-fishing is still widely viewed as effete and there are no salmonids to give it full meaning, that increasingly these days I find myself switching to other tackle when conditions seem to say to. And I knew now that trying to roll a six-weight tapered line across that angry air would lead to one sorry tangle after another.

We put our gear together and walked down to the beach, where the lone fisherman looked around and greeted as affably enough, though without slowing or speeding his careful retrieve of a lure. A full-fleshed, big-headed, rather short man with a rosy Pickwickian face, in his middle or late sixties perhaps, he was clearly enough no local. Instead of the stained and rumpled workaday attire that most of us hereabouts favor for such outings he had on good chest waders, a tan fishing vest whose multiple pouch pockets bulged discreetly here and there, and neat little tweed porkpie hat that ought to have seemed ridiculous above that large pink face but managed somehow to look just right, jaunty and self-sufficient and good-humored. He was using a dainty graphite rod and a diminutive free-spool casting reel, the sort of equipment you get because you know what you want and are willing to pay for it, and when he cast again, sending a tiny white-feathered spinner bait nearly to the cliff across the way with only a flirt of the rod, I saw that he used them well.

Raising my voice against the rapids' hiss and chatter I asked him if the fish were hitting.

"Not bad," he answered, still fishing. "It was slow this morning when the weather was nice, but this front coming through got things to popping a little. Barometric change, I guess."

Not the barometer but the wind had me wishing I'd mustered the sense to change to heavier clothing when the soft morning had disappeared. It muffled the pool's water darkly, working against the surface current.

Younger Daughter, I recalled, had cagily put on a down jacket, and when I looked around for her she was already thirty yards down the beach and casting with absorption, for she was and is disinclined toward talk when water needs to be worked. My Pickwickian friend being evidently of the same persuasion, I intended to pester him no further, though I did wonder whether he'd been catching a preponderance of crappie or of sand bass and searched about with my eyes for a live bag or stringer, but saw none. When I glanced up again he had paused in his casting and was watching me with a wry half-guilty expression much like one I myself employ when country neighbors have caught me in some alien aberration such as fly-fishing or speaking with appreciation about the howls of coyotes.

"I hardly ever keep any," he said. "I just like fishing for them."

I said I usually put the sandies back too, but not crappie, whose delicate white flesh my clan prizes above that of all other local species for the table and, if there are many, for tucking away in freezer packets against a time of shortage. He observed that he'd caught no crappie at all. "Ah," I said, a bilked gourmet. Then, liking the man and feeling I ought to, I asked if our fishing there would bother him.

"No, hell, no," said Mr. Pickwick. "There's lots of room, and anyhow I'm moving on up the river. Don't like to fish in one spot too long. I'm an itchy sort."

That being more or less what I might have said too had I been enjoying myself there alone when other people barged in, I felt a prick of conscience as I watched him work his way alongside the main rapids, standing in water up to his rubber-clad calves near the shore, casting and retrieving a few times from each spot before sloshing a bit farther upstream. It was rough loud water of a type in which I have seldom had much luck on that river. But then I saw him shoot his spinner-bug out across the wind and drop it with precision into a small slick just below a boulder, where a good thrashing sand bass promptly grabbed it, and watched him let the current and the rod's lithe spring wear the fish down before he brought it to slack shallow shore water, reaching down to twist the hook deftly from its jaw so that it could drift away. That was damned sure not blind fishing. He knew what he was doing, and I quit worrying about our intrusion on the beach.

By that time Younger Daughter, unruffled by such niceties, had caught and released a small sandy or two herself at the head of the pool, and as I walked down to join her she beached another and held it up with a smile to shame my indolence before dropping it back in the water. I'd been fishing for more than three times as many years as she had been on earth, but she often caught more than I because she stayed with the job, whereas I have a longstanding tendency to stare at birds in willow trees, or study currents and rocks, or chew platitudes with other anglers randomly encountered.

"You better get cracking," she said. "That puts me three up."

I looked at the sky, which was uglier than it had been. "What you'd better do," I told her, "is find the right bait and bag a few crappie for supper pretty fast. This weather is getting ready to go to pieces."

"Any weather's good when you're catching fish," she said, quoting a dictum I'd once voiced to her while clad in something more warmly waterproof than my present cotton flannel shirt and poplin golfer's jacket. Nevertheless she was right, so I tied on a light marabou horsehead jig with a spinner—a white one, in part because that was the hue jaunty old Mr. Pickwick had been using with such skill, but mainly because most of the time with sand bass, in Henry Fordish parlance, any color's fine as long as it's white. Except that some days they like a preponderance of yellow, and once I saw a fellow winch them in numerously with a saltwater rod and reel and a huge plug that from a distance looked to be lingerie pink. . . .

I started casting far enough up the beach from Younger Daughter that our lines would not get crossed. The northwest wind shoved hard and cold and the thin rain seemed to be flicking more steadily against my numbing cheeks and hands. But then the horsehead jig found its way into some sort of magical pocket along the line where the rapids' forceful long tongue rubbed against eddy water drifting up from the pool. Stout sand bass were holding there, eager and aggressive, and without exactly forgetting the weather I was able for a long while to ignore it. I caught three fish in three casts, lost the feel of the pocket's whereabouts for a time before locating it again and catching two more, then moved on to look for another such place and found it, and afterward found some others still. I gave the fish back to the river, or gave it back to them: shapely, forktailed, bright-silver creatures with thin dark parallel striping along their sides, gaping rhythmically from the struggle's exhaustion as they eased away backward from my hand in the slow shallows.

I didn't wish they were crappie, to be stowed in the mesh live bag and carried off home as food. If it wasn't a crappie day, it wasn't, and if satisfactory preparation of the sandies' rather coarse flesh involves some kitchen mystery from which our family's cooks have been excluded, the fact remains that they're quite a bit more pleasant to catch than crappie—stronger and quicker and more desperately resistant to being led shoreward on a threadlike line or a leader. In my own form of piscatorial snobbery, I've never much liked the sort of fishing often done for them on reservoirs, where motorboaters race converging on a surfaced feeding school to cast furiously toward its center for a few minutes until it disappears, then wait around for another roaring, roostertailed race when that school or another surfaces somewhere else. But my basic snobbery—or trouble, or whatever you want to call it—is not much liking reservoir fishing itself, except sometimes with a canoe in covish waters at dawn, when all good roostertailers and waterskiers and other motorized hypermanics are virtuously still abed, storing up energy for another day of loud wave-making pleasure.

In truth, until a few years ago I more or less despised the sand bass as an alien introduced species fit only for such mechanized pursuit in such artificial waters. But in a live stream on light tackle they subvert that sort of purism, snapping up flies or jigs or live minnows with abandon and battling all the way. It isn't a scholarly sort of angling. Taking them has in it little or none of the taut careful fascination, the studious delicacy of lure and presentation, that go with stalking individual good trout, or even sometimes black bass and bream, but it's clean fine fishing for all that.

Checking my watch, I found with the common angler's surprise that nearly three hours had gone a-glimmering since our arrival at the beach, for it was after four. Younger Daughter and I had hardly spoken during that time, drifting closer together or farther apart while we followed our separate hunches as to where fish might be lying. At this point, though, I heard her yell where she stood a hundred yards or so downshore, and when I looked toward her through the rain—real rain now, if light, that gave her figure in its green jacket a pointillist haziness—I saw she was leaning backward with her rod's doubled-down tip aimed toward something far out in the deep pool, something that was pulling hard.

If she had a mature striper on her frail outfit there wasn't much prayer that she'd bring him in. But I wanted to be present for the tussle that would take place before she lost him, and I hurried toward her shouting disjointed, unnecessary advice. She was handling the fish well, giving him line when he demanded it and taking some back when he sulked in the depths, by pumping slowly upward with the rod and reeling in fast as she lowered it again. She lost all that gained line and more when he made an upriver dash, and he'd nearly reached the main rapids before we decided that he might not stop there and set off at a jogtrot to catch up, Younger Daughter reeling hard all the way to take in slack. But the run against the current tired him, and in a few minutes she brought him to the beach at about the point where we'd met Mr. Pickwick. It was a sand bass rather than a striper, but a very good one for the river. I had no scale along, but estimated the fish would go three and a half pounds easily, maybe nearly four.

"I'm going to keep him," she said. "We can boil him and freeze him in batches for Kitty, the way Mother did one time. Kitty liked it."

"All right," I said, knowing she meant she felt a need to show the rest of the family what she'd caught, but didn't want to waste it. The wind, I noticed, had abated somewhat but the cold rain made up for the lack. "Listen," I said. "I'm pretty wet and my teeth are starting to chatter. Aren't you about ready to quit?"

A hint of mulishness ridged up along her jawline. "You could go sit in the truck with the heater and play the radio," she said.

I gave vent to a low opinion of that particular idea.

"There's his hat," she said. "The man's."

Sure enough there it came, the tweed porkpie, shooting down the rapids upside down and half submerged like a leaky, small, crewless boat, and no longer looking very jaunty. It must have blown off our friend's head somewhere upstream. Riding the fast tongue of current to where the pool grew deep, it slowed, and I went down and cast at it with a treble-hooked floating plug till I snagged it and reeled it in.

"I guess we can drive up and down and find his car, if we don't see him." I said. "It's a pretty nice hat."

She said in strange reply, "Oh!"

The reason turned out to be that Mr. Pickwick was cruising downriver along the same swift route his hat had taken but quite a bit more soggily, since his heavy chest waders swamped full of water were pulling him toward the bottom as he came. He was in the lower, deepening part of the rapids above us, floating backward in the current—or rather not floating, for as I watched I saw him vanish beneath surging water for five or six long seconds, surfacing enormously again as his large pink bald head and his shoulders and rowing arms broke into sight and he took deep gasps of air, maintaining himself symmetrically fore-and-aft in the river's heavy shove. He stayed up only a few moments before being pulled under again, then reappeared and sucked in more great draughts of air. It had a rhythmic pattern, I could see. He was bending his legs as he sank and kicking hard upward when he touched bottom, and by staying aligned in the current he was keeping it from seizing and tumbling him. He was in control, for the moment at any rate, and I felt the same admiration for him that I'd felt earlier while watching him fish.

I felt also a flash of odd but quite potent reluctance to meddle in the least with his competent, private, downriver progress, or even for that matter to let him know we were witnesses to his plight. Except that, of course, very shortly he was going to be navigating in twelve or fifteen feet of slowing water at the head of the pool, with the waders still dragging him down, and it seemed improbable that any pattern he might work out at that extremely private point was going to do him much good.

Because of the queer reluctance I put an absurd question to the back of his pink pate when it next rose into view. I shouted above the hoarse voice of the water, "Are you all right?"

Still concentrating on his fore-and-aftness and sucking hard for air, he gave no sign of having heard before he once more sounded, but on his next upward heave he gulped in a breath and rolled his head aside to glare at me over his shoulder, out of one long blue bloodshot eye. Shaping the word with care, he yelled from the depths of his throat, "NO!"

And went promptly under again.

Trying to gauge water speed and depth and distances, I ran a few steps down the beach and charged in, waving Younger Daughter back when she made a move to follow. I'm not a powerful swimmer even when stripped down, and I knew I'd have to grab him with my boots planted on the bottom if I could. Nor will I deny feeling a touch of panic when I got to the edge of the gentle eddy water, up to my nipples and spookily lightfooted with my body's buoyancy, and was brushed by the edge of the rapids' violent tongue and sensed the gravel riverbed's sudden downward slant. No heroics were required, though—fortunately, for they'd likely have drowned us both, with the help of those deadweight waders. Mr. Pickwick made one of his mighty, hippo-like surfacings not eight feet upriver from me and only an arm's length outward in the bad tongue-water, and as he sailed logily past I snatched a hold on the collar of his many-pocketed vest and let the current swing him round till he too was in the slack eddy, much as one fishes a lure or a fly in such places. Then I towed him in.

Ashore, he sat crumpled on a big rock and stared wide-eyed at his feet and drank up air in huge, sobbing, grateful gasps. All his pinkness had gone gray-blue, no jauntiness was in sight, and he even seemed less full-fleshed now, shrunken, his wet fringe of gray hair plastered vertically down beside gray ears. Younger Daughter hovered near him and made the subdued cooing sounds she uses with puppies and baby goats, but I stared at the stone cliff across the Brazos through the haze of thin rain, waiting with more than a tinge of embarrassment for his breathing to grow less labored. I had only a snap notion of what this man was like, but it told me he didn't deserve being watched while he was helpless. Maybe no one does.

He said at last, "I never had that happen before."

I said, "It's a pretty tough river when it's up."

"They all are," he answered shortly and breathed a little more, still staring down.

He said, "It was my knees. I was crossing at the head of this chute, coming back downriver. They just buckled in the current and whoosh, by God, there we went."

"We've got your hat," Younger Daughter told him as though she hoped that might set things right.

"Thank you, sweet lady," he said, and smiled as best he could.

"That was some beautiful tackle you lost," I said. "At least I guess it's lost."

"It's lost, all right," said Mr. Pickwick. "Goodbye to it. It doesn't amount to much when you think what I . . ."

But that was a direction I somehow didn't want the talk to take, nor did I think he wanted it to go there either. I was godawfully cold in my soaked, clinging, skimpy clothes and knew he must be even colder, exhausted as he was. I said I wished I had a drink to offer him. He said he appreciated the thought but he could and would offer me one if we could get to his car a quarter-mile down the shore, and I sent Younger Daughter trotting off with his keys to drive it back to where we were. The whiskey was nice sour-mash stuff, though corrosive Skid Row swill would have tasted fine just then. We peeled him out of the deadly waders and got him into some insulated coveralls that were in his car, and after a little he began to pinken up again, but still with the crumpled shrunken look.

He and I talked for a bit, sipping the good whiskey straight from plastic cups. He was a retired grain dealer from Kentucky and what he did mainly now was fish. He and his wife had a travel trailer in which they usually wintered on the Texas coast near Padre Island, where he worked the redfish and speckled trout on the bays with popping gear or sometimes a fly rod when the wind and water were right. Then in February they would start a slow zigzag journey north to bring them home for spring. He'd even fished steelhead in British Columbia—the prettiest of all, he said, the high green wooded mountains dropping steeply to fjords and the cold strong rivers flowing in from their narrow valleys. . . .

When we parted he came as close as he could to saying the thing that neither he nor I wanted him to have to say. He said, "I want . . . Damn, I never had that happen to me before." And stopped. Then he said, "Jesus, I'm glad you were there."

"You'd have been all right," I said. "You were doing fine."

But he shook his strangely shrunken pink head without smiling, and when I turned away he clapped my shoulder and briefly gripped it.

In the pickup as we drove toward home, Younger Daughter was very quiet for a while. I was thinking about the terrible swiftness with which old age could descend, for that was what we'd been watching even if I'd tried not to know it. I felt intensely the health and strength of my own solid body, warmed now by the whiskey and by a fine blast from the pickup's heater fan. If on the whole I hadn't treated it as carefully as I might have over the years, this body, and if in consequence it was a little battered and overweight and had had a few things wrong with it from time to time, it had nonetheless served me and served me well, and was still doing so. It housed whatever brains and abilities I could claim to have and carried out their dictates, and it functioned for the physical things I liked to do, fishing and hunting and country work and the rest. It had been and was a very satisfactory body.

But it was only ten or twelve years younger than the old grain dealer's, at most, and I had to wonder now what sort of sickness or accident or other disruption of function—what buckling of knee, what tremor of hand, what milkiness of vision, what fragility of bone, what thinness of artery wall—would be needed, when the time came to push me over into knowledge that I myself was old. Having to admit it, that was the thing. . . .

Then, with the astonishment the young bring to a recognition that tired, solemn, ancient phrases have meaning, my daughter uttered what I hadn't wanted to hear the old man say. She said, "You saved his life!"

"Maybe so," I said. "We just happened to be on hand."

She was silent for a time longer, staring out the window at the rain that fell on passing fields and woods. Finally she said, "That's a good fish I caught."

"Damn right it is," I said.

Weather

By *Thomas McGuane*

BACK IN THE EARLY SEVENTIES, WHEN I WAS EDITING *SPORTS AFIELD*, I read a piece on permit fishing in *Sports Illustrated* by a name that was new to me at the time, Thomas McGuane. The article was called "The Longest Silence," and its power has stayed with me over the years, through many, many rereadings.

Over the years since, I have not had the opportunity to meet Tom McGuane, despite the fact that many of my friends know him well, and I have only fished with Tom on his printed pages. But what fishing that has been! And novels and short stories that take me places I want to go. Even a movie that he wrote, *The Missouri Breaks*.

McGuane's interest in fishing has never wavered over the years, and his articles have followed his experiences and observations from Alaska to Patagonia. All the while he has continued to produce engaging novels and short stories, and in 1999 a nonfiction collection of stories called *Some Horses* published by The Lyons Press. The ranch life McGuane lives out in Montana furnishes the setting for *Some Horses*, as it has for some of his novels. Also published in 1999, by Knopf, was McGuane's new anthology of fishing stories, *The Longest Silence: A Life In Fishing*.

That McGuane has paid his dues in learning the ropes and tools of flats fishing will be obvious to you when you read my favorite of all bonefish stories. The story exemplifies the kind of prose of which the *New York Times* would someday say, "His sheer writing skill is nothing short of amazing."

Here is a man who can pole a flats boat, saddle and ride a bronc, rope cattle, and then sit down to write what's on his mind with the sensibilities of a true poet. Some other men may be able to do all those things, but there damn sure aren't very many.

— ❧ —

Sitting up in the pilot house, we could see with our own eyes that a serious storm was coming. The Weatherfax hadn't shown a good picture of it the day before, but you could see it on the radar, streaming through above Cuba, across Grand Bahama, and now it was on top of us. Chris went forward to the windlass while Phil laid down another hundred feet of chain between us and the anchor. The slight shifts in the boat's position were revealed in the apparent movement of the sandy bottom under deep, clear, pale-green tropical water. We were on good holding ground. There wasn't really much to worry about though it couldn't help the fishing. And there were the compensations of a tropical squall: the supercharged atmosphere of deep, humid wind, the unpredictable tide slipping through the roots of heaving mangroves. It was interesting weather.

We were in a remote part of the Bahamas, a long way from even the smallest village. There were so many small cays and deep green cuts that if things abated at all, we could get in a lee somewhere and go on looking for fish. Meanwhile, we hung on our anchor, transom directed at the low, broken coast, covered in spindly pines well spaced in their sandy footing by incessant sea winds.

At the last village we'd bought bread from the local bakery. The people were cheerful and smiled quickly. Most had little to do. Their modest gardens were ruled by stingy rainfall; commercial fishing seemed reduced to supplying a hotel or two. The people were scattered along the roads that left the village, strolling or carrying sacks. Coconut palms bowed over the roadway, and as one of my companions said to me, a coconut did not reach a great age here. These pedestrians weren't the first poor natives to roam the luxury home sites of the future.

The boat was owned by a friend of mine, and in his foresight and wisdom she was equipped with good electronics, shipboard refrigeration, and comfortable places to eat and sleep. And she carried two bonefish skiffs in davits. Phil, her captain, also acquitted himself as a cook, and the night we ate all the fresh mangrove snappers or the night we had all the crawfish and black beans illustrated the compensations of life on that part of the South Atlantic, which seems at once a global dropoff and shelf of copious marine life, a buzzing cross-section of the food chain with fishermen briefly at the very top. One could raise the poetry as a nonconsuming naturalist, but who besides the angler crawls to the brook at daybreak or pushes his fragile craft to the head of the tide to come out on the flood with the creatures that breathe the water?

The weather broke and we began to fish, poling the skiffs among the myriad small cays in the fragrance of mangrove blossoms, the ceremony of angling holding our minds on all the proper things. Bananaquits, the active little Bahamian honey creepers, flitted along the sandy shore. At one small cay we disturbed a frigate bird rookery, iridescent black birds, the males adorned with red inflated throats. They pushed off the branches of mature mangroves and soared with the amazing low-altitude slowness that their immense wingspans allowed, practically at a walk. For a moment the skiff seemed surrounded by magnified soot, then they climbed steeply and soared away.

We spotted two nice fish well back in the mangroves in inches of water, their backs out of the water as they scoured around the bases of the bushes for crustaceans. Their silvery brilliance was startling. We stopped the skiff and watched. They didn't seem to want to come out, so I decided to give it a try. I cast the fly into a narrow space between the mangroves and watched the two fish circle toward it. I moved the fly slightly and the first fish darted forward and took. I set the hook and the bonefish roared out of there so fast that for a brief moment the small mangroves swept low by the pressure of my fly line and the fish was off.

At the edge of a turtlegrass flat I hooked a bigger fish that forced a sheet of water up my leader with the speed of the line shearing the water. At about a hundred yards into his run, the hook broke. Now, that's very rare. I chatted less with my companion and more to myself and tried to stare through the water to the bottom or concentrate on the surface for the "nervous water" of approaching schools. We found one right at the edge of the mangroves. I hoped if I could hook one here, it would head for open water. I made a rather long cast that fell just the way it was supposed to. One strip and I was solid tight to a good fish. He ran straight at the boat and I had fly line everywhere as he passed us and stole line, causing it to jump up off the deck in wild coils that were suddenly draped around my head and shoulders. The fish was about to come to the end of this mess. When he did, I felt the strange sensation of my shorts rising rapidly toward my shoulder blades. At the point they came tight in my crotch, the leader broke with a sharp report: The line had hooked the button of my back pocket. My companion was hunched over the push pole in a paroxysm of laughter. I looked at him, I looked at the open sea, I tied on another fly.

I was in that state of mind perhaps not peculiar to angling when things seem to be in a steep curve of deterioration, and I had a fatal sense that I was not at the end of it. Bonefish are ready takers of a well-presented fly but once hooked, they are so explosive that getting rid of slack line and getting the fish on the reel can produce humiliating results. Their speed and power are so far out of proportion to their size that a bonefish, finally landed, seems to have gone through a magical reduction from the brute that burned line off against the shrieking drag to the demure little fellow one holds in one's hand while gently removing the fly. With his big round eyes and friendly face the bonefish scarcely looks guilty of the searing runs he just performed. And the fastest individuals are the ones that look fat, bright little pigs that root around the shallows. They're almost always moving, and if they rest, they prefer to get in among the mangrove shoots where barracuda can't get a straight run at them. Their reactions to anything overhead are instantaneous, so one good way of locating fish is to watch a low-flying cormorant cross the flats; every bonefish touched by the bird's shadow will explode to a new position, then resume feeding. You slip up to where you have seen them move and perhaps you make a connection, the slow-stripped fly line jumping rigid in a bright circle of spray.

After a wonderful meal of roasted razorback hog, garden vegetables, and big in-season Florida tomatoes, I sat up listening to my host's wonderful stories of life in the thirties: training fighting cocks in Bali while recovering from malaria, roading birds from his bicycle, tossing roosters from the balcony of his hotel to the bellhop down below to build up their stamina. Once, when he was waiting to catch the flying boat to the

Orient, his plane was so late that he went to Idaho to learn to skin in the meantime. And I enjoyed his cultural views: "The Italians are my favorite! They adore their little pope! Then they put on their condoms and fuck everything in sight!"

Afterward, I went up on the foredeck and sat next to the windlass to watch the full moon rise. We were in a small tropical sea trapped between the Atlantic and the Caribbean. The Gulf Stream, that great violet river, poured northward just beyond my view, regulating the temperature of the world. Once the moon was up, it appeared as a fixed portion of the universe while the clouds and weather of planet Earth poured over its face. I thought of all the places and times in my amusing life I had looked to a full moon for even one suggestion I could do something with. I thought about John Cheever stating that man made a better traveler than a farmer and how the motion of clouds against the face of the moon always made me crave motion or pine for the sound of waves breaking on an empty shore. Or how Roger Taylor said a boat was meant to improve your position for watching the weather, or how Hemingway said, "Always put in the weather." Weather on the Gulf Stream included the northern gale when we were headed to Cuba on my sloop *Hawksbill*: winds that built the seas up so high that the spreader lights thirty feet above the deck lit the waves from the side, and the big graybeards with their tops blowing off chased us high over the stern until they caught us and knocked us down at three o'clock in the morning. Weather is one of the things that goes on without you, and after a certain amount of living it is bracing to contemplate the many items not dependent upon you for their existence. But tonight the moon shone broadly on the tropical sea. I could make out the radio faintly from the wheelhouse; Reba McEntire, Roseanne Cash, Tammy Wynette, the big girls were out on world airways. I was supremely happy.

I had a good night's sleep. By the time we arose and went hunting fish, I had a healthier view of loose fly line, the messages from the moon, and my place in the universe. It was as if the bonefish were in one room and I was in another: it was just a matter of opening the door in between. And indeed, one nice, round fish, swimming along where a snapper-filled creek poured onto the flat, came to my fly at the end of the long cast. And I landed him.

Listen to this Tale of Woe

By Philip Wylie

THE LATE PHILIP WYLIE WROTE MORE THAN 100 *SATURDAY EVENING Post* stories about the Florida charter-boat fishing captains "Crunch" and "Des" from the 30s into the 50s. Collected into several books, these tales are but a portion of the prodigious literary output of this incredible man. Wylie also wrote straight-forward non-fiction articles and books on his passion for saltwater big game fishing, which he pursued all his life. In addition, he authored several novels and the legendary, iconoclastic *Generation of Vipers*, a non-fiction attack on American hypocrisies.

In the introduction to the collection of her father's best stories, *Crunch & Des, Classic Stories of Saltwater Fishing*, published by Lyons and Burford in 1990, Karen Wylie Pryor references a passage so typical of the kind of writing readers came to expect from a Wylie story. It is a description of a marlin that, in Wylie's words, "bounded out of the water, immense and shocking. Silver and blue. A fish with a bill like a baseball bat and eyes the size of teacups. Enraged."

To select one Philip Wylie story from such an abundance of great tales isn't really fair to the body of his work as a whole. But choosing one is about as close as any editor can ever come to having a sure thing, a cinch to delight readers.

My choice is one that many readers might have missed, since it is not one of the "Crunch and Des" tales. "Listen to this Tale of Woe" originally appeared in *True Magazine*, the publication that first printed many of Wylie's fishing tales and journalistic social barbs.

Fishing is mostly tough luck. "The big ones get away" is its basic slogan. And the bigger the fish an angler seeks, the tougher his misfortune is likely to be. A universal belief that fishermen are philosophers is explained by that circumstance: they have to be. A man unable to take a philosophical attitude toward the tribulations of life certainly couldn't enjoy a sport which requires immense patience, and a sport in which the reward for patience is often a titanic battle ending in utter defeat.

The calamities that may befall an angler who whips a brook trout are fairly limited. He can, to be sure, fall into a deep pool and drown; he can step on a rattlesnake or in a hornet's nest; he can concentrate so hard on a fighting trout that he fails to evade a bull charging across a pasture. (Once, in this last situation, I was obliged to abandon fishing and dive over a barbed-wire fence into a brook to escape a rushing bull.) But when a man takes himself out to sea with vastly heavier gear, he greatly increases the likelihood of misfortune even though he is reasonably safe from bulls, hornets and serpents.

Consider, for example, an expedition made by me many years ago to the famed island of Bimini in the British West Indies. Fishing on the good ship *Neptune*, with Harold Schmidt, a redoubtable guide, I put in a solid week trying for blue marlin. A week becomes a long time, when you rise with the dawn and come back to shore at sunset, when the sea is a daylong brazen glare of tropical sunshine and the brightwork on the boat becomes too hot to touch and when, after seven solid days, you haven't had a single bite. Under such conditions one is likely to grow restless and to reflect that one is spending a great deal of time (not to mention money!) doing exactly nothing in a fairly painful manner.

My mind was running in such a vein when, in the middle of the seventh afternoon, one of the big bonefish baits splashing along from an outrigger was hit suddenly and hard. "Barracuda," Harold yelled from up on the canopy.

A man set for blue marlin is not interested in catching barracudas. They merely spoil baits, as a rule, without becoming hooked—for even a large 'cuda seldom grabs a whole 5-pound bonefish; he snatches perhaps half, cutting it in two.

I had rushed to the heavy rod when the fish splashed at the bait, setting it in the gimbal of the fighting chair. I reeled in the bisected bait so we could put on another. But, as it came near the boat, the 'cuda swiped at it again. So I decided to try to catch the 'cuda as a kind of consolation for days of doing nothing at all. I threw the big reel on free spool—letting the line run out again. The bait drifted back and sank. That was to give the 'cuda plenty of time to pick up the last fragment of bonefish—which contained the hook.

When I thought I'd "dropped back" far enough for the 'cuda to devour the bait, I threw on the drag. There was, in this process, a period of about a fifth of a second in which I did not have a hand on the rod or reel but merely supported the tackle with my knee. One hand was resting on the free-spooling reel as a light brake, to prevent backlash. The other, very briefly, was used to snap on the brake or, as some anglers say to put the reel "in gear."

During that fraction of a second, however, as I got the reel in gear, the line came tight. It tightened, in fact, with a violence and suddenness I had never before experienced. The heavy rod was yanked clear of my knee. I snatched at it and my fingers actually grazed it; a tenth of one second of additional time might have allowed me to get a grip on it. But there wasn't even that extra split instant. The rod leaped from the gimbal. The reel turned over in the air and whacked mightily against the transom in the stern. Then the rod and reel bounced high and seemed to hang suspended in the sunshine for a moment before falling into the *Neptune*'s foamy wake.

I was on my feet at once. I saw the tackle—there was $600 worth of it—settling in the cobalt Gulf Stream. I saw something else presently. A tremendous blue marlin, deep-hooked, surged fifteen feet into the air not fifty feet astern! It made, in the ensuing moments, half a dozen sky-stabbing jumps in the attempt to shake my hook. Failing, it vanished, dragging behind it the $600 worth of tackle. That night I radiophoned to Miami for a new rod, reel and line.

Any marlin fisherman will understand what had happened, and how I had blundered. That marlin had been following my bait, deep down, out of sight, when the 'cuda cut in from the side and hit. Barracuda—and the invisible marlin—had then chased the mutilated bait together as I reeled in. When I dropped back, however, the marlin, not the 'cuda, took the bait. And, having seized it close to our stern, the marlin turned about and headed for parts unknown at full speed.

Just then, just *exactly* then, I'd slapped on the drag—and failed to keep a firm grip on the rod. I could have managed to hold the rod with my knee if the 20- or 30-pound barracuda had been hooked. But the force of 400 or 500 pounds of blue marlin taking off at perhaps 30 miles an hour relieved me of the tackle. We found later that the reel had hit the transom so hard it loosened twelve two-inch screws in mahogany!

Hard luck enough for one trip? Not at all! The very next day on a different rod (we were waiting for more marlin gear to come over by plane that afternoon) I hooked a palpably big fish. Mrs. Wylie, who was fishing beside me, hooked one, also. We fought our double-header (without knowing the identity of the quarry) for about a half hour before we began to see that when her fish ran, mine did, and when I got line back from my fish, she got line; when her fish tore off in a new direction, mine took the same path. So we realized we had both hooked the same fish. That is a fairly common piscatorial hardship and an irritating one, since a catch made on two rods doesn't count as anybody's prize.

After perhaps an hour, we saw our fish—a big hammerhead shark. We weren't interested in catching shark. But we were interested in testing the steel rod which had been sent to me for that purpose by a tackle manufacturer. So my wife deliberately broke her line and I fished alone simply to see how much pressure the rod could stand. It stood a lot. Before long I was working on that shark with my drag screwed up tight, bending way back, like a man shoveling dirt over his head. I expected, of course, to break the line at some point in this experiment—for it was only 15-thread, with (in those days) a breaking strain of 45 pounds.

But it was the rod that ultimately snapped. It snapped with a loud sound when bent almost double. And I felt a sharp pain in my left foot. The hollow steel shaft had broken in two in the middle. I still hung onto the butt. However, while so drastically bent, the rod had acted as a bow, the taut line as a bowstring, and the tip had broken off to become an arrow. The "arrow" was driven down into the top of my foot. It made a circular cut, a cross section of the rod, and only bone stopped the down-thrust. Blood was flowing freely on the Neptune's deck and we put in for shore. To this day I bear a circular scar which looks as if it had been made by a miniature cooky cutter. The shark? In the excitement, or during the subsequent first aid, it got away.

End of bad luck? Not entirely. Two days later I hung another uniden-tified but very large fish and fought it all afternoon through squall-driven rain and past half a dozen roaring waterspouts. Night fell and new squalls appeared. The lights of Bimini were lost to view and we were obliged to break off the fish to avoid disaster—disaster in pitch-black, tempestuous seas which heaved around us and thundered frighteningly over nearby snaggle-toothed coral reefs. On that particular trip, in fact, we caught only a single fish. But, in all fairness, I should add that it was a white mar-lin, taken on light tackle, that it weighed 99 pounds and is still the record in its tackle class for the Rod and Reel Club of Miami Beach.

Experiences of this sort ultimately started a train of thought in my mind. They seem unusual and some are. For instance, I do not know any-body else who's had a broken rod driven partway through his foot. But I saw my brother hurt himself badly (and lose a gigantic jewfish) when his rod broke and the force with which he'd been pulling drove the shattered butt against his forehead hard enough to cut it open. Had the break been an inch lower, he'd have lost an eye. But during the period when I was publicly belittling myself for losing a blue marlin owing to carelessness with a rod, Helen Lerner, one of the world's best big-game fisherwomen, told me that the identical accident had befallen her and that she, too, had contributed an expensive rod and reel to the briny deep. Furthermore, her rod had been sighted—rusted beyond use—a year later, in the reefs off Bimini. The hooked marlin had evidently swum through that area and the trailing tackle had caught in the coral, after which the fish had been able to free itself by pulling out all the line and breaking it.

In fact, whenever I told an angler of my misfortunes, I was told in turn of disasters similar, or greater, or funnier. There was, for example, a member of the above-mentioned club who one day went fly fishing, in waders, on the flats of the Bay of Florida. He dragged in the water behind himself a gunny sack in which he put his fish, with a view to keeping them alive and thus fresh. The sack was tied around his waist so as to leave his hands free. In it, as he waded and cast his flies, he accumulated a nice mess of snappers, groupers, jack and so on.

He was quite surprised when the sack of fish trailing behind him suddenly pulled so hard it sat him down—in about twenty inches of wet ocean. He stood up and was pulled down again. That time, however, he perceived it was neither a miracle nor the combined effort of his caught fish which explained his embarrassment. A very large shark—a shark so big its dorsal fin and back stood well out of water—had taken the fish-filled gunny sack in its mouth. Understandably, though perhaps unwarrantedly, my fellow club member feared his little fishes might be regarded as mere hors d'oeuvres and that he might become the shark's main dish. He therefore untied the rope that attached the sack to his middle and abandoned his catch to the shark. During the time employed by the shark in ripping up the gunny sack, my friend made fast, splashy tracks for shore.

People who go fishing for large tarpon seem to be especially beset by misfortune. Only a few days ago, I read an account of two anglers who were engaged in a serious tarpon duel. It was at first "serious" merely owing to the fact that it involved a large wager on the biggest fish taken. The two competitors angled indecisively for some days and then, minutes apart, each hooked a whopper. One man was fishing in a rowboat; the other fished hard by in the stern of a cruiser.

The man in the small boat had battled his tarpon fairly close to defeat when the tarpon being fought by his colleague jumped aboard. In coming into the dinghy, the tarpon knocked down the embattled angler, damaged his rod and broke his line. Old angling hands would probably have called this "no contest" and continued the duel. But the two gentlemen in question took a different view. The man aboard the cruiser insisted that, even though his fish had jumped into the rowboat, it was "fair caught"—and he won the stakes. The man who was knocked down by it—though he'd lost his own hooked fish—insisted that, since the tarpon had pinwheeled aboard his craft, he had caught it! Newspaper accounts did not give the final decision on this subject—but it certainly constitutes hard luck of a most bizarre sort.

Hard luck! It's the litany of angling! One morning, off Miami, after many days of marlin trolling, a big "blue" rose behind my bait, followed it for a quarter of a mile, and then lunged, bill out, tail cutting the sea to foam. It was a sure strike, the start of a hard strike, a pretty fair bet that we'd hook him. And then, just as the marlin opened his mouth to gulp the bonefish, coming from nowhere, a pelican dived with folded wings, beat the marlin by a foot, and flew off with the bait—until the line came tight and yanked it from the great bird's bill. The marlin, apparently overwhelmed with chagrin at so ignominious an event, made no effort to take a second bonefish we were trolling on the other outrigger. It departed. We saw no more marlin on that expedition.

Among tuna fishermen, a favorite tale of woe concerns the Cat Cay Tuna Tournament where, every year in the spring, some of the ablest and most obdurate deep-sea anglers in the world compete during the annual run of "horse mackerel." The huge fish swim north along the Bahamas edge of the Gulf Stream in large schools, moving close to the surface. It is easy to sight them but often extremely difficult to present them with a bait which they will take. I have stood in the stern of a boat moving fast enough to keep just ahead of schools of 400- and 500-pounders, offering them whole fish as bait and live fish, cut strips of fish, squid, feathers of various colors, and so on—and failed to get a single fish to turn from his group toward any lure.

In so hotly fought a contest as the Cat Cay tourney, a single fish may mean victory. Hence the moment when a tuna is distracted from a school and decides to take a bait is highly important—and tensely dramatic. One year, a contestant who for days had not been able to induce a tuna to hit, finally got a fish to swing away from its migrating brethren. A strike, at long last, was virtually assured. Unfortunately, at that crucial moment, the mate—an intent young man—bent a little too far forward in the effort to view the exciting, smashing hit. He fell overboard directly in front of the fish. Not being a man-eater, the tuna scrammed. And the luckless angler lost his opportunity.

Long ago, as I've said, matters of this sort set me thinking. I had been made, by that time, a director of the corporation which manages the annual fishing tournament of the Miamis, Coral Gables, and surrounding suburbs and towns. This is said to be the biggest fishing derby in the world and so far as I know, the claim has never been contested. After all, there are some 600 odd species of fish in Florida waters, of which most are edible and many are game. These fish are in general abundant. And hundreds of thousands of people annually go in quest of them.

The prizes for the varied game species are valuable and there are several for each sort of fish, as the fishing method and the tackle used determine the classifications of winners. Some anglers fly cast, some bait cast, some use spinning gear and some troll with light lines or the heaviest lines obtainable. As the years had passed I had observed that for every catch which won a prize there were uncountable tales of disaster, ignominy and rugged misfortune.

So, a dozen years ago, I suggested to the tournament committee that these people, valiant even if unsuccessful, should also have a shot at a prize of some sort. There ought to be, I said, a consolation reward for the hapless man or woman or child who had not the biggest fish but rather the toughest luck of the whole tournament. The committeemen, being anglers, took a sympathetic view of the idea, and, ever since, a silver cup has been awarded annually. It is called the Philip Wylie Hard Luck Trophy, and I have never been certain that I liked the connection of my name with misfortune, though I will yield to few in the matter of bad breaks at fishing. This prize is, I believe, the only one of its kind in the world, not a "booby prize" but an award for grim effort in the face of a most hopeless predicament.

People amongst Miami's myriads of tournament entrants "compete" for the Hard Luck Trophy by the following method: if they believe their luck has been spectacularly bad, owing to circumstances surpassing the normal expectation of an informed piscatorial pessimist, they are invited to write out the details of their misfortune. At the end of the tournament, a board judges these accounts (which must be attested by others) and the cup is awarded. Needless to say, the trophy has elicited some somber tales.

For it is tough to win the tough-luck trophy. In fact, it is tough to try to decide, as a yearly judge, whose luck was foulest. For ordinary misfortune doesn't even count in such a contest. Every season, for instance, dozens or scores or perhaps hundreds of people, unused to the routine difficulties of deep-sea angling, enter a hard-luck story without realizing it is a "normal" trial, to the old hand.

Thus, in 1941, the first year of the contest, the cup did not go to applicant R. A. Langley of Milton, Massachusetts. He hung what he at first assumed was the bottom of the sea. But it moved. In fact, it fought so tirelessly and so savagely that his companions in the cruiser began to ask for transportation elsewhere before the unknown monster should be boated. The fish finally showed—a tiger shark, "estimated" at possibly 1,500 pounds and "guaranteed" to go over 1,000. Mr. Langley didn't catch the shark; it finally straightened out his heavy steel hook as if it had been a bent pin—and escaped. But straightened hooks are not regarded by old hands as particular misfortunes—any more than frozen reels.

Many an angler—including your correspondent—has lost a fish that would have been a world record because, during the battle, the cease-less in-and-out running of line under tension gradually spreads apart the flanges of a reel until they jam—or freeze—against the sides.

The final contest for the hard-luck trophy that first year (if memory serves me correctly) was between Mr. Joe Nieser's $100 dinner and Mr. Jim Scully's two-hour world record.

Mr. Nieser, while fishing from the Venetian Causeway (which connects Miami and Miami Beach) caught a 6-pound pompano on very light tackle. An old fishing hand, well aware that the catch was excellent for the gear used, Mr. Nieser carefully weighed his prize on the scales in his tackle box. Then he hurried home. Three guests were due for dinner. In view of the fact that fresh pompano is among the greatest of delicacies, the fish was cut in filets, served, and eaten. During the meal, Mr. Nieser choked. His pompano had not been weighed *officially* and according to the rules. He rushed to the phone. Sure enough, it would have been an all-time tournament record. But it was not even eligible—it was digesting. H. H. Hyman, chairman of the committee, calculated later for the benefit of the anguished Mr. Nieser, that his prize pompano would have been worth more than $100, hence the meal had cost the angler $20 a portion—as well as a tournament record.

Mr. Nieser applied for the hard-luck cup. So did a famed and skillful angler named Jim Scully, whom I happen to know. Jim longed above all things to have his name inscribed on the IGFA world-record rolls. And one afternoon while fishing over the reefs off Florida, he took a 53-pound amberjack on 4/6 tackle—gear hardly heavier than that used by black-bass fishermen in fresh water. Jim kept the IGFA record charts in his tackle box. He scanned them. Sure enough, his catch qualified as a world record! He was being cheered and toasted by his companions on board the fishing cruiser when one of them, a Mr. Bert Harborn, also using 4/6 tackle, hooked another amberjack. It had taken Jim two hours to whip his fish on such light gear; Bert took about as long, only—and it was an important only—his fish weighed 58½ pounds. So Jim's name was not inscribed on the rolls of fame. The unprecedented thing had happened: world record had fallen twice on the same day, from the same boat.

The next year, Sam Holden of Ottawa, Canada, was the chief contender. Mr. Holden hired a charter boat and fared forth innocently to fish. Somewhere off the alabaster skyline of Miami he hung, battled and boated a white marlin which he brought in with elan, weighed and hung on the fish rack for all to see. It weighed 130 pounds. This marlin was bigger than any tournament winner in the previous several years and looked to be a sure first. Word got around on the following morning, however, that Mr. Holden's marlin was ineligible because it had been "mutilated by a shark." Judges rushed to the scene and, sure enough, a pound or so of marlin had been devoured—by what proved to be a stray cat roaming the docks during the night! Mr. Holden's relief was soon dashed. For he found he had caught the marlin on a charterboat that was not eligible to compete in the tournament. So his fish was ruled out. But it was eligible for a different, currently running competition, the George Ruppert Fishing Contest—with a $250 first prize.

This litany of disaster has continued down the years and their annals are crowded with unspeakable misfortune.

There is the case of Ernie Woolfe, a noted angler and a Miami Beach realtor. He took a 10-pound bonita on spinning gear, one day—weighed it and measured it and sent for judges to inspect it and denote it as what it was: a record. Before they arrived (and while Ernie was phoning proudly to his folks) a mate—new to the business—cut the prize up for strip baits! *No* record.

A recent winner of my Hard Luck Trophy didn't catch a fish at all. His name is Norman Theriot. During the 1950 tournament he had found and staked out a spot where some especially large barracuda and jack crevalle hung out. On the last day of the tournament, with very light tackle, Norman, in a skiff, went out to do what he was sure he could: break the records in a class or two. He made one cast, got one enormous strike— and then—because it was a windy morning—some men in the sea in a skiff nearby overturned. One of the men drowned immediately. Norman, by a homeric feat of swimming, of wading in seas that surged over him, of running his own small skiff in surf, rescued the other two, resuscitated them, and finally got aid for them on the lonely beach where he'd brought them ashore. He didn't get a record, but he did get the Hard Luck Cup— and the Carnegie Medal.

Another worthy, fishing on a drawbridge, hung one of those "lost monsters" and fought it for half an hour. Then a bell rang and the drawbridge started up. The man jumped to terra firma and continued his struggle. However, owing to the position of the fish, the river and the canted bridge, his line now sawed back and forth across a lamp post. Finally it was frayed in two—and the fish escaped.

In the record is another yet more somber tale. An angler caught a world-record tarpon while fly fishing from the bank of some nameless Florida estuary. He slew the fish, weighed it on his own scales, noted it went several pounds over the current record, and set it in the shade while he continued his sport. When the sun sank, he went back to the spot to retrieve his prize—and found its tail vanishing between the jaws of a large alligator!

Lines that lead from busy anglers to desperate fish and run out for 300 or 400 yards are often cut by the prows of majestic freighters which plow south along the golden sands of Miami's shore, just inside the north-racing Gulf Stream. But one of the saddest stories I ever heard concerned a nameless Keys gladiator who was casting in the old days from a trestle on the railroad line that once ran to Key West. Inadvertently, he let his backcast dribble into the sea. It was thereupon seized by a big tarpon. He whirled about to give battle—and stepped back quietly. A Florida East Coast train was bearing down, whistling. The gentleman's line was parted by its locomotive!

Then I recall the case of the fellow who went fishing and was *himself* caught. There were three men in the skiff—plug casting. One of them, Tom Dupree, a Miami pioneer and realtor (real-estate men seem to get mixed up often in these events) gave a mighty swing and planted all three of the triple-hook gangs on his plug in the scalp of a companion. The leader was cut. It was seen that a long trip back to the cruiser and a certain amount of minor surgery by another member of the party (who, luckily, was a doctor) would be required. But the thrice-hooked angler insisted that the blow had deadened his nerves and that he felt no pain. So he went on fishing the rest of the afternoon—and won all the bets of that day. Mr. Dupree insists the man won all wagers, owing to the fact that the plug, dangling from his skull, "flashing like a Christmas-tree ball and jingling with every cast," unnerved everybody else and spoiled their skill. Possibly so. Anyhow, it didn't hurt. I should know—I was the guy caught.

The Intruder

By Robert Traver

"Nick did not like to fish with other men on the river," Ernest Hemingway wrote in "Big Two-Hearted River." "Unless they were of your party, they spoiled it."

The secret fear that lurks at the heart of every trout angler is of paradise that might be lost—good fishing in seclusion, so hard to come by that it requires guarding desperately if it is to survive the onslaught of the crowds. Finding and fishing "secret" trout waters, streams, and ponds that beckon like some angling El Dorado in the backcountry, is a theme that occurs often in the angling works of Robert Traver, the pen name of the late John Voelker. A Michigan attorney and judge, Voelker both fished and wrote passionately. He loved old fishing cars that could hack it in the bush, brook trout, small rivers and ponds, his buddies, and "bourbon out of an old tin cup."

"The Intruder" is from his first book of trout pieces, *Trout Madness*, and is justifiably famous, having been included in several anthologies. Our publisher, Nick Lyons, had the privilege of publishing Judge Voelker's second fishing anthology, *Trout Magic*, and it was my own distinct pleasure to run some of those stories at *Sports Afield* when I was editor there. Judge Voelker's professional background provided the basis of the best-selling novel, *Anatomy of a Murder* (by Robert Traver), which was made into a successful and popular movie with James Stewart in the leading role.

$\sim$

It was about noon when I put down my fly rod and sculled the little cedar boat with one hand and ate a sandwich and drank a can of beer with the other, just floating and enjoying the ride down the beautiful broad main Escanaba River. Between times I watched the merest speck of an eagle tacking and endlessly wheeling far up in the cloudless sky. Perhaps he was stalking my sandwich or even, dark thought, stalking me. . . . The fishing so far had been poor; the good trout simply weren't rising. I rounded a slow double bend, with high gravel banks on either side, and there stood a lone fisherman—the first person I had seen in hours. He was standing astride a little feeder creek on a gravel point on the left downstream side, fast to a good fish, his glistening rod hooped and straining, the line taut, the leader vibrating and sawing the water, the fish itself boring far down out of sight.

Since I was curious to watch a good battle and anxious not to interfere, I eased the claw anchor over the stern—*plop*—and the little boat hung there, gurgling and swaying from side to side in the slow deep current. The young fisherman either did not hear me or, hearing, and being a good one, kept his mind on his work. As I sat watching he shifted the rod to his left hand, shaking out his right wrist as though it were asleep, so I knew then that the fight had been a long one and that this fish was no midget. The young fisherman fumbled in his shirt and produced a cigarette and lighter and lit up, a real cool character. The fish made a sudden long downstream run and the fisherman raced after him, prancing through the water like a yearling buck, gradually coaxing and working him back up to the deeper slow water across from the gravel bar. It was a nice job of handling and I wanted to cheer. Instead I coughed discreetly and he glanced quickly upstream and saw me.

"Hi," he said pleasantly, turning his attention back to his fish.

"Hi," I answered.

"How's luck?" he said, still concentrating.

"Fairish," I said. "But I haven't raised anything quite like you seem to be on to. How you been doin'—otherwise, I mean?"

"Fairish," he said. "This is the third good trout in this same stretch—all about the same size."

"My, my," I murmured, thinking ruefully of the half-dozen-odd barely legal brook trout frying away in my sun-baked creel. "Guess I've just been out floating over the good spots."

"Pleasant day for a ride, though," he said, frowning intently at his fish.

"Delightful," I said wryly, taking a slow swallow of beer.

"Yep," the assured young fisherman went on, expertly feeding out line as his fish made another downstream sashay. "Yep," he repeated, nicely taking up slack on the retrieve, "that's why I gave up floating this lovely river. Nearly ten years ago, just a kid. Decided then 'twas a hell of a lot more fun fishing a hundred yards of her carefully than taking off on these all-day floating picnics."

I was silent for a while. Then: "I think you've got something there," I said, and I meant it. Of course he was right, and I was simply out joy-riding past the good fishing. I should have brought along a girl or a camera. On this beautiful river if there was no rise a float was simply an enforced if lovely scenic tour. If there was a rise, no decent fisherman ever needed to float. Presto, I now had it all figured out. . . .

"Wanna get by?" the poised young fisherman said, flipping his cigarette into the water.

"I'll wait," I said. "I got all day. My pal isn't meeting me till dark—'way down at the old burned logging bridge."

"Hm ... trust you brought your passport—you really are out on a voyage," he said. "Perhaps you'd better slip by, fella—by the feel of this customer it'll be at least ten-twenty minutes more. Like a smart woman in the mood for play, these big trout don't like to be rushed. C'mon, just bear in sort of close to me, over here, right under London Bridge. It won't bother us at all."

My easy young philosopher evidently didn't want me to see how really big his fish was. But being a fisherman myself I knew, I knew. "All right," I said, lifting the anchor and sculling down over his way and under his throbbing line. "Thanks and good luck."

"Thanks, chum," he said, grinning at me. "Have a nice ride and good luck to you."

"Looks like I'll need it," I said, looking enviously back over my shoulder at his trembling rod tip. "Hey," I said, belatedly remembering my company manners, "want a nice warm can of beer?"

Smiling: "Despite your glowing testimonial, no thanks."

"You're welcome," I said, realizing we were carrying on like a pair of strange diplomats.

"And one more thing, please," he said, raising his voice a little to be heard over the burbling water, still smiling intently at his straining fish. "If you don't mind, please keep this little stretch under your hat—it's been all mine for nearly ten years. It's really something special. No use kidding you—I see you've spotted my bulging creel and I guess by now you've got a fair idea of what I'm on to. And anyway I've got to take a little trip. But I'll be back—soon I hope. In the meantime try to be good to the place. I know it will be good to you."

"Right!" I shouted, for by then I had floated nearly around the downstream bend. "Mum's the word." He waved his free hand and then was blotted from view by a tall doomed spruce leaning far down out across the river from a crumbling water-blasted bank. The last thing I saw was the gleaming flash of his rod, the long taut line, the strumming leader. It made a picture I've never forgotten.

That was the last time ever that I floated the Big Escanaba River. I had learned my lesson well. Always after that when I visited this fabled new spot I hiked in, packing my gear, threading my way down river though a pungent needled maze of ancient deer trails, like a fleeing felon keeping always slyly away from the broad winding river itself. My strategy was twofold: to prevent other sly fishermen from finding and deflowering the place, and to save myself an extra mile of walking.

Despite the grand fishing I discovered there, I did not go back too often. It was a place to hoard and save, being indeed most good to me, as advertised. And always I fished it alone, for a fisherman's pact had been made, a pact that became increasingly hard to keep as the weeks rolled into months, the seasons into years, during which I never again encountered my poised young fisherman. In the morbid pathology of trout fishermen such a phenomenon is mightily disturbing. What had become of my fisherman? Hadn't he ever got back from his trip? Was he sick or had he moved away? Worse yet, had he died? How could such a consummate young artist have possibly given up fishing such an enchanted spot? Was he one of that entirely mad race of eccentric fishermen who cannot abide the thought of sharing a place, however fabulous, with even one other fisherman?

By and by, with the innocent selfishness possessed by all fishermen, I dwelt less and less upon the probable fate of my young fisherman and instead came smugly to think it was I who had craftily discovered the place. Nearly twenty fishing seasons slipped by on golden wings, as fishing seasons do, during which time I, fast getting no sprightlier, at last found it expedient to locate and hack out a series of abandoned old logging roads to let me drive within easier walking distance of my secret spot. The low cunning of middle age was replacing the hot stamina of youth. . . . As a road my new trail was strictly a spring-breaking bronco-buster, but at least I was able to sit and ride, after a fashion, thus saving my aging legs for the real labor of love to follow.

Another fishing season was nearly done when, one afternoon, brooding over that gloomy fact, I suddenly tore off my lawyer-mask and fled my office, heading for the Big Escanaba, bouncing and bucking my way in, finally hitting the Glide—as I had come to call the place—about sundown. For a long time I just stood there on the high bank, drinking in the sights and pungent river smells. No fish were rising, and slowly, lovingly, I went through the familiar ritual of rigging up: scrubbing out a fine new leader, dressing the tapered line, jointing the rod and threading the line, pulling on the tall patched waders, anointing myself with fly dope. No woman dressing for a ball was more fussy. . . . Then I composed myself on my favorite fallen log and waited. I smoked a slow pipe and sipped a can of beer, cold this time, thanks to the marvels of dry ice and my new road. My watching spot overlooked a wide bend and commanded a grand double view: above, the deep slow velvet glide with its little feeder stream where I first met my young fisherman; below a sporty and productive broken run of white water stretching nearly a half-mile. The old leaning spruce that used to be there below me had long since bowed in surrender and been swept away by some forgotten spring torrent. As I sat waiting the wind had died, the shadowing waters had taken on the brooding blue hush of evening, the dying embers of sundown suddenly lit a great blazing forest fire in the tops of the tall spruces across river from me, and an unknown bird that I have always called simply the "lonely" bird sang timidly its ancient haunting plaintive song. I arose and took a deep breath like a soldier advancing upon the enemy.

The fisherman's mystic hour was at hand.

First I heard and then saw a young buck in late velvet slowly, tentatively splashing his way across to my side, above me and beyond the feeder creek, ears twitching and tall tail nervously wigwagging. Then he winded me, freezing in midstream, giving me a still and liquid stare for a poised instant; then came charging on across in great pawing incredibly graceful leaps, lacquered flanks quivering, white flag up and waving, bounding up the bank and into the anonymous woods, the sounds of his excited blowing fading and growing fainter and then dying away.

In the meantime four fair trout had begun rising in the smooth tail of the glide just below me. I selected and tied on a favorite small dry fly and got down below the lowest riser and managed to take him on the first cast, a short dainty float. Without moving I stood and lengthened line and took all four risers, all nice firm brook trout upwards of a foot, all the time purring and smirking with increasing complacency. The omens were good. As I relit my pipe and waited for new worlds to conquer I heard a mighty splash above me and wheeled gaping at the spreading magic ring of a really good trout, carefully marking the spot. Oddly enough he had risen just above where the young buck had just crossed, a little above the feeder creek. Perhaps, I thought extravagantly, perhaps he was after the deer. . . . I waited, tense and watchful, but he did not rise again.

I left the river and scrambled up the steep gravelly bank and made my way through the tall dense spruces up to the little feeder creek. I slipped down the bank like a footpad, stealthily inching my way out to the river in the silted creek itself, so as not to scare the big one, my big one. I could feel the familiar shock of icy cold water suddenly clutching at my ankles as I stood waiting at the spot where I had first run across my lost fisherman. I quickly changed to a fresh fly in the same pattern, carefully snubbing the knot. Then the fish obediently rose again, a savage easy engulfing roll, again the undulant outgoing ring, just where I had marked him, not more than thirty feet from me and a little beyond the middle and obliquely upstream. Here was, I saw, a cagey selective riser, lord of his pool, and one who would not suffer fools gladly. So I commanded myself to rest him before casting. "Twenty-one, twenty-two, twenty-three . . ." I counted.

The cast itself was indecently easy and, finally releasing it, the little Adams sped out on its quest, hung poised in mid-air for an instant, and then settled sleepily upon the water like a thistle, uncurling before the leader like the languid outward folding of a ballerina's arm. The fly circled a moment, uncertainly, then was caught by the current. Down, down it rode, closer, closer, then—clap!—the fish rose and kissed it, I flicked my wrist and he was on, and then away he went roaring off downstream, past feeder creek and happy fisherman, the latter hot after him.

During the next mad half-hour I fought this explosive creature up and down the broad stream, up and down, ranging at least a hundred feet each way, or so it seemed, without ever once seeing him. This meant, I figured, that he was either a big brown or a brook. A rainbow would surely have leapt a dozen times by now. Finally I worked him into the deep safe water off the feeder creek where he sulked nicely while I panted and rested my benumbed rod arm. As twilight receded into dusk with no sign of his tiring I began vaguely to wonder just who had latched on to whom. For the fifth or sixth time I rested my aching arm by transferring the rod to my left hand, professionally shaking out my tired wrist just as I had once seen a young fisherman do.

Nonchalantly I reached in my jacket and got out and tried to light one of my rigidly abominable Italian cigars. My fish, unimpressed by my show of aplomb, shot suddenly away on a powerful zigzag exploratory tour upstream, the fisherman nearly swallowing his unlit cigar as he scrambled up after him. It was then that I saw a lone man sitting quietly in a canoe, anchored in midstream above me. The tip of his fly rod showed over the stern. My heart sank: after all these years my hallowed spot was at last discovered.

"Hi," I said, trying to convert a grimace of pain into an amiable grin, all the while keeping my eye on my sulking fish. The show must go on.

"Hi," he said.

"How you doin'?" I said, trying to make a brave show of casual fish talk.

"Fairish," he said, "but nothing like you seem to be on to."

"Oh, he isn't so much," I said, lying automatically if not too well. "I'm working a fine leader and don't dare to bull him." At least that was the truth.

The stranger laughed briefly and glanced at his wrist watch. "You've been on to him that I know of for over forty minutes—and I didn't see you make the strike. Let's not try to kid the Marines. I just moved down a bit closer to be in on the finish. I'll shove away if you think I'm too close."

"Nope," I answered generously, delicately snubbing my fish away from a partly submerged windfall. "But about floating this lovely river," I pontificated, "there's nothing in it, my friend. Absolutely nothing. Gave it up myself eighteen-twenty years ago. Figured out it was better working one stretch carefully than shoving off on these floating picnics. Recommend it to you, comrade."

The man in the canoe was silent. I could see the little red moon of his cigarette glowing and fading in the gathering gloom. Perhaps my gratuitous pedagogical ruminations had offended him; after all, trout fishermen are a queer proud race. Perhaps I should try diversionary tactics. "Wanna get by?" I inquired silkily. Maybe I could get him to go away before I tried landing this unwilling porpoise. He still remained silent. "Wanna get by?" I repeated. "It's perfectly O.K. by me. As you see—it's a big roomy river."

"No," he said dryly. "No thanks." There was another long pause. Then: "If you wouldn't mind too much I think I'll put in here for the night. It's getting pretty late—and somehow I've come to like the looks of this spot."

"Oh," I said in a small voice—just "Oh"—as I disconsolately watched him lift his anchor and expertly push his canoe in to the near gravelly shore, above me, where it grated halfway in and scraped to rest. He sat there quietly, his little neon cigarette moon glowing, and I felt I just had to say something more. After all I didn't own the river. "Why sure, of course, it's a beautiful place to camp, plenty of pine knots for fuel, a spring-fed creek for drinking water and cooling your beer," I ran on gaily, rattling away like an hysterical realtor trying to sell the place. Then I began wondering how I would ever spirit my noisy fish car out of the woods without the whole greedy world of fishermen learning about my new secret road to this old secret spot. Maybe I'd even have to abandon it for the night and hike out. . . . Then I remembered there was an uncooperative fish to be landed, so I turned my full attention to the unfinished and uncertain business at hand. "Make yourself at home," I lied softly.

"Thanks," the voice again answered dryly, and again I heard the soft chuckle in the semidarkness.

My fish had stopped his mad rushes now and was busily boring the bottom, the long leader vibrating like the plucked string of a harp. For the first time I found I was able gently to pump him up for a cautious look. And again I almost swallowed my still unlit stump of cigar as I beheld his dorsal fin cleaving the water nearly a foot back from the fly. He wallowed and shook like a dog and then rolled on his side, then recovered and fought his way back down and away on another run, but shorter this time. With a little pang I knew then that my fish was a done, but the pang quickly passed—it always did—and again I gently, relentlessly pumped him up, shortening line, drawing him in the familiar daisy hoop of landing range, kneeling and stretching and straining out my opposing aching arms like those of an extravagant archer. The net slipped fairly under him on the first try and, clenching my cigar, I made my pass and lo! lifted him free and dripping from the water. "Ah-h-h . . . " He was a glowing superb spaniel-sized brown. I staggered drunkenly away from the water and sank anywhere to the ground, panting like a winded miler.

"Beautiful, *beautiful*," I heard my forgotten and unwelcome visitor saying like a prayer. "I've dreamed all this—over a thousand times I've dreamed it."

I tore my feasting eyes away from my fish and glowered up at the intruder. He was half standing in the beached canoe now, one hand on the side, trying vainly to wrest the cap from a bottle, of all things, seeming in the dusk to smile uncertainly. I felt a sudden chill sense of concern, of vague nameless alarm.

"Look, chum," I said, speaking lightly, very casually, "is everything all O.K.?"

"Yes, yes, of course," he said shortly, still plucking away at his bottle. "There . . . I—I'm coming now."

Bottle in hand he stood up and took a resolute broad step out of the canoe, then suddenly, clumsily he lurched and pitched forward, falling heavily, cruelly, half in the beached canoe and half out upon the rocky wet shore. For a moment I sat staring ruefully, then I scrambled up and started running toward him, still holding my rod and the netted fish, thinking this fisherman was indubitably potted. "No, no, no!" he shouted at me, struggling and scrambling to his feet in a kind of wild urgent frenzy. I halted, frozen, holding my sagging dead fish as the intruder limped toward me, in a curious sort of creaking stiffly mechanical limp, the uncorked but still intact bottle held triumphantly aloft in one muddy wet hand, the other hand reaching gladly toward me.

"Guess I'll never get properly used to this particular battle stripe," he said, slapping his thudding and unyielding right leg. "But how are you, stranger?" he went on, his wet eyes glistening, his bruised face smiling. "How about our having a drink to your glorious trout—and still another to reunion at our old secret fishing spot?"

The Music of the Spheres

By John Gierach

BEGINNING WITH *TROUT BUM* IN 1986, JOHN GIERACH'S BOOKS HAVE been snapped up by the reading public like "daiquiris in hell," as Ernest Hemingway once described how his *For Whom the Bell Tolls* was selling. Before he wrote *Trout Bum*, Gierach had written *Fishing the High Country*, a fine book, delivering everything the title promises, written in the straightforward style of most outdoor-subject books of that time. But *Trout Bum* was something different. Here was a rollicking, free-spirited account of a man's fishing passions without a single promise to teach the reader a thing. Gierach decided to let the chips fall where they may and to mine the ground few others had bothered to work: Storytelling, as opposed to teaching. If the reader picked up some useful information along the way, that was fine too.

The Gierach style that emerged in *Trout Bum* has continued through *The View From Rat Lake* (from which this story is taken), *Dances With Trout*, *Where the Trout Are All As Long As Your Leg* (published by Nick Lyons), and others. While most of John Gierach's stories are based on trout fishing, there are some on bass, panfish, grayling, and other species. This tale of bass fishing on ponds with fly rods and float tubes belongs among the best things I've ever read about bass fishing. "Trout Bum" that he is, John Gierach knows a good thing when he tries to catch it, and as you will see here he is certainly no stranger on bass waters.

It's toward the end of May; shirtsleeve warm most days, but still cold— rather than "cool"—as night comes on. The cottonwoods, willows, and dogwoods are leafed out and some grasses are up, but it all looks new and almost edibly tender. The efficient, hard greens of summer are yet to come; it will happen imperceptibly, but one day there it will be. Great Blue herons fish in the shallows, and a few Canada geese are still on the nests, though most are now out on the ponds towing dirty yellow goslings behind them.

You've been fishing the warm water for a month now, having been skunked, or nearly so, the first few times out. But that's part of it. The spawning of the bass and panfish starts early. Well, not "early," really; exactly on time, in fact, but sooner in the year than you have ever been able to get used to.

It's a holdover from childhood, reinforced by outdoor photography and magazine stories. This kind of fishing is supposed to take place in hot weather, complete with mosquitos, but when you look at your slides of past seasons, you see your friends in jackets and wool hats standing among brown cattails catching bluegills.

The spawning bluegills are easy. They'll hit any wet fly, nymph, or streamer they can get their small mouths around. All you have to do is find them, and that's not too hard, either. They spawn in the same spots season after season, and you've been fishing these ponds for many years.

The largemouth bass are on the beds at about the same time, and, although it's not quite like shooting fish in a barrel as some say, they can be found and they can be caught. There's some debate over the ethics of this. Some say spawning fish should be left alone ("How would you like it?"), but you have yet to make your mind up on that one. In a sense it does seem unfair, but then you've been told by warm-water fisheries managers that bass seldom spawn successfully here in Colorado because of the skittish, fitful spring weather. The water warms, but then a cold front comes in and it cools down again. Or it snows, or cold snow-melt water pours in, or something. A change of only a few degrees can, and often does, kill the eggs. Most Colorado bass fisheries are put-and-take in one way or another. The fish are residents of these ponds and plenty wild enough, but few were actually born here.

From a management point of view, it's okay, but usually after a few trips you begin to feel cheap taking them off the beds like that, even though you're releasing them. They fight sluggishly, seeming puzzled, or maybe even resigned, and they don't even hit from aggressiveness so much as from a kind of housecleaning instinct. You cast a fly onto the bed and the fish picks it up to move it out.

Among these bass are some of the biggest examples of the species you'll see all year, but once you've seen a few, it's enough. You return to the bluegills, who nail a fly harder in the spring than at any other time of year, taking them on the 2-weight rod so they can show off. Then you hunt up some pumpkinseeds for no other reason than that they're so pretty. Sometimes they're in with the bluegills, but you know of two places where they'll be off by themselves.

This is all near shore, including the bass, but then you climb into the float tube and go looking for the crappies spawning in deeper water. This is a bit more cerebral, since you're no longer sight-fishing to fish you can clearly see, but working deep, maybe even with a sink-tip line, in up to eight feet of water. The fly is a size 6 Weedless Wooley in bright yellow; a new pattern, but an old idea. "Crappies like yellow," everyone's granddad used to say, and all those grandpas were right. Maybe they were right about a lot of things, but that's the one that has stayed with you.

It's spring and everything is mating. Remember the lady biologist you met out here once who was busy studying the sex habits of the frogs? She explained how the males just jump on anything, trying one thing and then another until something submits. And then she gave you that look that seemed to say, "Just like you, right?"

But forget about sexual tension for the moment. As if there were some justice, the first fishing of the season is predictable and it's here. It's almost as if there were some reward for having come through the winter without wigging out. It was a long winter of working, tying flies and watching crooked and/or stupid politicians on television. At one point you caught yourself feeling sorry for anyone in government who made a practice of telling the truth because there's no good reason to believe him. You found yourself missing Jimmy Carter. Remember that interview?

"What are you going to do now, Mr. President?"

"I think I'm going to learn to be a really good fly-fisherman."

You understood that to be significantly different than just saying, "I'm going to go fishing."

Now, regardless of the placement of the equinox on the calendar, it has become summer. The fish have finished their reproductive business and have moved out of the shallows. They're hungry, and, as luck would have it, lots of things to eat have recently been born.

They'll lurk in the deeper water during the heat of the day, feeding casually as opportunities present themselves. They can be caught then, but it's a lazy, time-consuming kind of fishing. Not bad at all, you understand. In fact, there are days when you're genuinely up for it.

You settle in the belly boat under a wide-brimmed hat. Between the chapeau, full beard, and sunglasses, the only part of your face that's exposed to the sun is your nose, and this you slather with suntan lotion—the waterproof kind. With better than half of you beneath the water line, you'll stay pleasantly cool.

The selection of a streamer takes what would appear, to an observer, to be some thought, but "thought" isn't quite the right word. You gaze into the streamer box, which, because it's early in the season, is still nearly full of flies, looking for some sign. Bright colors with lots of wafting marabou and tinsel to catch the light? Or maybe a more sedate, more lifelike eel or bucktail bait fish pattern? How about the meaty, mechanical-looking weedless crawdad? Maybe the rubber worm copy tied with the six-inch strip of rabbit skin.

There have been days when the right fly seemed to crawl from the box into your hand saying, "I'm the one," and there were days when it was right, but this time none of them speak. Nothing you know—or suspect—about bass clicks with anything you know about fly tying, so you fall back on "bright day, bright fly." That's something else a lot of grandpas used to say.

You pick a big one because, well, because what the hell? The same reason you used when you chose a small one last time. What you're trying to do is tempt intuition into your corner, even though intuition seems to have stopped off for a few drinks today.

The leader tippet is 2x (6-pound test) just in case. The big bass are rare, but they're here—somewhere. You could reasonably go even heavier, perhaps, but even the 2x muffles the action of the fly. You used a streamer with lots of marabou so that the breathing of the materials might make up for the wire-stiff leader. This is only logic, but it might attract a real insight.

Much is made of logic in fly-fishing these days, especially when it comes to trout, but the bass-fisherman is still often faced with trying to decide whether his fish will eat a red and white thing as opposed to a bright yellow thing when there's no discernible reason why he should bite either.

During the course of fly selection you and your belly boat have drifted out from shore. The light from the blue sky is flat and shadowless, and the surface of the water shows not a single crease from any movement of the air. Still, you have somehow drifted ten feet and would, if you sat perfectly still in the belly boat, apparently end up on the far bank in an hour or so. The pace of fishing at midday is a little quicker than that, but not much.

The cast is made quartering off to the northwest, toward the deeper water. The weighted fly lands with an audible "blip," pulling the leader down with it as it sinks in the clear water. The monofilament leaves the top in jerks as a section of it hangs up on the surface film until the increasing angle of the descending fly pulls it under. You should have thought to rub it with mud while you were still close enough to shore to get a handful. Then again, what's the hurry?

You watch the leader, knowing that a bass will sometimes be taken with curiosity about a slowly sinking fly and hit it. Or maybe—more likely, in fact—a kittenish young panfish with a mouth too small to take the hook will give it a tug. The fruitless noodling of a baby bluegill can affect the leader in the same way as the mouthing of a five-pound bass. The times when you strike and miss, you assume it was the former, but you're never sure.

With the leader sunk almost to the tip of the floating fly line, you begin to paddle the flippers, very slowly. You'll troll down the deep slot at the laziest speed possible; just enough to keep the fly moving. The bottom here is no more than ten feet down, with the weed tops closer yet to the surface. You want the supposedly weedless streamer to go just into the vegetation where a little bait fish would hide. There are no natural contours to the bottom here, just what was left by the steamshovels that took the gravel out decades ago, but there's a kind of logic to that, too. You'll troll about 200 yards down the slot to the south, then back to the north, then take the arm pointing pretty much west, and then back to where you are now. If it takes less than an hour, you're going too fast.

With the sun high and the weather hot, the bass are sulking in the places that are the most comfortable for them. They're waiting for things to be more to their liking and are probably in something of a funk. You try to picture it in terms you can understand. Imagine yourself when you're like that. You will not respond positively to razzle-dazzle, but a needling suggestion—that could work.

Thinking "Slowly," you begin up the pond. There are geese and some coots in the water with you, seemingly unconcerned with your presence as long as you're at a safe distance. The heron was a different story; being one of the spookiest of birds, he heaved off on his great, long wings as soon as you came in sight. That's why waterfowl hunters use copies of them as confidence decoys. Supposedly ducks know that, too.

The original plan for today had been to meet two belly boating friends here at about five in the afternoon for a few hours of bass bugging. It had, however, been one of those late spring/early summer afternoons when warm weather was still a fresh and joyous thing tugging at your mammalian consciousness. The fishing gear had been assembled and loaded in the truck by lunchtime. That left four and a half hours before it would be time to leave. There was plenty of work to do, but with this virulent a case of pond fever, it would have taken you that long to get comfortable in the desk chair.

On the drive out to the ponds, threading the dirt county roads away from the foothills and out onto the flatlands, you decided it would be a good idea to be on the water at something less than the ideal time of day for fishing. Instead of just arriving at the right moment (and congratulating yourself on your exquisite sense of timing) you would be able to watch it evolve from the bright, siesta doldrums of midday to those hours just before and after sunset when the fish, as they say, "move." You tell yourself it will be both educational and spiritually uplifting, as all imaginative excuses for goofing off are.

A few hours after you first stepped into the water, you're back on shore using the belly boat as an easy chair. The chest waders are rolled down below your knees so you can air out a bit. Neoprene waders are great for belly boating—streamlined and comfortable—but you *can* get a little ripe in them. It's suppertime: a half-hour rest break, the high points of which are a sandwich, apple, candy bar, and several long, luxurious slugs of water from the canteen. A cup of coffee would hit the spot, but the truck, with the camp stove and coffee pot, is parked nearly a mile away.

That, in fact, is one of the things that makes this your favorite pond. Of all the odd little bodies of water here, this is the farthest one from where you have to leave the car. It's not unusual to be alone on it, at least during the week, which is considerably more than can be said for what are known as the "front ponds." It's nameless, but you and your friends have come to call it The Bass Pond so as to distinguish it from all the other bass ponds.

Speaking of bass, you managed to take three little ones and one about a foot long while trolling; more than you expected. Then you switched to a size 12 Hares Ear Soft Hackle and took some small bluegills. After that it was break time, so you'd be fresh when your friends arrived. They're due in a half-hour, which means they should have been here by now. Any second now they'll be coming over the rise through the tall grass with float tubes strapped to their backs.

Soon the pond will move into its evening program. The bass and the larger panfish will come out of the deep water to nose into the shallows. This they'll do to the music of the spheres—the turning of the planet that drops the sun, slants the light, cools the water, and brings the fish to the surface. The catching of the first fish of the day on a floating bug is an ordinary, predictable event that still has a certain cosmic significance.

Your friends arrive, talking and waving in anticipation. They can see you came early and have been fishing. They understand and approve of this, calling you a sneaky son of a bitch and accusing you of spooking the pond, before they ask how you did.

"Got a couple," you say in your best understated Gary Cooper drawl, avoiding their eyes so as to give the impression that it was actually more than "a couple," but you're too modest to brag. It's a standard working man's gambit that stops short of actually lying and always works.

Your friends hustle into waders and flippers and string up their fly rods as you casually clip the still wet, plastered streamer from your leader and hang it on the drying patch, threading it deeply into the sheepskin. The only disadvantage to barbless hooks is that they'll sometimes jiggle loose from things like drying patches and hatbands to vanish into that yawning void where lost flies go.

You tell yourself you'll put the streamer back in the box where it belongs as soon as it's completely dry—maybe in an hour or so—while noticing that the drying patch holds at least a dozen flies left over from last season.

From this collection you pick a little pencil popper. It's a size 6, store-bought job with a long, thin, cork body, feather tails, and long rubber legs. The back of it is painted in a kind of frog spot pattern with eyes. You had just about given up on bugs like this, figuring that the fish can't see what's on the top anyway; that it's just a bit of fanciness designed to catch fishermen. But then there was that study, the one that said the bug resting on the surface bent the surface film in toward it, refracting the light so that the fish would see the bottom of the bug as it actually was with the top lying in a sort of halo around it. It could be true, and the bugs *are* real pretty.

This is such a standard bug for you now that you finally broke down and ordered several dozen of them, in assorted fancy color schemes, from the factory where they're made in Ohio. They're hard to find out here in the West. It's considered a panfish bug, but that, it took you almost ten years to realize, is little more than a matter of nomenclature. Bass like them. In fact, they prefer them to the larger bugs so often that you've begun to change your ideas about fly-fishing for largemouths.

The smaller bug is more like what the fish would be eating on a day-to-day basis. We like to think of bass waiting with ominous, predatory composure for the opportunity to eat a muskrat, but they couldn't actually do that, could they? They have to eat what comes along, and this thing splits the difference between damselfly, dragonfly, grasshopper, moth, and baby frog.

Also, you have begun to think, eating these things involves less of a commitment—less of a *decision*—from the bass than attacking a bullfrog or duckling. The fish seem to take them more casually and sooner, too;

after less teasing. The biggest bass you've seen caught in this state—about 8 pounds—was taken on a popper a size smaller than the one you've just tied on your leader. It wasn't taken by you, of course, but by a friend you loaned a fly to. Sure, it was your idea and your fly, but he caught the big fish. Remember, fairness is a human idea largely unknown in nature.

The three of you waddle down to the water and cast off into the pond in your tubes. It is still what most would call "daytime," but the shadows of the cottonwood grove where the owl lives are leaning into the pond, and, although the air hasn't cooled enough for you to wiggle into the sweater yet, it is about to cool, and that gives you the intellectual equivalent of a slight chill. The social chatter is over now. From here on out, the talk between you will be technical and, with any luck, congratulatory.

When the fleet was launched, you just happened to be in the middle, and your partners now naturally peel off to the left and right, leaving you headed for your favorite weed bed. It angles out from the cattail marsh along a spit of gravelly sand that drops off sharply to what passes here for deep water. The fish like this. They prowl from the dark water up into the cover of the weeds at this time of day without ever having to offend their nocturnal sensibilities.

Did you subconsciously jocky for this position when you started? Did your friends, just as unconsciously, allow you your spot? You'll never know. It just seemed to happen.

It's early yet; not quite dark enough, but the light is bouncing off the water now instead of slicing in and below your dangling butt; the evening has already begun. The fish are hungry, that is, they're *supposed* to be hungry now. Sometimes an evening goes by with no action. You don't know why this happens, although you have determined that it is not, as some say, the phase of the moon.

That determination was made somewhat scientifically, and you're proud of it. Last year you got your hands on a lunar chart, one of those that farmers use. In it you could look up any day of the year and find it to be, for instance, a good day to plant corn, a good day to "kill noxious growths," but a bad day for slaughtering hogs and for fishing.

If accurate, this information could have been invaluable. It could have made you the hottest bass fly-fisher in the county, especially since this down-home, *Farmers' Almanac* style of celestial mysticism is largely out of fashion now.

But how to test it? If you fished only on good days, you would surely prove the theory because you'd catch some fish. It would be the classic self-fulfilling prophecy. Even if you fished on what were supposed to be good, bad, and indifferent days, you could still unconsciously skew the results because, to be honest, you *wanted* to believe it.

What you came up with was this: you just fished as usual, that is, as often as possible, without looking up the days on the chart beforehand. You made a mark on your calendar for every expedition—A+ for a good day of fish catching, A- for a poor day, and a 0 for one that was so-so.

After six weeks of this came the day of revelation. You sat down with the calendar and the moon chart and found, lo and behold, no noticeable correlation. Conclusion: the music of the spheres is still probably real, but it's not a simple melody.

Having approached within casting distance of your weed bed, traveling backwards in the belly boat, you scissor the flippers to achieve a smart about-face and scan the water. It's calm and unbroken, which is okay; the fish won't really be charging around for a little while yet. You cast the bug to within inches of the weeds in front of you, and, before you have a chance to give it the first tantalizing twitch, it goes down in the kind of vigorous but dainty rise peculiar to bluegills. It's a good fish, about the size and shape of your hand, a keeper that puts slightly more than a laughable bend in the bass rod. Nice.

A further advantage of the small bugs is that the good-sized panfish can also take them. You are not one of those fishermen who feel they have to change gears in their emotional transmissions when they go from bluegills to bass. They're members of the same family living together in the same water. Bass will eat bluegills, but adult panfish will also eat newborn bass. One is nothing but a larger or smaller version of the other, and full grown examples of either are completely satisfactory.

With the bluegill released, you cast again, this time farther to the right. There are nearly always bass here, but they are not in predictable spots. There's no sunken stump, deadfall, or other textbook example of where the big one should be hiding. You don't really know how they behave down there below the weed tops, but, in order to give yourself a handle on it, you picture them cruising moodily, sometimes backing into the weeds to lurk. They are a nasty, aggressive fish with a seemingly uncharacteristic shy streak.

The way you move them to a floating bug is by needling. Sure, there are evenings when they'll nail a popper the way that bluegill just did, but those are usually the smaller ones. The big bass are, for reasons that are unclear, considerably more reticent.

It's not unlike playing with a house cat. You know the game, the one with the shoelace. The adolescent cat is easy; flip the lace out onto the floor and she jumps on it. This is so easy, in fact, that it's only fun for a few minutes. The adult cat is a little harder. The string itself isn't enough, it also has to act right. The most difficult is the old cat—the seven-pound, sixteen-year-old spayed calico. Her predatory instincts are intact, but she's seen it all, having killed and eaten, in her time, everything from grasshoppers to baby rabbits. Roll cast the shoelace to where she's sleeping and she will open one eye just wide enough to register her boredom with such a clumsy and obvious ruse.

In can take twenty minutes to get her to bat at the string, and during most of that time the shoelace should lie still on the floor, twitching and crawling just often enough to hold her interest. If you're not up for it, she can wait you out. If you get impatient and wiggle the thing hard right in her face, she'll get up and find a soft place to sleep where she won't be bothered by the likes of you.

Her psychology is as much like that of a big bass as any creature you're likely to meet, and she hits the string in the same way the bass hits the fly: without completely buying the idea that it's real.

The bug has landed on the water with a splat, and the last of the rings it started have dissipated. By tightening the line you're holding in your left hand, you give the fly the subtlest possible jerk—the spark of life.

Was that a slight bulge in the weeds just off to the left? Maybe. There's often no hint at all that a bass is approaching, but sometimes there's just a little bit of one. Without anything you could point to as a clear indication, the surface of the warm water can seem to vibrate before a strike; an effect a musician/fisherman friend once referred to as "basso profundo."

In times past, when the light and the angle were just right, you've seen bass creep to within inches of a floating bug and then hang there looking at it, apparently thinking it over. Admit it. With all the evidence to the contrary, you've come to believe that bass think. What else would they be doing at a time like that?

You've also learned that, as satisfying as it seems at the moment, twitching the bug is the wrong thing to do. At the worst, it will spook the fish and you'll never see him again. At best, it will set off a whole new line of speculation in his chilly little brain. If he's there at all, he'll bite the thing in his own good time. You can't rush him.

You wait for long minutes and nothing happens. Is a fish looking at the fly now or not? How are you supposed to know? You twitch the bug again—tentatively, cautiously—and yes, just the shadow of a wake seems to approach it now. Yes. Maybe. It might have been a ripple from the wind, but there is no wind; not a breath of it.

The sky is still blue, but it's darkening. The sun is no longer on the water anywhere on the pond. There's a liquid "whoosh" behind you as a pair of geese land, but you don't look.

No question about it, something is about to happen.

Now I Lay Me

By Ernest Hemingway

BY THE TIME HE INCLUDED "NOW I LAY ME" IN HIS NEW BOOK OF short stories, *Men Without Women*, in the autumn of 1926, Ernest Hemingway's prose had already earned him international literary acclaim. Two books of stories—*Three Stories & Ten Poems* and *In Our Time*—and the novel *The Sun Also Rises* were testaments of his relentless dedication to his prose which had started when he arrived in Paris in the winter of 1921–22. Then he had been a successful and resourceful journalist, willing to work hard on his fiction through months and years of struggle and rejection.

In making his mark in the world of fiction, Hemingway had already reached deep into two of his favorite preoccupations, war and fishing.

In the winter of 1923–24, Hemingway began writing a short story that used his boyhood and teenage years of trout fishing in Michigan as the setting and background. The original draft was called "Black River" but actually described a stream resembling the Fox River, not the Black. Hemingway had fished both rivers extensively, but was not interested in writing a factual trout-fishing narrative, but creating an original world and unique experience. And his character Nick was pursuing not only trout, but something much deeper. Hemingway had been wounded as an American Red Cross ambulance driver in Italy in World War One, hit with mortar fire while distributing candy and cigarettes to troops. He had lived the role of the returning wounded veteran, and the memories were very much a part of his thinking while writing his fishing story. As he would later say in *A Moveable Feast*, "The story was about coming back from the war but there was no war in it."

In the end of the summer of 1924, Hemingway's fishing short story had reached 100 pages in length and was titled, "Big Two-Hearted River," a name Hemingway chose from another river he knew simply because he liked the dramatic flair of the words. The river he had been describing all along in his story was his reinvention of the Fox.

In the draft of that time, the story contained a long section near the end in which Nick reflects on art and writing. To quote a few lines from the original manuscript: "He [Nick] wanted to write like Cezanne painted. . . . Cezanne started with all the tricks. Then he broke the whole thing down and built the real thing . . . He, Nick, wanted to write about country so that it would be there like Cezanne had done it in painting. You had to do it from inside yourself. There wasn't any trick. Nobody had ever written about country like that."

There was much more of this sort of thing in the original story, cut by Hemingway, when the story eventually appeared in his breakout book of short stories, *In Our Time*, without the section on art and writing. [To read portions of the original manuscript, see *The Nick Adams Stories*, Preface by Philip Young, Scribners, 1972. For the best and most complete Hemingway biographies, see the five Hemingway books written by Michael Reynolds.]

Today, of course, "Big Two-Hearted River" is one of Hemingway's most celebrated fishing stories, along with "The Old Man and the Sea" and magazine articles like "On the Blue Water." [The new book, *Hemingway On Fishing*, edited by Nick Lyons and being published by Lyons Press, is a landmark work in gathering Hemingway's fishing stories and articles in a single book.]

Unless you are a particularly keen or scholarly Hemingway reader, "Now I Lay Me" just might be a story that sneaked past you unnoticed. Written before he started his ultimate novel based on his war experience, *A Farewell To Arms*, "Now I Lay Me" foreshadows the first-person style and tone that eventually made *Farewell* so great, as Hemingway plumbs the depths of his painful memories of hospitalization after being wounded by mortar fire. On nights when he cannot sleep, he clings to visions of the trout streams of the past. And they serve him well.

That night we lay on the floor in the room and I listened to the silk-worms eating. The silk-worms fed in racks of mulberry leaves and all night you could hear them eating and a dropping sound in the leaves. I myself did not want to sleep because I had been living for a long time with the knowledge that if I ever shut my eyes in the dark and let myself go, my soul would go out of my body. I had been that way for a long time, ever since I had been blown up at night and felt it go out of me and go off and then come back. I tried never to think about it, but it had started to go since, in the nights, just at the moment of going off to sleep, and I could only stop it by a very great effort. So while now I am fairly sure that it would not really have gone out, yet then, that summer, I was unwilling to make the experiment.

I had different ways of occupying myself while I lay awake. I would think of a trout stream I had fished along when I was a boy and fish its whole length very carefully in my mind; fishing very carefully under all the logs, all the turns of the bank, the deep holes and the clear shallow stretches, sometimes catching trout and sometimes losing them. I would stop fishing at noon to eat my lunch; sometimes on a log over the stream; sometimes on a high bank under a tree, and I always ate my lunch very slowly and watched the stream below me while I ate. Often I ran out of bait because I would take only ten worms with me in a tobacco tin when I started. When I had used them all I had to find more worms, and sometimes it was very difficult digging in the bank of the stream where the cedar trees kept out the sun and there was no grass but only the bare moist earth and often I could find no worms. Always though I found some kind of bait, but one time in the swamp I could find no bait at all and had to cut up one of the trout I had caught and use him for bait.

Sometimes I found insects in the swamp meadows, in the grass or under ferns, and used them. There were beetles and insects with legs like grass stems, and grubs in old rotten logs; white grubs with brown pinching heads that would not stay on the hook and emptied into nothing in the cold water, and wood ticks under logs where sometimes I found angle-worms that slipped into the ground as soon as the log was raised. Once I used a salamander from under an old log. The salamander was very small and neat and agile and a lovely color. He had tiny feet that tried to hold on to the hook, and after that one time I never used a salamander, although I found them very often. Nor did I use crickets, because of the way they acted about the hook.

Sometimes the stream ran through an open meadow, and in the dry grass I would catch grasshoppers and use them for bait and sometimes I would catch grasshoppers and toss them into the stream and watch them float along swimming on the stream and circling on the surface as the current took them and then disappear as a trout rose. Sometimes I would fish four or five different streams in the night; starting as near as I could get to their source and fishing them down stream. When I had finished too quickly and the time did not go, I would fish the stream over again, starting where it emptied into the lake and fishing back up stream, trying for all the trout I had missed coming down. Some nights too I made up streams, and some of them were very exciting, and it was like being awake and dreaming. Some of those streams I still remember and think that I have fished in them, and they are confused with streams I really know. I gave them all names and went to them on the train and sometimes walked for miles to get to them.

But some nights I could not fish, and on those nights I was cold-awake and said my prayers over and over and tried to pray for all the people I had ever known. That took up a great amount of time, for if you try to remember all the people you have ever known, going back to the earliest thing you remember—which was, with me, the attic of the house where I was born and my mother and father's wedding-cake in a tin box hanging from one of the rafters, and, in the attic, jars of snakes and other specimens that my father had collected as a boy and preserved in alcohol, the alcohol sunken in the jars so the backs of some of the snakes and specimens were exposed and had turned white—if you thought back that far, you remembered a great many people. If you prayed for all of them, saying a Hail Mary and an Our Father for each one, it took a long time and finally it would be light, and then you could go to sleep, if you were in a place where you could sleep in the daylight.

On those nights I tried to remember everything that had ever happened to me, starting with just before I went to the war and remembering back from one thing to another. I found I could only remember back to that attic in my grandfather's house. Then I would start there and remember this way again, until I reached the war.

I remember, after my grandfather died we moved away from that house and to a new house designed and built by my mother. Many things that were not to be moved were burned in the back-yard and I remember those jars from the attic being thrown in the fire, and how they popped in the heat and the fire flamed up from the alcohol. I remember the snakes burning in the fire in the back-yard. But there were no people in that, only things. I could not remember who burned the things even, and I would go on until I came to people and then stop and pray for them.

About the new house I remember how my mother was always cleaning things out and making a good clearance. One time when my father was away on a hunting trip she made a good thorough cleaning out in the basement and burned everything that should not have been there. When my father came home and got down from his buggy and hitched the horse, the fire was still burning in the road beside the house. I went out to meet him. He handed me his shotgun and looked at the fire. "What's this?" he asked.

"I've been cleaning out the basement dear," my mother said from the porch. She was standing there smiling, to meet him. My father looked at the fire and kicked at something. The he leaned over and picked something out of the ashes. "Get a rake, Nick," he said to me. I went to the basement and brought a rake and my father raked very carefully in the ashes. He raked out stone axes and stone skinning knives and tools for making arrow-heads and pieces of pottery and many arrow-heads. They had all been blackened and chipped by the fire. My father raked them all out very carefully and spread them on the grass by the road. His shotgun in its leather case and his game-bags were on the grass where he had left them when he stepped down from the buggy.

"Take the gun and the bags in the house, Nick, and bring me a paper." he said. My mother had gone inside the house. I took the shotgun, which was heavy to carry and banged against my legs, and the two game-bags and started toward the house. "Take them one at a time," my father said. "Don't try and carry too much at once." I put down the game-bags and took in the shotgun and brought out a newspaper from the pile in my father's office. My father spread all the blackened, chipped stone implements on the paper and then wrapped them up. "The best arrow-heads went all to pieces," he said. He walked into the house with the paper package and I stayed outside on the grass with the two game-bags. After a while I took them in. In remembering that, there were only two people, so I would pray for them both.

Some nights, though, I could not remember my prayers even. I could only get as far as "On earth as it is in heaven" and then have to start all over and be absolutely unable to get past that. Then I would have to recognize that I could not remember and give up saying my prayers that night and try something else. So on some nights I would try to remember all the animals in the world by name and then the birds and then fishes and then countries and cities and then kinds of food and the names of all the streets I could remember in Chicago, and when I could not remember anything at all any more I would just listen. And I do not remember a night on which you could not hear things. If I could have a light I was not afraid to sleep, because I knew my soul would only go out of me it if were dark. So, of course, many nights I was where I could have a light and then I slept because I was nearly always tired and often very sleepy. And I am sure many times too that I slept without knowing it—but I never slept knowing it, and on this night I listened to the silk-worms. You can hear silk-worms eating very clearly in the night and I lay with my eyes open and listened to them.

There was only one other person in the room and he was awake too. I listened to him being awake, for a long time. He could not lie as quietly as I could because, perhaps, he had not had as much practice being awake. We were lying on blankets spread over straw and when he moved the straw was noisy, but the silk-worms were not frightened by any noise we made and ate on steadily. There were the noises of night seven kilometres behind the lines outside but they were different from the small noises inside the room in the dark. The other man in the room tried lying quietly. Then he moved again. I moved too, so he would know I was awake. He had lived ten years in Chicago. They had taken him for a soldier in nineteen fourteen when he had come back to visit his family, and they had given him me for an orderly because he spoke English. I heard him listening, so I moved again in the blankets.

"Can't you sleep, Signor Tenente?" he asked.

"No."

"I can't sleep, either."

"What's the matter?"

"I don't know. I can't sleep."

"You feel all right?"

"Sure. I feel good. I just can't sleep."

"You want to talk a while?" I asked.

"Sure. What can you talk about in this damn place."

"This place is pretty good," I said.

"Sure," he said. "It's all right."

"Tell me about out in Chicago," I said.

"Oh," he said, "I told you all that once."

"Tell me about how you got married."

"I told you that."

"Was the letter you got Monday—from her?"

"Sure. She writes me all the time. She's making good money with the place."

"You'll have a nice place when you go back."

"Sure. She runs it fine. She's making a lot of money."

"Don't you think we'll wake them up, talking?" I asked.

"No. They can't hear. Anyway, they sleep like pigs. I'm different," he said. "I'm nervous."

"Talk quiet," I said. "Want a smoke?"

We smoked skillfully in the dark.

"You don't smoke much, Signor Tenente."

"No. I've just about cut it out."

"Well," he said, "it don't do you any good and I suppose you get so you don't miss it. Did you ever hear a blind man won't smoke because he can't see the smoke come out?"

"I don't believe it."

"I think it's all bull, myself," he said. "I just heard it somewhere. You know how you hear things."

We were both quiet and I listened to the silk-worms.

"You hear those damn silk-worms?" he asked. "You can hear them chew."

"It's funny," I said.

"Say, Signor Tenente, is there something really the matter that you can't sleep? I never see you sleep. You haven't slept nights ever since I been with you."

"I don't know, John," I said. "I got in pretty bad shape along early last spring and at night it bothers me."

"Just like I am," he said. "I shouldn't have ever got in this war. I'm too nervous."

"Maybe it will get better."

"Say, Signor Tenente, what did you get in this war for, anyway?"

"I don't know, John. I wanted to, then."

"Wanted to," he said. "That's a hell of a reason."

"We oughtn't to talk out loud," I said.

"They sleep just like pigs," he said. "They can't understand the English language, anyway. They don't know a damn thing. What are you going to do when it's over and we go back to the States?"

"I'll get a job on a paper."

"In Chicago?"

"Maybe."

"Do you ever read what this fellow Brisbane writes? My wife cuts it out for me and sends it to me."

"Sure."

"Did you ever meet him?"

"No, but I've seen him."

"I'd like to meet that fellow. He's a fine writer. My wife don't read English but she takes the paper just like when I was home and she cuts out the editorials and the sport page and sends them to me."

"How are your kids?"

"They're fine. One of the girls is in the fourth grade now. You know, Signor Tenente, if I didn't have the kids I wouldn't be your orderly now. They'd have made me stay in the line all the time."

"I'm glad you've got them."

"So am I. They're fine kids but I want a boy. Three girls and no boy. That's a hell of a note."

"Why don't you try and go to sleep?"

"No, I can't sleep now. I'm wide awake now, Signor Tenente. Say, I'm worried about you not sleeping though."

"It'll be all right, John."

"Imagine a young fellow like you not to sleep."

"I'll get all right. It just takes a while."

"You got to get all right. A man can't get along that don't sleep. Do you worry about anything? You got anything on your mind?"

"No, John, I don't think so."

"You ought to get married, Signor Tenente. Then you wouldn't worry."

"I don't know."

"You ought to get married. Why don't you pick out some nice Italian girl with plenty of money? You could get any one you want. You're young and you got good decorations and you look nice. You been wounded a couple of times."

"I can't talk the language well enough."

"You talk it fine. To hell with talking the language. You don't have to talk to them. Marry them."

"I'll think about it."

"You know some girls, don't you?"

"Sure."

"Well, you marry the one with the most money. Over here, the way they're brought up, they'll all make you a good wife."

"I'll think about it."

"Don't think about it, Signor Tenente. Do it."

"All right."

"A man ought to be married. You'll never regret it. Every man ought to be married."

"All right," I said. "Let's try and sleep a while."

"All right, Signor Tenente. I'll try it again. But you remember what I said."

"I'll remember it," I said. "Now let's sleep a while, John."

"All right," he said. "I hope you sleep, Signor Tenente."

I heard him roll in his blankets on the straw and then he was very quiet and I listened to him breathing regularly. Then he started to snore. I listened to him snore for a long time and then I stopped listening to him snore and listened to the silk-worms eating. They ate steadily, making a dropping in the leaves. I had a new thing to think about and I lay in the dark with my eyes open and thought of all the girls I had ever known and what kind of wives they would make. It was a very interesting thing to think about and for a while it killed off trout-fishing and interfered with my prayers. Finally, though, I went back to trout-fishing, because I found that I could remember all the streams and there was always something new about them, while the girls, after I had thought about them a few times, blurred and I could not call them into my mind and finally they all blurred and all became rather the same and I gave up thinking about them almost altogether. But I kept on with my prayers and I prayed very often for John in the nights and his class was removed from active service before the October offensive. I was glad he was not there, because he would have been a great worry to me. He came to the hospital in Milan to see me several months after and was very disappointed that I had not yet married, and I know he would feel very badly if he knew that, so far, I have never married. He was going back to America and he was very certain about marriage and knew it would fix up everything.

The Marquesas

By John N. Cole

OUR FLATS FISHING EPISODES CONTINUE, THIS TIME WITH TARPON ON the agenda—although out there on the tidal reaches on the shoulders of the vast depths you're liable to run into almost anything that swims, from fifteen-foot hammerhead sharks to snappers to barracuda.

John Cole subtitles his *Fishing Came First* collection of stories, which Nick Lyons published in 1989, "A Robust Memoir." The book lives up to that promise without even breathing hard and, in fact, is one of my favorite fishing books ever. Not surprising, any of that, considering the source.

John Cole lives and writes in Maine on subjects that take him just about everywhere. And what he writes gets published, in important national magazines like *Sports Illustrated*, *Harper's*, and *The Atlantic Monthly*. And in books, fifteen of them by my last count. Reading reviews and notices of Cole's books has about all the surprise of watching a red light turn green. You know just what's coming—every time. Gushes of unbridled praise from every side.

Now here is a fish worth writing about, and we have the right man for the job. You're going to finish this one wanting to go tarpon fishing. And wanting to read more of John Cole.

———

FEBRUARY 29, 1988

The Marquesas Keys are a wonderful mystery. Some Key West historians will tell you the ring of small islands about twenty-five miles southwest of Key West is the only atoll in the Atlantic. I have never been to the islands of the Pacific, but I have seen enough aerial photographs of atolls to know that they mark the graves of long ago volcanos or mountains that sank beneath the sea. A lagoon shimmers at the center of a round, geologic crown of rock and coral: all that's left of the rim of an ancient volcanic peak.

The Marquesas, the popular argument goes, are the remnants of just such a prehistoric drama, a geologic anomaly that rose from the primeval sea far from its brethren in what is now Mexico. Other folks have other thoughts about the unique formation that marks the end of the necklace of keys and hummocks draped along the meeting ground of the Atlantic and the Gulf from Key West to the Tortugas. Some reason that the ring of coral sand and marl was formed in an earthquake. "Mexico is not that far off," they say, "and earthquakes have been happening there for centuries."

Knowing nothing of geology, and less about the genesis of the Marquesas, I can believe the theory I like best. And there is one. Jeffrey tells me there are informed Keys mariners who believe the Marquesas are the child of a meteor—some giant fragment of infinity that plummeted from outer space, or perhaps from another universe. So far removed in time that its fiery flight went unmarked by any being, the visitor from the unknown hurled itself into the warm salt seas of the shoals that rise on the western rim of the Boca Grande Channel. Blazing, hissing, smashing into its final grave, the meteor's calamity left its own mile-wide mark on the sea floor, an almost perfectly round depression wreathed by a circle of islands and hummocks forced from the center of the meteor's impact just as mud squeezes from around a boot sole pressed into a puddle.

Tended by a millennia of solitude, the raw material pushed from the sea bottom acquired its dry-land biota. First the tiny plants that are children of wind-blown seeds, then the mangroves, propagated by currents and sea-bird droppings. And finally the maturing greenery that is south of Florida's horticultural signature: impenetrable tangles of mangrove roots, scrub pine, sawgrass, and dozens more species and sub-species of green, growing vegetation that defies human perambulation and appears consummately designed to protect every anonymous marl hillock from the kind of heedless human exploration that's so often memorialized by the extinction of the very places that once held mystery in their grasp.

Bulldozers, of course, can make an instant mockery of mangroves. In moments, lowered blades eradicate the work of eons, sparing nothing, not even the only salt-sea memento of a dying meteor's final flight. That could have happened, probably would have happened if the Marquesas and their sister keys to the north had not been protected by the Department of the Interior, which has recently stamped "National Wildlife Refuge" across every map of the watery territory that stretches from Fort Taylor at the end of Key West's Southard Street to Fort Jefferson in the Tortugas. I am no fan of the Federal bureaucracy, but each time I look southwest from any Key West vantage point, and every time I navigate those azure waters in any sort of craft I write a silent note of gratitude to Nat Reed and everyone else in Interior's Washington labyrinth who engineered the decisions and agreements that have become such an effective shield for what is, I'm certain, the globe's largest submerged national park and wildlife refuge. There is, on Woman Key's northeast corner, witness to what might have happened if Interior had not acted. Not that David Wolkowsky built himself an ugly retreat; he did not. His elevated, wood-framed and wood-sheathed house at the edge of a crescent of pure white beach is a graceful and sensitively sited structure: the only one between Key West and the Marquesas, built before the territory was taken out of public circulation. But each time I pass it, it shouts to me of a future these keys might have known.

We will not hear its voice today. We are, Jean and I and Jeffrey, aboard his Waterlight on a course through the Lakes, the interlocked stretch of shoal channels on the north side of the line of keys that follow the reef from Key West to Boca Grande Key at the northern rim of Boca Grande Channel. David's house faces south, and besides, we are a mile or more north of Woman Key racing across turtle grass flats in water so clear and so smooth I can see individual blades of grass waving in the current.

How lucky I am. When I made this date with Jeffrey a week ago, there was no way of knowing what our weather would be. Like February everywhere, the month in Key West arrives with surprises. One dawn will open the curtains on a dark melodrama acted by rolling clouds stuffed with rain and thunder. Others torment the sea and land with winds like those that pushed Jeffrey and me into the lee of Archer Key just three days ago. I have been remembering that day and more as I waited for this one.

Because this one was memorable even before it arrived. I had Jean's promise that she would come with me to the Marquesas, the scene of adventures that come to a fisherman only if he is blessed by the fates—adventures that are as vivid in my history as any I have lived. Each has been narrated to Jean in detail, each has been retold to others as Jean listened, wondering I'm sure how many times a tale can survive retelling. This two-week visit to Key West would not go by, I promised myself, without a trip to the Marquesas with Jean.

But only if the weather is right: that was an addendum to my pledge. Jean is not a complainer; she would have made the trip in any weather Jeffrey considered navigable. But I know she is a creature of the land, not a spirit of the sea. She endures every discomfort in the service of her garden; she will politely refuse almost every invitation that involves leaving port.

But given this day's splendor, even an earth mother is exhilarated by the sea. We are afloat on a shimmering mirror of a cloudless sky. At thirty knots, the *Waterlight* glides like raw silk pulled across a polished table. Today, earth's reassuring firmness reaches to encompass a sea as smooth as a meadow in May. Jean's soul rests content.

Over the decades of my wage-earning work as a journalist I would, in times of particular drudgery, push away from my desk and confide to my co-workers that I was on the brink of abandoning not only my job but my home community and my entire life's routine. Asked what I would do and where I would go I would say with considerable conviction that I would start over on some island in the Carribbean set at the center of the finest fishing waters on the planet. "I will," I told my listeners, "spend my days in a small boat afloat on a crystal sea where fish flash bright greetings under a tropic sun."

"Yes, that sounds fine," those skeptics would reply, "but how long do you think you can do that before you get bored."

And my answer was always the same. "I'll try it for twenty-five years, and then take a second look."

Each time I told that ritualized tale, I saw myself at the center of a shoal-water universe, alone with my fish and my fishing. Soon the fancy became a dream, a dream I began to want desperately to come alive.

And today, I tell myself, it has. And today, I tell myself, I know what I said is true: I can do this for the rest of my life, however long or short it may be, and be truly happy doing it. And happiest when Jean and Jeffrey are with me.

When we reach Boca Grande Key and make the turn that starts us across Boca Grande Channel, I am now and at last positively certain of this day's mercies and splendors. The region's entrance to the Gulf of Mexico from the Straits of Florida and the southern Atlantic, this channel is like so many places where two headstrong waters meet. Even on windless days, the surface surges with restless tides and currents ebbing and flowing across Boca Grande Channel's four miles. Pushing two seas together in such relatively narrow confines and in such relatively shoal water is a process sure to encounter resistance. With no room to run, the two seas meet here in an endless turbulence that roils even windless waters. And when gales do blow, this is not an easy place to be. Odd-shaped swells approach from nowhere, rolling against wind and tide; even the most seaworthy boat and experienced helmsman cannot avoid a pounding. I have made the crossing several times with Jeffrey when the best I could do was hold on, grit my teeth, and pray that we would soon reach sheltered waters.

And while I prayed, I tried not to remember that the world's record hammerhead shark was taken from these very waters, a great and terrifying fish almost twenty feet long weighing more than a ton. There are others down there in the depths, I am certain, as massive as the meteor that's buried somewhere beneath the bottom of the Marquesas lagoon.

Today the channel is so wonderfully benign that as we cross I inform Jean of its hammerhead distinction. That's how certain I am of this day's good fortune.

Given my Marquesas history, I should be more restrained. On other fine days, other orchid mornings, I have cruised this same course across a well-mannered channel, my hopes flying like a banner in the dawn. Yet those very days kept a secret from me, a shock they delivered just as I began to believe I held paradise in my grasp.

Ten months ago four of us crossed Boca Grande on an early May morning as soft as a newborn kitten. Jeffrey, my brother-in-law John Graves, his wife, my sister Jane, and myself. Jeffrey seldom carries more than two fishermen; as he does so often, he gave me his blessing and made room. In return, I promised that John and Jane would do the fishing; it was, after all, their charter.

We were looking for tarpon, and Jeffrey brought us to the right place. The reefs, islands, hummocks, and dunes that define the Marquesas lagoon are not a perfect circle. The curving half-circle of land on the northeast quadrant is the largest single land mass: a single, sheltering arm that protects the lagoon from the northeast winds that prevail. To the southwest, its counterpart land arc is a series of small, and even smaller islands and hummocks. Both Gulf and Atlantic tides and currents sweep along the channels between these independent mangrove masses. Like arteries, the channels feed the shallow lagoon, circulating nourishing sea water across the mile-wide flats. Of these channels, the entrance to the largest is on the due-south curve of the Marquesas circle. Here where its entrance waters are almost ten feet deep, is one of the places where migrating tarpon move on their journey from the dark depths of the ocean to their shoal spawning grounds off the southern coast of Mexico.

Certainly not I, nor any of the fishing people I have spoken with, can come up with a dependable reason why tens of thousands of these huge and graceful silver fish should choose to navigate this single, small channel on their thousand-mile voyage to their mating and nursery destinations.

Look at the chart. A few miles southwest of the Marquesas, just beyond the Quicksand Shoals, there is a channel ten miles wide and more than a hundred feet deep that reaches all the way to the Dry Tortugas. Why haven't the tarpon made that their central passage? There they could find invisibility in the depths; here at the Marquesas, their wonderfully prehistoric, deep-sided, armor-scaled massive shapes glide like shimmering projectiles across the white sand of the channel mouth in water so stunningly clear I have, I swear, seen my reflection in a tarpon's dark globe of an eye as the fish soared under our bow.

I think John Graves is a year or so older than I. Because I've never asked, I do not know. I can, however, vouch for his gristle. A Marine lieutenant who fought and lost an eye in World War II, he is a Texas man in every sense of the weight that heaviest of states implies. His parents and grandparents are the same and John has written some of the finest, and it is so acknowledged, Texas history, Texas prose, and Texas anecdote that can be found in any library of contemporary history and literature. Unlike me, he is a scholar, albeit one who lives on a two-bit ranch he made for himself in a tiny town called Glen Rose a few miles southwest of Fort Worth.

Because he is a scholar, and because he has, in the latter years of his active outdoor life, taken on fly fishing as his mission, he was especially enchanted by the prospect of casting one of his hand-tied flies to the largest and most spectacular fighting fish a fly-caster can find. A husky, weathered man who looks like the rancher he also is, John makes his own fly rods on Sage blanks, mounting each guide and applying each coat of lacquer with as much patience as he gives to the individual well being of the cattle and the goats that are so superbly cared for in Glen Rose.

I have always been fond of John, primarily because we got off to a fine start. Before he married my sister Jane some thirty-five years ago, she was a New York City debutante, a properly educated young lady whose college years had cost the family a bundle. She knew a great many old-money sons and daughters and, I'm certain, Helen, our mother, harbored high hopes that Jane would, in Helen's words, "Marry well." Honestly defined, the phrase meant marrying old money.

Well, in Texas John Graves might be considered old money, but Texas is a young state and I'm certain my mother never had in mind a man who wore blue jeans to restaurants and hopped in his pickup truck with cow flop on his stable boots. Nor did she think that the best Jane could do would be to hook up with a man who planned on building his own house, limestone block by limestone block in a far corner of a state famous for its far corners. "But nobody knows him!" Helen often said; or "Who does he know?" John, as it turned out, had many close and distinguished friends when he met Jane, but, as Helen said, "They're no one we know, dear."

So I was anxious to see how the first encounters would develop when John arrived in New York for the wedding. He was, I had been advised, not a party man. Indeed, the odds were high, a mutual friend advised me, that John Graves would not appear at any of the various receptions and dinners that preceded the ceremony. But he did, and he won. He somehow made it clear by his demeanor and actions that while he obviously believed the city social scene to be something less than bullshit, he would, nevertheless, do what was proper and courteous on Jane's behalf.

He appeared at the gatherings, but he kept himself at a polite Texas remove. Helen had nothing to criticize and everything to be worried about. Her only daughter was quite clearly marrying a man who knew himself and his values well enough to be certain of his standards. John Graves could not and would not be easily moved away from those standards toward others, no matter how important those others might seem to his new mother-in-law.

I was, I must say, delighted. I still am. I think of those cocktail parties almost every time John and I meet.

Which we have done infrequently. Jean and I have visited the "ranch" in Glen Rose twice, and Jane has come east frequently. But John has not. His visit to Key West was the first time since he married Jane that I saw him outside of Texas. And it was the tarpon, not I, that brought him.

In the early morning of the second day of our three-day charter with Jeffrey, a tarpon took John Graves's brown Cockroach fly and slammed across the flats ripping more than two hundred feet of backing off the reel on the Number 9 Sage fly rod John had made for himself in the shed alongside his barn in Glen Rose. Two hours later in the high May sun that had, by then, heated the humid air to close to ninety degrees, the fish was still on and it was in better shape than John. At least, watching the sweat roll from his brow, I thought so. The tarpon could still jump; John could hardly move. Looking at his steely gray hair along the nape of his seasoned neck, watching the hard-knuckled and calloused hands kink and curl from the cramps that came from holding the rod for 120 minutes or more, seeing him blink his one good eye to clear the sweat from his vision, I realized that this was a fight the fish might win.

But John Graves hadn't changed in thirty-five years. Just as stubborn, just as ornery, and just as proud as he had always been, he hung in there. Three hours and ten minutes after the tarpon first ate the fly, Jeffrey released him. Although the ninety-pound fish was weary, it did not need as much caring as many tarpon Jeffrey has revived and released.

"That's a lovely rod, John," said Jeffrey, after the tarpon had vanished in the channel, "but I think it's a little light for this kind of fishing."

"Jeffrey," sighed John as he slumped to a seat, "you're right."

Cruising slowly through the channel from north to south, Jeffrey shut down the Yamaha when we reached the Marquesas' south shore and anchored in eight feet of water above a large patch of pale marl. The bowl-shaped depression gleamed under the one o'clock sun, a ladle of transparent tropical sea unmarred by vegetation, a coral dish as delicately vacant as a porcelain soup tureen polished and waiting on a mahogany sideboard. Jeffrey lowered his small mushroom anchor carefully and the *Waterlight* swung in the current on a surface as still as cut glass. In the windless torpor, each of our spirits slumped along with John. Released from the stretch of the tensions that had tugged for three hours, we were quite ready to do nothing but sit there, accepting the sun's potent presence while we regrouped for the afternoon.

"We'll have some lunch," Jeffrey said, opening his ice chest. "If a tarpon or two does cruise across this white spot, we'll see it coming. One of you should be ready to cast."

No one moved, so I took my rod from its brackets and laid it along the broad gunwale, Cockroach fly at the ready.

"Be sure you drink plenty of fluids," Jeffrey advised as he passed around ice water, beers, and jugs of Gatorade, "especially you, John Graves. In this sun, you can get dehydrated more quickly than you think."

Sitting on the casting deck, my legs draped over the bow so my toes just touched the water's surface, I joined the general silence as each of us foraged on our tunafish-salad sandwiches. In the flooding tide, the *Waterlight* swung on her mooring so her bow faced seaward; my view as I gulped my Gatorade reached to the southern horizon across an ocean as peaceful and green as a croquet lawn. Not a riffle stirred in the unusual afternoon calm, no short seas had been left by any long-gone gale, not even a vestige of a swell nudged the tranquil surface to announce its parent storm a thousand miles at sea.

Over my years of fishing, especially on those trips aboard the *Double Trouble* with Matty, I have become conditioned to scanning every sea for signals. Some flags raised from below are as dramatic and unmistakable as the black, new-moon crescent of a swordfish dorsal. Others appear more frequently: white puffs of feeding bluefish as they break water; raindrop patterns of tiny baitfish pursuing an invisible purpose; or the spreading V of a fish wake as some unidentifiable shape swims just beneath the surface. Since my first days on the water, I have been a lucky fish spotter; I have become accustomed to having others doubt my reports simply because they have not seen what my eyes recorded. Knowing this, I was careful not to overstate my case on that somnolent afternoon at anchor. But about a half-mile offshore, something unusual was happening. Of that, I was convinced.

Along the horizon a spreading banner of darker blue flowed like indigo spilled across a lime-green canvas. Some massive, submerged turbulence roiled the flawless surface, altered its refraction, and changed its hue.

"See that, Jeffrey," I called. "Is that a bunch of fish out there, or is it a breeze about to take hold?"

"I don't know," he answered, making it clear by his tone even he could not solve a mystery so distant, so ill defined.

I kept my eyes on the spreading strangeness. When a tarpon leapt free of the sea, a silver missile fired from a submerged ship, and hung there against the sky at least six feet above the horizon line, I gasped and shouted, my voice charged and the words tumbling even as the fish turned on its side in the air and crashed in a welter of white water.

"It's a tarpon, a big tarpon. Did you see it, Jeffrey, did you?"

By the time my question took shape and Jeffrey was framing his response, the query was rendered academic. From the dark pasture at least six tarpon leaped, and then six more and then others until an incredible tapestry was woven for us by countless giant silver fish. Like a surging school of bluefish or herring grown to monstrous dimensions, tarpon churned, jumped, rolled, pushed water, and leapt again and again, wanting, it seemed, to take wing, to depart the very sea they swam in.

"Sharks! Hammerheads!" Jeffrey yelled. "It's sharks chasing a big school of tarpon. They're driving them like sheep."

In our silence, watching, knowing even then that we were witness to a natural cataclysm few humans will ever see, we could hear a sound—a ripping, as if a vast cotton sheet was being torn from edge to edge. It was the sound of the sea's rending, the hiss of panic as hundreds of tarpon swam at their ultimate and desperate speed. As we watched and listened, the sound acquired new tones, more depth, until it became close to a roar, more like a waterfall's cascade than fabric pulled asunder.

Thrashing, pounding their tails convulsively in the hysteria of their flight, the school of thousands of great tarpon flailed the still surface so violently that the liquid rumble filled the air around us with an awesome echo of distant, rolling thunder. Driven closer to us by still unseen sharks, the silver and indigo mass began changing color under its dapple of white water that marked each breaking fish. A copper-burnt-orange rose began blooming at the center of the violence, spreading its somber petals until they, too, were a piece of the whole.

"That's blood," Jeffrey said. "Those fish are being torn to pieces."

A new sound made its entrance, one I knew immediately, one every boatman knows: the sibilance of a breaking sea, a wave on the approach. But here? Here in a dead calm.

The wave rolled toward us with surprising speed. Perfectly formed, gleaming in the shimmering sunlight, it crested at almost two feet, lifted the *Waterlight* as it surged under and past us and crumpled into white water as it stumbled against the shallows of the flats. It was a wave born of apocalypse, a creation of fear, a signal of massacre and futile flight, an echo of the final energies expended by slaughtered tarpon and their relentless butchers.

Herding their silver sheep, the sharks pressed toward the Marquesas shoals, knowing their work would be quicker once the tarpon were forced against the flats.

A dark dorsal, curved and blunt, cut the water as I watched and understood I was seeing a shark, not a tarpon. I was stunned by its speed. Peering from pulpits off Montauk, I have watched many sharks move out of harm's way. There was always a certain languor to their departure, as if they understood the immensity of the depths at their disposal. And I have watched sharks cruising the flats and witnessed their strikes at hooked and wounded fish. But even then, these predators moved with deliberate speed, certain of their ultimate success.

This hammerhead was a projectile. A roostertail of white water flared from its dorsal as emphatically as it would from a high-speed outboard. The massive shadow shape beneath raced across the bleached flats like a shaft of dark light. I could not absorb the concept; the notion that a submerged creature that large could move so quickly stunned me. There could, I knew, be no defense, no evasion of such startling speed. A new standard of wild behavior had been set. I watched and knew I would judge the flight of every other fish by the mark that shark etched in my memory.

Once pushed against the land, the tarpon scattered, followed by their pursuers. There was no longer a concentration of doom. Only the faltering copper rose still bloomed offshore to affirm the spectacle each of us knew had been ours alone, and would always be. We could, we knew, return to this place, to these Marquesas each May day for the rest of our lives and never witness such a spectacle again.

Nevertheless, I sought verification. "Have you ever seen anything like that?" I asked Jeffrey.

"No," he said, shaking his head, "no, never."

Sitting quietly, more weary now than we were before we anchored for lunch, we waited for our adrenalin rush to subside. It seemed almost surreal to be so taut in what is thought to be a torpid climate.

Within a half-hour, however, we had revived and chattered easily about the spectacle, John's long battle, and the tarpon's migratory mysteries.

Jane, I noticed, seemed restless.

"Can I slip overboard for a swim?" she asked Jeffrey, and then explained. "All those fluids you made sure we drank are beginning to get to me. I'll just hang on to the boat and do what I have to do, okay?"

"Sure, fine. Do what you need to, Jane. We'll make sure you get back aboard."

Jane stood, her mouth set firmly in that line of determination I know so well, sweat beading on her forehead above her large, brown eyes. I watched to see just how she would, in her late middle age, trim though she might be, negotiate her entrance to the waters of this Marquesas lagoon.

"John," she said to me, in a tone I also know well, "you don't have to watch my every move. Isn't there something else you can do?"

As I turned toward the bow, Jeffrey said, "You might want to wait a minute or two, Jane, before you go over. Look there, about six o'clock, coming toward the stern."

Following the line set by Jeffrey's extended arm we each looked toward the eastern edge of our coral-dish anchorage. There, outlined in dark and dramatic silhouette against the white sand was the distinctive profile of a large hammerhead moving directly toward the *Waterlight*. This fish was in no hurry. Quite the opposite. Apparently assured of its complete command of any situation, the shark took possession of the small lagoon. With sinuous, lazy motions as fluid as the currents it moved through, the hammerhead continued its sensual and silent advance until it was directly under our boat.

"God, isn't it beautiful," Jeffrey said in a half-whisper.

I judged the shark to be a foot longer than our flats skiff, which made it at least an eighteen-foot hammerhead, by far the most magnificent and terrifying I have ever seen. Its nearness was even more exceptional. In the sun's glare, I could see each of its luminous, green eyes at each end of the odd airfoil protuberances that extended from its snout. An oddity familiar to saltwater fishermen, the hammerhead's profile had sometimes seemed clumsy to me, a kind of genetic flaw, a handicap. But looking down at that fish less than four feet from us in water as clear as if it were distilled, the hammerhead's most distinctive feature seemed more awesome than awkward, fitting, not freakish.

Hesitating a moment in the darkness of the *Waterlight*'s shadow, the shark appeared to be deliberating its immediate choices. None of us made a sound. Then, with a subtle movement of its sweeping tail, the hammerhead glided across the lagoon onto the flats where we could see its dorsal above water and then back into the channel further west where it vanished in the darker, deeper unknowns.

Jane spoke first. "Jeffrey," she asked, "have you got a can, or a bucket or something I can use?"

During the next two days that John and Jane visited with us, staying in the small apartment built above a storage shed in the backyard of our rented home on South Street, I talked with John several times about our days on the water, sharks, and fly fishing. I learned that he was almost totally committed to the fly rod, using it even when angling for the small bass and perch in the creek running through his ranch and in his dug stock pond called in Texas style a "tank."

Typically, he had thought a great deal about that commitment. And, typically, he had assembled a scholar's library of information on every aspect of the skill. He had learned to make his own rods, tie his own flies, and research his own ichthyological data, and had even begun thinking about how he would convert a plain, empty boat hull into a flats skiff. He is a fellow who goes all the way with his avocations.

I was ready to listen to his ideas. "It's an infirmity without a cure, fly fishing," he said at one point. "But it's also a pretty deep field of study, bottomless really, which I guess is why it attracts a lot of bookish types, including ex-professors like me. The first symptom is a desire to cast a fly nicely like somebody you've seen somewhere, maybe on a trout river in the Rockies. To lay the line out straight to a reasonable distance, and have the fly land where you want it to. And that may be the easiest part of the whole damned business."

"Ah, yes," I said with some bitterness. "Very easy indeed."

"Then you start throwing flies at fish," said John, "which arouses your curiosity about the kinds of water different species prefer, and what they like to eat. Which in turn, unless you're careful, leads you into trying to imitate what they eat with hair and fur and feathers and tinsel and thread."

"Fly tying," I said.

"By then there is no escape, and all the rest of it follows. Building rods that will help you cast better, you hope. Messing with boats. Learning about knots and splices and tapered lines and leaders, not to mention all the kinds of fish there are to read about and try to catch, one species after another. All of it follows the simple, fatal fact that you once admired the motions of some lunatic sloshing around in cold river water and waving a thin pole in the air."

"You're sorry you got involved, then?"

"Hell, no, I'm not," John said. "What I'm sorry about is that it took me this long to get around to trying it in salt water. Except that it's great to be hitting a whole new realm of the sport. You know something? At our age, there is no earthly way you and I are going to live long enough to learn all there is to know about this kind of fly fishing. Isn't that a pretty thought?"

"I may have had some prettier ones from time to time," I answered. "What about other kinds of fishing?"

"Fishing's fishing," said my brother-in-law. "I don't mind throwing a baited hook at catfish when I want one to eat. Sometimes I'll switch to spinning gear if the wind gets to blowing a gale. But it's not the same; it's not as good."

"After watching you and Jeffrey fly fish, I'm inclined to agree with that," I said. "But I still don't know *why* the other ways aren't as good."

"Well, they're fine unless you're a diseased fly man, I guess. I don't know why I believe fly fishing is better, not really. It's got something to do with grace, I think—with handling rather simple tools that feel good and get to working like a part of you, so that using fly tackle is an active and satisfying thing even when you don't catch anything. It's cleaner, too, somehow, and single fly hooks with the barbs mashed down are a hell of a lot easier than trebles on fish that break off, or the ones you bring in and release. I don't often keep them any more, do you?"

"No, not often," I said, thinking that my answer didn't matter much at that point. It had been a while since I'd brought a fish near enough to have to make a decision. "I believe most of what you say, John, except that I don't find fly casting to be nearly as easy as you seem to think it is. And I've got a bunch of good spinning rods and reels."

"Keep on using them," John said, and then grinned. "But if you'll learn how to throw a fly right, I bet you'll be giving that spinning gear to Roger. Get some books and videos and practice casting on the grass or somewhere. Did you ever see that casting tape of Lefty Kreh's?"

"Yeah, I've seen it," I said, telling him the same lie I'd told elsewhere. Watching me fly cast on the Upsalquitch, in Alaska, on the Leirasveit or the Kennebec, a half-dozen other fly fishermen had asked the same question. Evidently, all I had to do was pick up a rod to indicate I was seriously lacking in instruction. Shit, I told myself now, I don't need to watch a television tape to learn how to cast a fly. But I knew it could help, and that made me even more angry with myself.

"Well, it's a good piece of teaching," he said. "I wouldn't nudge at you about this except that I know you've got the bug. Practice, damn it; decent casting doesn't amount to much. Practice every day. It'll just come to you at some point and you'll wonder why it ever seemed hard. Grace, Brother John, grace will come to you from on high. Amen."

"Amen, Brother John," I said.

Jane and John left early the next morning. That afternoon, I took my big tarpon fly rod down to the White Street pier and practiced. Hey, give it a shot, I told myself. Who knows, you might even catch a tarpon.

A month later, I was still trying and had just one chance left. Knowing Jean and I were due to leave for Maine late that June, I arranged a final trip to the Marquesas with Jeffrey. Roger came with us on a majestic morning just three days before the summer solstice—long days that arrived in the small hours and lasted until even the most continental visitors had finished their alfresco dinners on the Bagatelle's verandah.

We were up at four, bumping each other in the cramped kitchen, making certain we had packed proper lunches. Since he left high school, Roger has not spent many nights sleeping. Which does not mean he is alert at dawn. On the contrary, his nocturnal ramblings along Key West's restless streets and his silent and determined alcohol intake set him up for sunup surliness. But fishing dulls his churl, and knowing he could rest for an hour once we set our course from Garrison Bight gave him hope.

Like a marionette whose strings go slack, he rolled with the *Waterlight*'s turns, eyes closed, blond-haired head nodding like a sunflower in a breeze. His gentle face with its button nose and boy's mouth looked, as always, angelic in repose—an altar boy at rest. Which is, I suppose, why an altar boy's disguise has so often been used by scoundrels.

I wanted to nudge the slim figure, give him no peace, make him able to receive the glorious messages that dawn was sending us. Even as Jeffrey peered west through the dark, sweeping the sea for the few modest markers that line the all but invisible trail through the lakes, I could look off our stern and watch the dawn's pale tints dilute the darkness on the eastern horizon. Soon enough light had spilled to silhouette morning wings as herons, gulls, and comorants began their early errands. Alone in my world of sound, speed, and genuine solitude I wanted, as I always do on that journey through the water wilderness, to take someone's hand, to share the glories we alone were being given.

But Roger was not about to be that person. His concentration on recuperation was absolute and he did not stir until Jeffrey throttled down and began to use his quiet electric motors to move us along the Marquesas' southern shore where tarpon sometimes gather early on a new day. I made Roger fish first. My perversity sprang partially from my knowledge of the weight of his beer-battered head and my feeling that there were indeed tarpon to be had. I wanted to see Roger react to a strike that stripped two hundred feet of backing off his spinning reel.

In twenty minutes, Jeffrey had put us alongside a school. The fish were daisy-chaining in a casual circle, quite unaware of their visitors. Roger, however, was overly aware of the lumbering, coppery shoulders that emerged from an ocean that had yet to become blue with daylight. In the windless dawn, the sibilant hiss of the fish sounded soft on the morning as the tarpon exhaled air from their flotation bladders. Even their sliding silver emergence and entry to and from the sea could be heard, that most fragile sound of those ultra-smooth, silver-scaled torsos sliding along the warm salt surface.

"Cast now!" Jeffrey said, his crisp voice cutting the paralysis Roger and I shared as we watched the splendid pageant just off our bow.

Raising his rod, Roger's arm pivoted in the school's general direction, but no plug hit the water.

"Shit," Roger said, flipping the bail that he had forgotten and casting again.

"Reel slowly," Jeffrey called from the stern.

Roger stopped reeling and the red-and-white plug wobbled to the surface, followed by a wide-open tarpon mouth as large and as dark as a black bushel basket. "Oh, God," Roger said, then yanked hard. Soaring free of the surface, the plug whipped empty air above Roger's head, snapped back, wrapping line around the rod tip on its rebound. Reaching for the tip, Roger tried to untangle the mess of monofilament, then put the rod on the deck when he realized the complexity of his problem. As he worked, frowning and fumbling, tarpon circled like porpoises for a few more moments and then vanished as gentle ripples radiated from the scene of their dawn frolic.

Gentle Jeffrey said nothing. Unlike so many professional fishing guides, who, I suppose, sometimes feel demeaned by their for-hire status, he never tries even to the score by criticizing an inept fisherman. He does just the opposite: he tries harder to make sure that fisherman is successful.

Poling the *Waterlight* along the south shore, past the entrance to the deepest channel, Jeffrey let his skiff drift into the same coral serving dish we had anchored in four weeks before. I had not forgotten the hammerhead, nor the venue of its visit.

"We'll try it here a few minutes, Roger," Jeffrey said. "Be ready to cast when I tell you. These fish will be traveling, not daisy-chaining."

Sighing with remorse at his earlier showing, Roger stood at attention on the bow casting platform. Believing that I had given him a fair opportunity to hook up, I picked up my fly rod and stood at the stern quarter, just in case. Jeffrey stayed in the bow, ready to instruct if and when he saw a fish turn Roger's way.

Incredibly, as I stared off to the northern sky, my eyes caught the movement of three shapes heading toward us off the flats, not from the deeper water as Jeffrey anticipated.

They came closer, moving steadily, but not quickly. The composure of their procession told me that they had not seen our boat, or, if they had, they judged it no threat.

On they came. I began shaking. My knees, as they always do when I see large fish, deserted their structural purpose. I had trouble staying upright. Even if I had wanted to, which I did not, I could hardly have gotten a word past my tight windpipe.

The tarpon, because that is what they definitely were, never swerved or hesitated. They were, I could tell, going to glide just a few feet from where I stood.

I began swinging my rod in its casting arc, stripping line as I did. Any idiot could cast far enough to reach these fish, I told myself. For Christ's sake, they were practically under our stern.

There were three of them. The two in front were smaller. The single fish, a few lengths back, looked immense. I cast in their general direction.

My fly flopped on the water. By the time it sank to the tarpons' depth, the two lead fish had already moved too far toward the bow. But that third fish found a Cockroach sinking slowly just in front of its mouth. Opening its maw, the tarpon inhaled my fly. I saw it vanish.

When I did, I yanked hard. The fish kept swimming, and that's what saved me. It was the tarpon's progress, not my strike, that did the deed. Before the fish recognized the fly for what it was, its own forward motion snapped the hook against the corner of its jaws.

"Hey!" I yelled, "Hey!"

Spinning, Jeffrey turned toward the stern, saw what was happening, saw the fish dash under the bow and saw the bend in my rod.

Then each of us watched open-mouthed as the tarpon jumped clear less than twenty feet off the bow, crashing back in an awkward, sideways tumble that sounded like a cellar door thrown overboard.

Then that fish took off.

"It's a big fish, a big fish, John!" Jeffrey yelled from the brink of his composure.

"Get up here in the bow," he called as he cleared a path. Holding my rod so its tip pointed at the sky, I edged forward, stepped up onto the platform. The fish made it easier than it might have been. Its run appeared endless, unswerving, and fast. Line disappeared from the Fin-Nor flycasting reel a generous soul had given me, and I began to be certain the backing would vanish entirely. Nothing I could do could stop the fish, not with a twelve-pound-test tippet tied between the shock leader and my flyline. There was no surge, no struggle. Line left me as if the other end was fast to a heavily loaded trailer truck cruising a throughway downgrade at seventy miles an hour.

Just when I was certain that tarpon's first run was also my last, the fish jumped. I could not comprehend the distance. At first, I thought it was some other fish, not mine. Far to the west, on the way to the Tortugas, the tarpon leapt free and clear, hung there and crashed back.

The line went slack.

"He's off," I said.

"No. No." Jeffrey said. "He's headed straight back this way. Reel, John. Reel as fast as you can."

I tried. I turned the crank as fast as my hand and wrist would respond to my brain's message. I could not catch up to the fish. Slack line curved on the water's surface.

"Reel! Reel!" Jeffrey yelled.

I did, desperately. Then, pressure, wonderful pressure. The encounter continued. I could feel the fish; it could feel me. Once again, we were joined. What I'd said to my father was right: fishing should come first.

"Flyline coming in," Jeffrey called.

I had retrieved all the backing. My aching arm told me it had been a job.

Just as the flyline began to build on the reel, the tarpon turned and began another run: the same truck on the same throughway.

This time, it hit a wall. The reel stopped turning, the rod bent sharply, too sharply. I watched, knowing disaster had been born in that instant of silence. The rod snapped back in my hand like a tree branch bent and released. This time each of us knew the fish was free.

"What happened?" Jeffrey asked.

Looking at the reel I knew. When the fish had turned and run toward me, and when I was reeling in as fast as I possibly could, the slack in the line had looped back on itself. I had, in fact, wrapped a free-floating loop of backing around the reel. On its next run, the tarpon had gone as far as that loop. Wrapped around the line, it became an instant brake, a stop as effective as any knot. The tippet, as it was designed to do, broke under the pressure. My tarpon was free. My giant tarpon, gone.

"A big fish," Jeffrey said. "A very big fish."

"Hey," I said, "it took my fly. I cast to it by myself and it took my fly. That's the first tarpon that's ever done that."

Nine months ago, that happened, and I can still see that fish leaping against the sky, almost as far off as the Tortugas.

We are fishing inside the lagoon today, in barracuda country. When February's northeast winds chill the deeper waters of the channels, barracuda congregate in the thin water of the Marquesas flats favoring circles of pale sand free of turtle grass and seaweed. From his perch on the poling platform above the stern, Jeffrey looks for their motionless cigar shapes;

these fish take the sun as studiously as a Manhattan broker on his first day alongside a Miami Beach hotel pool.

"Fish at twelve o'clock," Jeffrey calls. "He's out of casting range, but let me know when you can see him."

Staring, peering straight ahead, I see the barracuda's shadow profile suspended above the golden sand. "I see him. I see him." I raise my rod and begin false casting, the lime-green tassel whipping back and forth.

"Cast now," Jeffrey tells me, and I do.

The line collapses on the surface as if it spilled from an overhead slop jar. The fly is nowhere near the fish.

"Pick it up and cast again," Jeffrey says. "He's still right there."

I yank too hard on my retrieve. The fly pops from the surface headed straight for me. I duck as it wraps itself around the rod. By now, the *Waterlight*'s easy momentum has brought the boat too close and the barracuda glides off.

Jeffrey says nothing, keeps poling, keeps looking.

Half-an-hour later, after a discouraging series of flawed and fruitless casts, I think I detect a note of weary resignation in Jeffrey's words, encouraging though they may be. He has, after all, put me within casting range of a half-dozen sturdy barracuda, all of whom are still at large and at ease.

"Fish at ten o'clock," he calls, "moving toward eleven."

I see the fish, and I cast. The fly lands almost where I want it to go, but I begin stripping line, trying to retrieve it as fast as possible so I can try the cast a second time.

"He sees the fly," Jeffrey calls. "He's after it. Here he comes. Keep stripping. Strip as fast as you can."

Now I can see the push of water racing behind my fly as the barracuda gets up to speed. Then I see the fish. It is less than twenty feet from our bow and racing.

I keep stripping. I watch as the barracuda opens its mouth and eats my fly. I expect the fish to strike the boat. It turns and runs a few feet, then jumps. The sun flashes on its sides of mottled silver.

"Look at that jump," yells Jeffrey. "Get him on the reel, John. Get him on the reel."

As the fish runs across the flats, I keep tension on the flyline with my left hand. In moments, the slack is taken.

"You got him on the reel. Good boy," Jeffrey yells.

The fish makes several jumps, at least three fine runs, and then I have it beside the boat: my first barracuda on a fly. Jeffrey leans over the gunwale and cautiously removes the hook. After a motionless moment, the barracuda waves its tail gently and moves off at a measured pace across the flats.

Jeffrey walks forward and shakes my hand. "Congratulations, Cap," he says. "That was a good fish, about fifteen pounds."

Jean is smiling as I put down my rod and slide onto the seat beside her.

"How about some lunch?" asks Jeffrey. Not waiting for our answer, he opens a cooler and passes around sandwiches and cold juice. Staked off, the *Waterlight* is the only boat inside the Marquesas lagoon, we are the only human souls in sight. Because I know this is a wilderness preserve and because Key West is more than twenty miles northeast, I feel privileged, lucky to be in this wild and distant place on such a sparkling adventure on such a fine, sun-drenched day.

"There," I say to Jean, as I remember John Graves's words, "I've caught a barracuda on a fly. Next will come a tarpon, then a bonefish, and then a permit. Isn't that a wonderful agenda to have in front of me. It took me sixty-five years to get this far. I'm going to have a shitload of fun traveling the rest of the way."

And we hold hands.

Down to Zero

By Ted Leeson

WHEN NICK LYONS WAS PREPARING TO PUBLISH TED LEESON'S *THE Habit of Rivers* in 1994, almost everyone connected with book and magazine publishing knew a new gun was in town. Everyone who saw even portions of the book unleashed praise at its most lavish, with expressions such as "unusual grace and power"... "the wonder never ebbs, from beginning to end"... "eloquent"... "brilliant." And the best news of all was that *The Habit of Rivers* deserved every word being written and said about it.

Today Ted Leeson's book still occupies the lofty pinnacle of respect it earned back when first published. An English teacher at Oregon State University when he wrote the book, Leeson makes the trout, salmon, and steelhead waters of the Pacific Northwest seem as familiar as our nearby streams, and the fishing itself seem almost illuminated by some universal bond of understanding and sharing between anglers.

If you have not had the opportunity to read Ted Leeson until now, you might be questioning whether or not this rather expansive buildup to the piece is a little overcooked. Fear not! Ted Leeson delivers on every promise we've made.

―∾―

The Deschutes again. The circus has left town, its only vestiges the crumbling shucks of long-gone salmonflies and empty husks of paper and aluminum cast off by departing campers, exuvia of the hatch now dessicating in a summer sun. The desert air grows hard and dry as a white stone. The tenuous greens of spring fade from the slopes, trickling downhill and collecting in the narrow fringe of vegetation that still thrives at the river's edge. Under a cloudless sky, the landscape browns like a baking loaf.

Days lengthen into indefiniteness. In scrubby draws, quail and chukar hide out. Coyotes sleep in dens. Trout hug the shady banks and the shadowed lees of rocks, waiting for evening.

In this steep country, the sun sets prematurely, dropping early below the high butte on Webster Flat. But the day itself lingers in the heat rising from volcanic dust, the resinous odor of sagebrush, and in the glow of the rimrock still lit by the sun. Through a long dusk, light climbs the ochre and gray canyon rocks and is mirrored in the river hundreds of feet below, suffusing the landscape from top to bottom with a golden-bronze light that tints whatever it touches. You wade in the reflection of a reflection, and the coppery water streams against your legs like something molten.

It is a serenely beautiful light, but damned hard to see in. Standing shin-deep among thick, wavering tendrils of ranunculus, I can just make out a pair of geese herding four goslings to the point of the island for the night. Caddis flutter everywhere, lighting on the back of my hands and crawling over my glasses. In the dim metallic twilight, the first few rings appear, expanding concentric zeros of rising trout. They are barely perceptible on the riffly seam between the channel and flats, like intermittent bits of sense snatched from radio static. Fly and tippet raised in silhouette against the sky, I work in two dimensions to thread one to the other and eventually manage a questionable knot.

Before long the river is spattered with rises, vague bullseyes I can't seem to hit because I can't see where my fly lands. The last light settles on the river in a pale cross-current streak, and as on so many June evenings before, I wade up or down to center this foot-wide window of lightness over a few working fish, their ripples black against the faint flush. The casts are guesses of distance and drift, and I strike at every rise. Mostly there's just empty air and a headstart on the next backcast, but now and again, I meet the resistance of something solid that surges without pause to the middle of the river and leaps in the darkness. A big trout here—and most of them are—will instantly quarter down and out, and gaining the main current, can spool you in half a minute. Long before that, this one breaks the leader.

On other days, I'd stick with it, losing at last the dwindling June light and fishing by sense and sound. Tonight, without the pang of opportunity foregone, I wade out and watch the last of the rises, and beyond them the long, unruffled expanse of a summer that will gloss these first few hours.

At an early age I more or less consciously concluded that the things I was really interested in possessing could only be bought with time, not money, and that I would make it my business to trade the one for the other whenever possible. Whether this implied a kind of wisdom or a kind of laziness is a question I've always sensed wouldn't bear much scrutiny. Nevertheless, in the cunning, Confucian way that life sometimes works itself out, I seem to have been given precisely what I'd asked for. I have at my disposal more uncommitted time than is ordinarily considered seemly for an adult, whereas money remains largely a theoretical concept. All in all, the circumstance is only slightly more equivocal than I supposed it would be.

The exact moment all this dawned on me is distinctly clear in my memory—a warm early-June morning at my grandmother's house in the farm country of southern Wisconsin. I was ten. School had let out the day before. I was sitting in a backyard that sloped and then leveled its way to the banks of Turtle Creek, a sluggish little mudhole that at the time I regarded as the most fascinating body of water on earth. It was for many years a place where I would inflict my curiosity on toads, frogs, chubs, crayfish, and all the usual victims of childhood's wanton and sadistic wonder.

Thinking of nothing at all, really, but lying in the cool, uncut grass, feeling the fineness of the day and how much of it lay ahead, I was struck immediately and altogether, the way a sonic boom seems to hit you with a pressure wave from all sides at once, that it wasn't just the promise of the creek that waited before me, or even the rest of the day, but the day after, and the day after that, stretching on into a distance I could scarcely contemplate. It wasn't some sudden first grip on the concept of "summer"—that, I understood entirely—rather, I was seized by the intuition of perfect open-endedness, the vision of a vast uncluttered plain of time over which my existence would move without keel or destination, frictionlessly propelled by the slightest puffs of whim or desire. The force of this awareness detonated in my mind a soft implosion of pure bliss that ran through me like a transfusion. A poor man's infinity, I suppose, but it was plenty to handle then, as it is now.

This sense of unfetteredness, of the future as a patient infinity, was for summer after summer a free-floating thing, though not a neutral one. It was charged like an ion, and the year I turned sixteen, drew into its orbit the attractive prospects of a driver's license and a not-so-nearby trout stream. My vast plain of time suddenly acquired a topography of hills and meadows, highways and gravel roads, open rivers and weedy spring creeks. The vista of summer changed from simply all-the-time-in-the-world to the decidedly more particular all-the-time-in-the-world-to-fish. Or so it seemed at first. Trout fishing, I was to learn, was a season. It had an opening, but it also had a closing, and this little-expected development significantly altered the view. My sense of open-endedness began to acquire the finitude of its object, as the onset of the trout season already implied its finish. I went at every conceivable opportunity. The fishing was often good and the days immensely happy, though now touched with a consciousness of their extent, in just the way that all powerful emotions seem to me now tinged with their opposites. At the time, I was well aware that things die, had even some notion of death, but this particular feeling of an end lurking within the fact of beginning was for a while the most palpable understanding I had of mortality.

September was the wall, the close of the season as incomprehensibly laid down by the Department of Natural Resources. It deposited me on the edge of a great black void, of eight-and-a-half lightless months of winter with nothing to hold on to but the none-too-sure conviction that next summer, another season would come. In the interim were the small facts of eternity and gym class. By December, I was deeply depressed; by April, given to minor psychotic episodes and kept marginally sedated by the narcotics of anticipation and tackle catalogs. When the trout streams finally opened, the soul-rinsing relief was inexpressible.

Though I eventually moved West for much different reasons, I have come to appreciate this one above all others: It rescued me from seasons. They exist here, to be sure, but less as a matter of calendars than of inclination and opportunity. Salmon, winter steelhead, whitefish, trout, shad, spring chinook, trout, smallmouth, summer steelhead, sea-run cutthroat, salmon—they overlap like the scales of fish, layered three and four deep on some rivers, the smooth skin of a year that is proof against a good many things. You fish with a psychic tilt, listing forward, the momentum of one season bearing you into the next, and the sense is overwhelmingly of beginning rather than ending.

It's a personal version of a cultural idea, I suppose—the West as a place of starting over, of renewal, a world always on the verge of opening out. Oregon was, and is, my "fresh green breast of the new world," though it grows a little less green every day. But outfitted with an open mind, warm waders, and semireliable transportation, it is possible to step into a consecutive series of new beginnings and, with the right kind of eyes, to see precisely the rarity there to be appreciated.

The sudden liberation from a sense of seasonal boundaries had two entirely serendipitous, if slightly contradictory, consequences. Old habits die hard, and some not at all. The lengthening days of summer for so long marked the onset of the fishing season that I found myself unable to abandon the idea altogether. Though I may have fished almost continuously for twelve months running, summer remains a psychological beginning. It is the newest start in this place of new starts, the zero point of my year.

And from here I survey the summer, and this summer in particular, in much the old way, as a horizon of pure possibility of indefinite tenure with a nearly ridiculous personal liberty and an unshackled sense of the lightness of existence. Summer shapes itself in my mind as a zero-gravity world where rivers and lakes, fly rods and landscapes, trout and highways, whim, will, happenstance, and all the time in the world drift freely, bumping gently together in endlessly recombinant and deeply pleasurable collisions.

When your chief engagement with the world of commerce is exchanging money for time, dollars become days. And lying in the cool, uncut grass on the bank of the Deschutes, I contemplate the venture capital of a summer's happiness stretched out before me, an unnumbered Swiss account of unnumbered sunny days that I intend to spend to the last nickel. I don't even mind squandering some. Like a lottery winner lighting victory cigars with a hundred-dollar bill, I burn a little time just watching the last few rises to the last few caddis on this first of evenings, and look forward to a summer as exquisitely functionless as the fishing that will fill it.

New waters or old? That is the summer question. They're filed side-by-side in a fisherman's mind like shelves of books. Some are familiar and well-thumbed, the favorite parts underlined with notes in the margin; stood on their spines, they fall open to the places you can quote from memory. Fishing them offers the delights of rereading—the intimacy of things already known and the small, subtle surprises of discovery within the familiar. Beside them are new lakes and streams, unknown quantities temptingly jacketed and attractively titled, loaned by friends or picked up on a hunch, their waters waiting to be read.

Deciding not to decide, I take down some of each. And as all rivers do, each eventually clarifies itself as one of the infinite variations on the single theme of moving water, the simplest of all ideas in countless permutation that makes all rivers at once perfectly individual and essentially alike. In incidental echoes, river is linked to river, event to event. They overlap, contacting at capricious points, coincidences of memory and sense—the sharp smell of sagebrush, the ratchet of a kingfisher, the feel of a hot wind or a heavy trout in the hand—until you cannot seize hold of one without the rest clinging to it.

Time, someone once said, is what keeps everything from happening at once. Its medium is motion, constant and cyclonic, in which events are held separate by the sheer force of ongoingness, like leaves in a fall whirlwind. Against the pressure of a summer sun, time slows; movement slackens; and the grains of recollection settle out into the thin, intervalless lamina of simultaneity.

Below Leaburg Dam, the south bank of the McKenzie River climbs steeply and is matched in pitch by the long wooden slide that sluices a boat from a small pull-off down forty feet to the river, or somewhere thereabouts. It looks like an old log flume and, on a dew-slick morning like this one, functions with the same ungovernable approximateness.

The launch can be a ticklish business by yourself, but this morning it is uneventful.

With their usual mandarin inscrutability, the Eugene Water & Electric people have cranked down the gates despite a recent rain. The water is low, and bedrock ribs and vertebrae poke everywhere through the skin of the river. It promises to be a rocky ride—not the bucking stuff of white-water, but an occasional African-Queen-style boat drag over gravelly shoals and stone shelves. I tie a line to the bow before pushing off and then dodge my way downriver between the rocks and the aluminum skid marks left by other low-water drifters.

Half-a-mile down, the water splits and files through three parallel slots, as uniform as furrows in the riverbed. The sun hasn't yet cleared the firs on the bank, and in the morning shade, I fish through a sequence of nymphs—#14 Hare's Ear on the point, #16 Pheasant Tail on the dropper; point fly off, #14 Muskrat on; dropper off, #18 Black A.P. on; point off. . . . It has all the appearance of a random exploration, but I know in advance exactly where it's all headed, the way you can spiral down to the point in a conversation, to prolong the pleasure or defer disappointment, knowing from the start you'll eventually get there.

I end up where I thought. On the dropper is a #16 Green Sparkle Pupa, a pattern that is sheer inspiration on some rivers, a waste of time on others, and a #14 Zug Bug on the point, a fly that has caught hundreds of trout for me, but one for which I haven't developed the slightest bit of affection. Immediately, I begin mopping up on little ones—small cut-throats, steelhead and salmon smolts—each a wonderfully precise minia-ture of what it may someday become.

With a few firm exceptions, fishing from boats holds little appeal. It has a certain industrial quality about it, a no-nonsense fixation on the business of catching fish, and I'd much rather drift from place to place, working the promising water on foot, which brings you closer to every-thing. Sometimes, though, casting from a boat can't be helped. The slower, unwadable pools are tinted a translucent emerald and transected by solid columns of light that exaggerate the sense of the water's depth. To a short leader and a sink-tip line, I tie an undesignated miscellany of marabou and hen hackle and chuck the whole unruly mess to one side, feeding line until fly and boat are synchronized in the same lazy drift. The technique is as craven as it sounds, modeled after the drift fisherman's practice of "boondoggling," a corruption of the term "boom-dogging," that came about in earlier times when long rafts of logs were herded down rivers. The tag ends of huge chains that bound the booms together dragged the river bottoms and stirred up everything, including the steelhead. Boat fishermen would follow (or "dog") the booms in hopes of finding takers among the agitated fish. With a distinctly regional penchant for the heavy-duty, boom-dogging was a cross between stoning the pool and the world's biggest San Juan shuffle, with all the genteel attraction of hunting pheasants behind a grain combine.

I set the rod down and, working under the assumption that an empty bladder is the devil's workshop, open a beer, hand-picked for the day and requiring the reassuring inconvenience of a bottle opener. Only a stout can measure up to the intensity of a summer noon, and Grant's Imperial, the issue of a Washington microbrewery, is nothing if not intense. It pours like used motor oil, has a potent bitterness and enough body to make solid food redundant. Not exactly the stuff one swills by the six-pack, it takes an hour to drink one properly, perhaps a bit longer with the hard-smoked trout I've packed along with it.

History being what it is, I count myself lucky to have been born into an age of renaissance in both fly fishing and serious brewing. In the right proportion, they resonate with unusual harmony in the pace and subtlety of their enjoyment. That some varieties of beer blend especially well with certain types of trout water seems to me a book-worthy subject, though the world is not yet ready for this. Or so I was told by a publisher to whom I mentioned the idea—over, incidentally, a tap of Blackhook Porter, the hands-down beverage for any editorial negotiation.

In mid-sip, the rod tip plunges deeply twice, strains to some invisible surge, and, before I can swallow, springs straight under a limp line and clatters hollowly against the gunnel. It is no less than I deserve.

On a day in late August, you don't need a physicist to tell you that light exerts pressure. You can feel it on your shoulders and the back of your neck, a pleasant weight that induces the kind of reverie always and best described as "thinking about nothing." I ship the oars and sip the beer. Unchecked, the boat drifts to an eddy on the left bank and idles there in slow, counterclockwise revolution, suspended beneath the long pause of a windless afternoon.

On a windless afternoon, I climb the flank of a canyon along a small coastal stream, shown to me years ago by a friend in exchange for the promise never to reveal its location. His caution, however understandable, was unnecessary. The 30% grade of crumbling rock, the pathless descent through a tangle of deadfalls, scrub, and dense patches of Himalaya vine have so far proven more than adequate to safeguard the place.

Nine hours ago, I picked my way down the slope with high hopes and a daypack to the little freestone creek. Its bouldery bed, brisk runs, plunge pools, and deep basinlike holes brought to mind similar streams I'd only recently left behind in the Blue Ridge and Allegheny Mountains of Virginia. Instead of wild brook trout, I found native coastal cutthroats, though in their way these two fishes are as much alike as the streams they inhabit. The cutts are small, beautifully formed fish with opalescent bellies, silver sides, and blue-green backs flushed with violet, indigo, and red. The orange slash beneath their gills is precisely the color of a spawning brook trout and, like them, the cutthroats are quick and nervous, but aggressive if not spooked, with a fondness for bright flies and shady water.

On my first trip to a coastal stream, I was struck by the similarity of the two species and of the places they are fished. And I still take pleasure in the accidental symmetry: The native brook trout of the ancient Appalachians and the wild cutthroats of the young Pacific Coast Range bookend the continent and bracket the world of my trout fishing.

The fish come easily, one or two ten-inch cutts from each little run and pool, jabbing fiercely against a resilient six-foot cane rod, lovingly if amateurishly built from the top two sections of an old Granger Favorite I bought for $8 at a rummage sale. I catch dozens of trout in the slow passage upstream. Scrambling over boulders, crisscrossing the water, wading through thick stands of ferns, trillium, wood sorrel, and wild bleeding heart that flourish in the damp shade, I travel three miles for every one of river, and once, boosting myself over a deadfall, settle my butt in banana slug half again as long as my hand.

Sitting on the shank of a fallen cedar, I eat lunch (a pair of stream-chilled Cold Spring Exports and a cellophane bag of some kind of cheese things). The trunk is massive, perhaps sixteen feet in circumference, and the root mass suggests it fell some time before the area was first logged at the turn of the century. Such a tree would never have escaped ax and oxen. The surface is bleached and smooth as whitened bone, but cedar endures like the mountains, and there is little doubt that beneath the weathering, its wood is sound and fragrant, good for another century at least. In the pool backed up by the deadfall, I soothe barked shins and wash the slug slime off my jeans.

The frothy water spilling into the head of this pool produces the largest trout of the day, a skinny thirteen-inch fish that I imagine was seeing its last season. Not many weeks before, in water much like this, I discovered the fresh carcass of a giant Pacific salamander, a prehistoric-looking creature a full foot long with a broad flattened head and tiny eyes. On a hunch, I wade the edges of the pool, poking among rocks and leaves, looking for a live one. Instead, under a sheet of peeled bark are two enormous millipedes with thick, hard, deeply segmented bodies, like finger-length sections of a gooseneck lamp.

They are a prefiguration. A month later on Fall River, the trout we've come for, big browns alleged to haunt the lower stretches, are apparently haunting someplace else, though we manage a few in the three- to four-inch class. Wading out for a rest, I upend an unsplit fire log for a seat and expose, amid the dust and rotting bark, two families of black widows. A pair of obsidian females scutters among several dozen small spiders, already with the distinctive body shape but not yet black, their abdomens a mottled glossy brown like tumbled agates. They seem as little inclined to bite as the fish.

Fall River cuts through the flows of basalt laid on the leveling slope of the eastern Cascades, and the stream threads its way among stands of fir and Ponderosa. Much of it is shallow, flowing thinly over sandy, troutless bottom and offers holding water only behind the many bankside sweepers. But it is one of the best places I know to see birds. There are tanagers here in enormous numbers, and from forest floor to canopy, woodpeckers drill incessantly.

Toward afternoon, I hook the only real fish of the day, a rainbow that darts from beneath a volcanic ledge to grab a nymph almost at my feet. Its thrashings on the surface of the narrow channel attract the notice of an osprey peering over the edge of a jackstraw nest built in a Ponderosa snag. The bird rocks for a moment on the edge of indecision, tempted by an easy meal but concluding, eventually, that I'm a little too close.

Sixty miles and six weeks away, the osprey on Davis Lake are not nearly so timid. Wings and tails flared to stall against the incoming breeze, they perch in freeze-frame on an invisible column of air and scan the water below. Then folding up, they spear fifty feet of air and shatter the lake amid casting fishermen and dimpling trout, taking fish one dive out of three and preening their feathers between tries. Six birds work the small lake at the same time.

The water is almost as clear as the air (all this before the lake was poisoned for rough fish), and pods of whitefish swim beneath the boat to forage among the reed beds like schools of mudding bonefish. Trout are mixed in, too—rainbows, some going six or eight pounds. We fish the margin of the weeds with 6X tippet and a tiny Pheasant Tail or Cates Turkey, studying the precise point where the leader slips beneath the surface film, waiting for the nervous flutter that may signal a take. We work hand-twist retrieves with a patient, glacial crawl that makes lake fishing, at best, the sport of monks and at worst a barbiturate daze. I venture this opinion after hours beneath a blazing afternoon—that river fishing is inherently more interesting, exacting more skill and invention, better for the soul and eye, less stultifying and more productive.

Later that night I dine on these words, and though well-spiced with irony and served with a clean Sierra Nevada Bock, they taste remarkably like crow. For at twilight, ginger midges appear. The lake is alive with rises, and from sunset to insensibility, we twitch #18 Blond Haystacks to quick, hard hits.

By the time it is over we need flashlights to beach the boat in the shallows beside camp. As the bow slides to a stop in the silt, the shoreline seems suddenly to dissolve in a quick, diffuse shiver, and just as quickly coalesce to solidity. In one of the more curious, small-potatoes spectacles I've seen, the beach is blanketed with a swarm of tiny toads that jump in unison at the sound of the boat. Each is a duplicate of the next, knobby, ambered-eyed halves-of-an-inch, the color of an old penny. A score of them would fit in a boot-track, and I skirt the shore for a quarter mile, each footstep sending up an explosive little cloud of toads. They must number in the tens of thousands.

They brought to mind the grasshoppers on the Williamson River—the same flurried, cross-hatched scattering, a net of movement cast in the grass to trap the eye with confusion. Hordes of them clicked like mussels in the sun. I took the hint and twitched small hopper patterns on twelve-foot leaders in the glassy stretches below Spring Creek, avoiding the meat bucket at Chiloquin and, it turned out, most of the trout.

Not a whisper of air disturbed the blank, blistering August afternoon that bridged the two ends of this very buggy day. In the morning chill, I sat in a camper with a steaming mug of coffee, watching hundreds of Tricos molting outside on the window glass, and waited for a spinner fall that never came. I fished hoppers during the hot afternoon, and dusk came with the audible, aggregate whine of a million mosquitos.

One of them sank an exploratory shaft into an already tender and inflamed swelling next to my watch band, and I hoped it was poisoned by residual venom. A few days before, at 7:20 p.m., while I was wading the North Umpqua, minding my own affairs, a sudden burning in my wrist triggered a violent, involuntary, full-body spasm. A yellow jacket lazily flew off from a reddening circle beside the winding stem of a watch that read 7:20. I dipped my arm in the cold water for half a minute, but couldn't spare more. Caddis were hatching all around me, and from bank to bank the river was pocked with rises.

I had come, as all do, to fish this holiest of water for steelhead. I cast without conviction when the sun was high, but in the evening, with the river blanketed in shadows and caddis, I began to think I might have blundered upon every steelhead fisherman's sweetest dream—the chance to take a bright sea-run fish on a dry fly and light trout tackle. Knotting on an Elk Hair Caddis, I dressed it with floatant and hope and covered rise after rise, beginning with the near bank and working slowly outward among deceptively swift currents and rocks of legendary slickness.

In the end, the steelheader's dream remained just that, but I caught some cutthroats, a few decently large, and fished the caddis, to me among the most agreeable of all hatches.

For reasons both historical and aesthetic, the mayfly is angling's glamor-bug. It garners most of the press and a lavish attention from fly tyers. No single group of insects has spawned more or more various patterns than the mayfly, from nymphs to spinners to the hyper-refinements of crippled emergers and stillborn duns. A mayfly is never just a mayfly. Show a single Pale Morning Dun to any serious fisherman, and he'll give you the full breakdown in an instant: *Ephemerella inermis*; #17 female imago; recently molted; slightly more reddish than the norm; with egg sac. Venture that it's a "little rusty mayfly" and you'll be hooted out of the corps. Our exactness defers as much to their beauty as necessity.

But most of the time, a caddis is just a caddis—maybe a "speckled caddis" or a "little black caddis," and it seldom goes much beyond that. Nevertheless, I have an abiding fondness for caddis and regard them as the preeminent fly of summer—reliable and prolific, an everyday workhorse, the utility outfielder of bugs. Were it a beer, it would Henry Weinhard's or Rolling Rock. Few insects can match the elegance of a mayfly, as precise and delicate as an origami bird. The caddis, however, is a fisherman's fly.

Though mostly dull grays and tans, some are strikingly patterned, and of these, none more so than a caddis I saw first when I came west—a big fly, an inch long, with tawny wings grained in shades of chestnut and gold, like a chip of burnished oak. Quite by accident, I came to know them better in a freshly painted outhouse at a campsite on the middle Deschutes. There on the wall, above a roll of toilet paper, wings and legs and antennae perfectly and symmetrically extended, one of these caddis had become stuck in the paint and dried there, every translucent detail of its anatomy visible over the background of pure white. Underneath it, in the neat, squared hand of a draftsman, was printed, "*Hesperophylax incisus.*" Back at the tent, I fetched a thick volume of aquatic entomology and returned to the privy, passing a group of rafters whose looks questioned just what I had in mind and just how long it was going to take. I found the identification accurate.

Some time later, I discovered the caption was the job of someone I distantly knew. Much of life depends from such coincidences. Despite our efforts to plot the cause and effect of events, history seems to rattle from one accident to another in a pachinko of chance associations.

Which is how I happen to be sitting on the South Jetty of Yaquina Bay, with the butt of an eleven-foot surf rod wedged in the rocks beside me. The first outdoor magazine I ever saw fell into my hands thirty years ago, and I read it at once from cover to cover, including a pair of run-of-the-mill fishing yarns that knit themselves together in my mind. The first concerned catching large trout on small flies and featured an inset photo of a gigantic rainbow with a tiny midge nearly invisible in its huge maw. The second was about surf-casting and pictured a lone angler in waders carrying an enormous red drum by the gill plates, its tail dragging in the sand of a deserted beach. The images were instantly and permanently yoked together. I'd never fly fished, and surf was a little hard to come by in Wisconsin, so I recognized no particular incongruity. Thirty years later, the one idea still clings compatibly to the other, following it around instinctively like one of Konrad Lorenz's geese, and the fact that it's only a synaptic fluke doesn't bother me.

Soaking chunks of mussel on the bottom of the bay, I'm hoping for ling cod (several months out of season); I'll take anything I can get. Today, it happens to be a few sculpins, a small rockfish, and a nice Dungeness crab that surrenders the bait before I can nab it. The wind shifts on the ebb tide and mounts nearly a full gale by afternoon. At the juncture of outgoing tidal currents and onshore gusts, the mouth of the jetty develops a heavy chop and dangerous rips. Charters wait offshore for a lull, then hurry in. I cast in the same lulls, but the power of the wind and plumes of cold spray drive me off. At home, I steam the rest of the mussels.

I fished in wind like this once on Chickahominy Lake, the kind of muddy, bleak, weather-whipped toilet I've seen only in eastern Oregon. One comes here strictly for the fishing, though often enough that is sufficient. In the morning, I was pinned inside my tent by a Hereford bull grazing the campsite; in the afternoon, my back to roaring wind, I cast stiffly to the tips of sunken sagebrush and caught fat rainbows on lethally weighted Woolly Buggers.

I drill one of these same flies into my ear on a breezy morning fishing the North Santiam. Daubing at a remarkable quantity of blood leaking from my ear lobe, I walk back to the car for some lunch, a sclerosis of bacon and avocado on pumpernickel and a bottle of Mt. Hood Hefeweizen, a thin, cloudy gruel of a beer made from wheat. But it chills well and takes the edge off a hot day. Laying out these provisions on the steel siderail of the bridge, I watch a fisherman in voluminous chest waders on the far bank, half-hidden in the shadow of the concrete abutment. He's holding a spinning rod bent nearly in half by the exertions of an apparently large fish in the deep, heavy current sweeping beneath the bridge.

When he loops up, I can tell he's shouting something, but the sound is lost in the rush of the river and in the rattles and grumbles of an ancient flatbed truck, headed my way down the edge of a vast field of strawberries. The engine stops, a door slams, and I'm joined on the bridge by the driver, an Hispanic farm laborer in his mid-fifties perhaps, with a skin like weathered elk hide and the broad cheekbones and nose I've seen in Mayan stone reliefs. He taps an open cigarette pack against his lower lip with a practiced gesture that slides out a single smoke just far enough to grab with his teeth, and lights it. By the fit of his work glove, I can tell he's missing the little finger of his right hand.

The fisherman below is clearly losing ground. A formidable chute runs between the midriver bridge piling and the concrete abutment on the bank that is blocking his passage downriver. The rod tip lunges rhythmically; each pulse exacts a squealing little burp from the reel and moves the fish a few feet farther away. From the other side of the bridge, we make out the flash of a sizeable steelhead, bright as a new dime and twisting in the current. No more than a hundred feet below the fish, the river gathers to the right and drops through a whitewater sluice that curves against an evil-looking rip-rap bank.

The driver smokes, I finish my sandwich and sip the beer, and it's obvious to both of us that the thing is about over, when the fisherman tugs at the drawstrings on his waders, raises his rod above his head with both hands, and steps into the channel. The river laps at his neck, though it is not as deep as I thought. He bobs downstream with just enough control to stay upright but not enough to influence his speed or direction, and disappears under the bridge.

Touching the cigarette for the first time with his muddy glove, my companion flicks an exclamatory ash and quietly exhales, "Cojones."

I respond with equal understatement, a stifled swallow and aborted laugh that ejects a fine spray of wheat beer out each nostril. This hurts, but amuses him highly, and we hurry to the other side of the bridge.

On schedule, the fisherman reappears, feebly sweeping his right arm to draw him to the bank. His circumstance is not yet dangerous, but getting there. Opening the bail on his reel to release line, he clamps the rod butt crosswise in his teeth and begins the clumsy dogpaddle of a man in swamped waders. At the edge of the current, he regains some footing and tightens the line, but the fish has already hit the tongue of the sluice and the monofilament parts like a rifle shot.

It is impossible to walk in brimful waders. Instead, the fisherman crawls on his hands and knees to the banks and bows his head to the ground. A few gallons of the North Santiam spill from his wader tops, and from our angle, he looks remarkably like a man puking. Stretching full-length on the bank, he slides his feet uphill to drain out the rest of the water and for a moment doesn't move. Then he reaches to his breast pocket, and with superb insouciance, puts on a pair of sunglasses and folds his hands neatly across his stomach.

My companion spits his cigarette into the river and returns to the flatbed. I drive upstream to Fisherman's Bend and creel a handful of hatchery trout with a death wish. That evening, I brine and smoke them, and will eat them in a few days, drifting down the McKenzie with a Grant's Imperial Stout beneath a windless afternoon.

Summer is as much a space as it is a time, though in the end these things behave in much the same fashion. In the bright, flat light of midday summer (the one shunned by photographers and painters), space collapses. Perspective-giving shadows shrink and with them the distinctions of remoteness and proximity. The landscape forfeits dimension as foreground and background merge, and the scene becomes as depthless as a canvas. It's a trick of the light, but what things are not?

The same sun beats down a sense of simple aliveness powerful enough to stop a clock. Time folds in on itself. Events are superimposed, an endless succession of images on a single emulsion that reproduces no space between then and now. Time telescopes into itself, and could you cross-section a season, summer would show the concentric rings of a tree trunk, expanding iterations of an archetype, like a riseform.

And like a riseform, summer pleases best in the evening. It is a curious fact of perception that the architecture of a summer day is not symmetrical. An astronomer, citing the constancy of bodies in space, can prove to you that the climb of a morning sun to the meridian and its descent to the western horizon are nearly mirror images of one another. They are equivalent events; a sunset is merely a sunrise played backward. But nothing could be further from the sense of these things. In a lifetime of fishing, I've watched thousands of sunrises, many of them more striking than sunsets, but their beauty is, above all else, momentary and transitory. The first soft flush of dawn hardens without pause to the light of common day. The rise of the sun is sudden and summary, no sooner begun than finished, a beautiful but businesslike preliminary to the business end of the day, its advance as headlong and steady as a cesium clock. I have never seen a lingering dawn.

But it is the essence of a sunset to linger. In imperceptible gradations, it fades to the indefinite and suspended duration of twilight, and dusk feels less an ending than an onset.

The geometry of a summer day is not a perfect hemisphere. It curves eccentrically and elongates time. There is a bulge in the day at evening, as there is in the year at summer, and it is shaped like the bend of the fly rod in my hand, arced to a trout that will in a moment break free into the dimming, gold-leaf currents of the Deschutes, where I will watch the last few rises to the last few caddis, down to zero, on a summer-solstice evening, at the best part of the best part of the year.

September Song

By Robert C. Ruark

ROBERT C. RUARK CREATED READING TREASURE FROM HIS EXPERIENCES
as a lad in North Carolina who learned to hunt and fish under the tute-
lage of his grandfather. Ruark's "The Old Man and the Boy" columns in
Field & Stream are classics in outdoor literature, evoking the fullest senses
of delight in seeing hunting and fishing through youthful, unjaded eyes.
(The columns have been collected in two books, *The Old Man and the Boy*,
and *The Old Man's Boy Grows Older*, Henry Holt and Company.)

Robert Ruark was a nationally known syndicated newspaper col-
umnist when he made his first safari to Africa in 1950. The experience
changed his life. He began writing *Horn of the Hunter*, the terrific book
that details the events of that safari, and decided to try a few pieces for
Field & Stream. The first was "The Brave Quail," regarded today as a classic piece on quail hunting, which appeared in December, 1951. There
were other articles in *Field & Stream* that began a relationship that led to
the creation of "The Old Man and the Boy" column. The income helped
Ruark shuck off his newspaper duties and pursue his deep interest in
Africa, which led to the best-selling novel *Something Of Value*. Later he
wrote *Uhuru*, *Poor No More*, and *The Honey Badger*. He also wrote many
other articles on hunting which have been collected in books.

"September Song," from *The Old Man and the Boy*, is one of many of
my Ruark favorites and brings to this particular collection a glimpse into
the world of easygoing, catch-as-catch-can fishing on the edge of the
sea. You can smell the salt air, hear the thump of the waves, and feel the
excitement of powerful fish melting line off your reel.

Ruark never knew that for him the outdoor life he loved so much and wrote so vividly about was to be short-lived. He died of illness in 1965 at the age of fifty. Many, many other writers have tried to write the type of nostalgic "remembering when" pieces that gave Robert Ruark millions of readers. None have ever taken his place.

When the autumn came to our coast, just a little ahead of the quail-shooting season, when all the summer visitors went away from Wrights-ville Beach and the gray-shingled little beach houses had their windows tacked shut against the northern gales, when the skies got as gray as the shingles and a wood fire was nice at night and all the little shops closed for the long, unprofitable off season—that was when the Old Man and I got into big business with each other.

"It makes a wonderful balance of nature," the Old Man would say, eying the woodpile speculatively, which made me know all of a sudden that he was going to suggest an ax and a small boy to wield it. "When the dodlimbed tourists leave, the bluefish cannot be very far behind. There was a book along those lines, I recall, called *If Winter Comes* or some such. Except I think the writer was reading more spring than bluefish into the script."

As I remember the Old Man, he never said anything at all that you couldn't walk away from three ways and still find a fresh idea in it. I got to where I could listen to him with only one ear, separating the meat from the philosophy, and it wasn't until a lot of years later when I grew up to be a man that I found I remembered more philosophy than meat.

"It is now Labor Day," the Old Man said. "Never quite understood why they call it that, since nobody works on the week end before the Monday they named it after. But on Tuesday the boys will all be gone, and the men will be left. And the bluefish, having watched carefully from Topsail, will come in to commune with the men. Bluefish do not like summer tourists. They like people who admire nor'easters and don't mind a little rain and a squall or so.

"The first thing we will do about bluefish," the Old Man continued, "is to catch a mess of them easy, so you can learn to appreciate the other way. It's too early for them to be inshore, in the sloughs, so we will go trolling for bluefish like the rich people do, and let the boat kill them. I got a connection in the Coast Guard. We will go to Southport and leave early in the morning with Cap'n Willis."

We went on the cutter, and we went out past Caswell, out from Southport, around Frying Pan Shoals. The driver of the boat—he had to be named Midyette, because nearly all Coast Guarders come from Okracoke Island, near Hatteras, and they're all named Midyette down there— tooled the little craft so close to the edge of the shoals you could touch sand with your left hand and see ten fathom of water to your right.

The water was as clear and cool blue as in Bermuda, and the sand as white. The bell buoy was just a little bit behind you, making mournful sounds, and the lightship was over there, as lonesome as the men who lived on her. The gulls wheeled and screamed, and the gannets prowled the water looking for small bait, and off from the sand shoals you could see the big red living shoals of menhaden—pogies, we called them—that the fishing fleet preyed on to make fish-scrap fertilizer.

Here was where the mackerel (we always called them Spanish mackerel) lived, and the kingfish or horse mackerel lived. And here was where the bluefish and the sea trout came into the shallows for the small mullet and the shrimp that swarmed off the rim of the shoals.

"This is silly fishing," the Old Man said. "Don't take any sense or skill at all. All you need is a rod and some line and a hook and piece of bone to make the hook look like a minnow. Heave her over, and the bluefish fight each other for the right to take it. The speed of the boat half-kills the fish, so it is just a matter of hauling them in. Try it and see for yourself."

He handed me a light bass rod, and I flipped the bone minnow over the stern. The line hadn't paid out twenty yards when there was a strike and the rod bent double. It was pretty tough reeling, what with the boat going one way and the fish trying to go another, but I hauled him in. It was a nice bluefish, about two pounds, steely blue in the sun, with his jaw mean-looking and pugnacious and his teeth sharp. He was the first of a hundred, some smaller, which we threw back, and some bigger. One was a four-pounder.

Later on we hooked into a school of mackerel—big, streamlined, speckly fellows that have a chin like a barracuda—and it was the same story. When we finished about 10:00 a.m., we had a boat full of fish—blues, mackerel, a few bonito, and a couple of big kingfish. We had enough fish to feed the whole Coast Guard station and half of the town. Like the Old Man said, it wasn't much sport after the first dozen. But there wasn't anything wrong with them in the skillet or on the little makeshift barbecue the Old Man rigged in front of the shack.

I feel real sorry for people who never had a chance at broiled bluefish or mackerel when the fish is so fresh you have to kill him before you clean him. Some say that blues and mackerel are too fat and oily, but there are some people who don't like snails or oysters and think carrots are just dandy. The way the Old Man cooked them, they tasted better than any fish has a right to taste. He just laid them on the grill over the hot coals and left them until you could see the skin blistering and cracking and turning gold and black, with the white showing through and the grease sizzling steadily onto the coals. When he finally took them off, he had to do it with a flapjack turner; they were so tender they just fell apart. He bathed them in about half a pound of butter per fish, poured vinegar over them, and then dusted them with black pepper. I ate about four pounds of fish before I quit.

Later on in the fall, after the first steady northers had begun to cut sloughs into the beaches and it was getting chilly in the afternoons, he announced one day after lunch that it was time to *really* go fishin'.

"We'll go to Corncake," he said. "I got a hunch the puppy drum are hungry and are in those sloughs stuffin' themselves on sand fleas. This is my kind of fishin'. It ain't murder—it's *fishin'*."

He dug out two big surf rods from under the house and got a big tackle box from his bedroom. We went down to the water front and bought some salt mullet—big ones, thickly crusted with salt—and set out. We took our time. The Old Man said it was no use fishing or hunting any time except real early in the morning or late in the afternoon, because even a fish or a jack rabbit had too much sense to bustle around in the heat of the day.

It was a gray, mean day, with the spume flying and the gulls moaning low and complaining. Along about 5:00 p.m. it was chilly enough for a sweater, and the water was cold on my bare legs. The Old Man spent the first hour trying to teach me to cast, with no bait on my hook. It looked so easy, the way he did it. It looked impossible, the way I did it. He would take the rod, wade out to over his knobby old knees, bring the rod back over his shoulder, with about four feet of line running free. Then he would bring the rod up and over in one single smooth motion, with a whip on the end of the cast. The line would sing through the reel, and the heavy, pyramid-shaped sinker would go whistling out to sea for maybe forty or fifty yards and fall with a plunk right where he was aiming in the slough. Then he'd reel in, very slowly, just enough to keep his line always taut.

When I did it I either threw the sinker into the water at my feet, or jammed the reel and threw the sinker away entirely, or had a backlash right in the middle of the cast. We spent most of the early afternoon unsnarling the reel or putting iodine on the fingers I cut and knocked and line-burned. But I expect young fellows learn pretty fast to do things with their hands, and by dusk I was still clumsy but getting the line out far enough to where at least some fish were. Then the Old Man took his sawbacked ripping knife and showed me how to cut the salt mullet in strips, slicing the inch-and-a-half strips diagonally across the fish. Next he showed me how to work the hook through the strips, weaving it back and forth until the mullet was firm and only the tip of the barb showed. The reason, he said, that we used the mullet instead of fresh bait or shrimps was that the salt had toughened the skin and she'd stay on the hook in rough surf, whereas the other stuff would work off every cast.

The Old Man used a long leader made out of wire, and he hooked two leaders, two hooks, and two baits onto each line. He grinned to himself, humming quietly as he fixed the tackle. His square hands with the broken, stubby fingers and with the old man's brown liver spots on the backs looked clumsy, but they weren't. Anything he handled, from a knife to a gun to a fiddle, was handled so swift and well that it looked easy.

It was growing dark when I stepped out into the icy gray water and cast. The line went out pretty well, the baits whirling through the air, and settled into a slough with a satisfactory chunk. I began to wind her up, to get the belly out of the line, when two bolts of lightning struck. The line screamed out of the reel, and I burned some more fingers before I could get the drag on. It was like being tied fast to two horses, each with his own idea about where he was headed. It seemed that whatever was on that line was going to pull me right into the ocean. But then I began to walk slowly backward, cranking a little bit, keeping the tension on the rod by holding the tip high, the reel close to my belly, and the rod jammed under my arm.

I finally backed up to where the dunes started and the sea oats grew, and I could see the fish coming out of the water, flopping and fighting even on the silver sands. They looked big, like live logs on the beach. I started toward them now, reeling in the slack, and went down to where they lay on the sand. They were both big bluefish, three or four pounds each. I felt like I had just played four quarters of football.

I played out pretty quick, because the rod and reel were heavy and every time I cast—when I didn't backlash—two big bluefish tied into me as soon as the sinker settled. It was taking me fifteen to twenty minutes to land the ones I landed. The ones I lost didn't take so long, and I lost a good deal more than I beached.

By black dark I was cold and wet and sore all over. My hands were cut and full of burning salt, and my back ached like a dissatisfied tooth. But I had caught maybe a dozen big blues, and once a ten-pound puppy drum with the big black spot on his silver backside.

After a while I built a fire out of some driftwood, and sat down to chew on some raw mullet—which tasted delicious—and to watch the Old Man work. The moon rose, about full, and it was like something I had never seen or imagined. The Old Man would wade out and cast into the slough. He would back up, and suddenly he would strike his rod, which would bend double. He would then begin that slow and dignified backward march up the beach, fighting the fish. I was fascinated, watching what eventually emerged from the dark seas onto the moonlit sands.

He fished until midnight. Once he hooked into two drum, and not puppies. One weighed twenty-two pounds, and the other twenty. He was nearly an hour getting them ashore, and when they finally slid up on the sand they looked as big as a couple of Coast Guard surfboats. He never took a line out of the sea without two fish on it. They were starving, I guess, because he never quit until he was exhausted, and they were still striking two at a time the second the bait hit. The Old Man has been dead a long time now, but I'll never forget the way he looked in the moonlight, horsing two channel bass onto the beach, with the birds screaming and the wind high.

"This," the Old Man said as we headed home with the car full of fish, "is what fishing can be like, where you earn your fish and don't kill him with a boat. I'd rather have two mad bluefish on the same line in a cold ocean than catch all the sailfish and marlin ever made. The only thing I know of that's better is a frisky Atlantic salmon in a cold Canadian stream, on about six ounces of fly rod. I hope you get a chance to try it some day when you're bigger."

I did get a chance when I got bigger, and it was twenty-eight pounds of salmon, and he worked me an hour and a half. But he never gave me what I got out of those first two bluefish in an angry autumn sea.

Now the summer was completely gone, and all the memories of the summer. The time of year I liked better than any other had started. You could tell in so many ways that the summer was finished—your legs didn't sweat the crease out of your Sunday pants any more, and there was just a little nip in the evening air. The dogs that had been listless and shedding hair in the sticky heat got into condition again without being dosed, and began to look hopefully at the tin Liz, like maybe a ride was indicated.

The milky smell of summer was all gone out of the air, and had been replaced by the smell of leaves burning and the tart odor of the last of the grapes. You could feel your blood sparkling inside you, no longer heavy with the summer lethargy. A hot breakfast—pancakes and sausage and eggs busted and mixed into the grits—tasted just fine. The leaves were beginning to crinkle a little on the edges, and the first norther that brought the marsh hens flapping up from flooded marshes had already come and gone. A few ducks—teal, mostly—were beginning to drop in.

I don't know if you remember clearly the unspoken promise of excitement that early autumn brings, just before frost comes to grizzle the grasses in the early morning; before the chinquapins are ripe in their burry shells, before the persimmons lose the alum taste that twists your mouth. It's sort of like the twenty-third of December—Christmas isn't quite here, but it's close enough to ruin your sleep.

This was the time when we went fishing seriously on the week ends—fishing in the cold gray sea that always carried a chop except in the long, smooth sloughs; fishing in the inlets, and fishing off a long pier that went away out into the ocean. It was called Kure's Pier, if I remember right, and it cost something, ten cents or two bits, to fish off it. I used to see a couple of hundred fishermen casting off the pier, and there was so much fishing courtesy around in those days that when a man hung into a real big channel bass all the fishermen on his side would reel in and let him work his fish to the shore.

But by and large there weren't many big ones snagged off Kure's Pier. The stuff ran little—two-pound blues and an occasional sea trout, the odd puppy drum and a whole lot of whiting, which we called Virginia mullet. The Old Man and I didn't crave company very much; we went farther down the coast from Carolina Beach past Kure's to old Fort Fisher, where the big guns used to be aimed against the Civil War blockade runners.

Down there we had the peculiar kind of solitude the Old Man loved and which I loved then, without ever knowing why we loved it. Oh, but that was a scary, desolate beach, the offset currents cutting great sloughs where the big fish lay. The silver-sandy beach came down from steep dunes as high as mountains, with just a fringe of sea oats. There weren't any houses as far as you could see. The bush was warped and gnarled by the winds that never stopped, the myrtle and the cedars and the little hunch-backed oaks twisted and tortured and ever buffeted. The thin screech of the wind was always there, and the water was cold. The rafts of sea ducks looked gloomy, and the birds always screamed louder there than on any other beach I can remember. The general air of age was heightened by the fact that you were always stumbling over an old cannon ball or a rusty saber, and the ghosts flew thick at nightfall.

We used to stop off at Kure's Pier once in a while, just to swap lies with fishing friends. We were an odd bunch, I'm forced to admit. The one I liked best was Chris—Chris Rongotis, or some such name as that—a flat-necked Greek who owned a café, naturally, in town. Chris lived to fish. The restaurant was strictly side-bar. Chris always had a joke for me, or a slab of "oppla pie" or "peenoppla pie" or "strumberry tsortcake" he'd fetched from the restaurant, and a thermos of the hottest coffee in the world. He would tell me what it was like back in Greece, and I learned three bars of the Greek national anthem. Chris just about died laughing at my Greek accent.

There were also a doctor and a dentist and a World War hero with most of himself shot loose. There were a Portygee and a Frenchman and a big blowsy old woman who wore pants and hip boots and cussed worse than anybody I ever heard when she lost a fish. I reckon it was my first real taste of the international set—except none of these internationals could have bribed their way into a parlor. The Portygee even wore big gold earrings and shaved every other Fourth of July.

If you snapped a rod or threw your last leader or ran plumb out of cut bait, somebody would come along and lend you a hand without appearing to be doing you a favor.

What I'm trying to do is tell you how nice it was in the fall, in late October and early November, when the big blues ran close ashore to feed off the minnows and the sand fleas. Looking back, I can't think of any real big fish we caught, or any lives we saved, or anything poetic or fancy. But this I do remember—an infection I caught which, if the good Lord is willing, I never aim to get cured of. That is the feeling of wonderful contentment a man can have on a lonesome beach that is chilling itself up for winter, sort of practice-swinging to get ready for the bitter cold that's coming.

We had a little weathered gray shingle-and-clapboard cottage rented for the fall fishing. It stuck up on a high bluff just between Carolina and Kure's Beach. If you stepped too spry off the front piazza, you would tumble right down onto the brown mossed-over rocks, which weren't so much rocks as case-hardened sand. There was a rough board step—more of a ladder, actually—that you had to climb up from the beach, about fifty yards straight up.

It wasn't very grand, I must say. It had a toilet and a ramshackle stove and a bedroom and a sitting room and a fireplace. The fireplace was what made it. This fireplace drew so hard that it dang near carried the logs straight up the "chimbley." That was how I pronounced "chimney" until I was about grown, and I still think "chimbley."

This place was home, castle, sanctuary. I mind it so clear, coming in off that beach in the black night. The surf would be booming spooky and sullen, sometimes wild and angry and spume-tossing when the wind freshened. Your feet in the heavy black rubber boots sank down into the squishy sand, and you had to pull them out with a conscious effort as you walked up from the firm, moist sand at the water's edge and slogged through the deep, loose sand to the first steep rise of bluff. You would naturally be carrying a heavy surf rod and a heavy reel and a tackle box, and were generally dragging a string of fish that started out about the size of anchovies and wound up weighing more than a marlin before you got 'em home.

There would be an ache all through your shoulders from casting that heavy line with the four-ounce sinker and the big slab of cut mullet. There would be an ache in the back of your legs from wading in and then walking backward to reel in the fish. There would be cramps in your cold, saltwater-wrinkled red fingers, and your nose would be pink and running. If anybody had snapped you on the ear, the ear would have fallen off. Your feet were just plain frozen inside those clammy rubber boots, and you were salty and sandy from stem to stern.

Somehow you wrestled your gear and yourself up the steep steps in the dark, and the door would open when you moved the wooden latch. The first fellow in lit the lamps, old smoky kerosene lamps, and there wasn't any quarrel about who fixed the fire. Among the Old Man's assorted rules was one unbreakable: you never left the house unless the dishes were washed, dried, and stacked, the beds made, the floor swept and—this above all—a correct fire laid and ready for the long, yellow-shafted, red-headed kitchen match to touch it into flaring life. The Old Man said you couldn't set too much store by a fire; that a fire was all that separated man from beast, if you came right down to it. I believe him. I'd rather live in the yard than in a house that didn't have an open fireplace.

One of the chores I never minded was being the vice-president in charge of the fire detail. I loved to straggle off in the mornings, with the sun still warm and bright before the afternoon winds and clouds chilled the beach, just perusing around for firewood. We had wonderful firewood—sad and twisted old logs, dull silver-gray from salt, big scantlings and pieces of wrecked boats, and stuff like that, all bone-dry and wind-seasoned. The salt or something caused it to burn slow and steady with a blue flame like alcohol burns, and the smell was salt and sand and sea grapes and fire, together. All you needed under it was a few tight-crumpled, greasy old newspapers that the bait had been wrapped in and a lightwood knot or two, and when you nudged her with the match she went up like Chicago when the old lady's cow kicked over the lantern.

With that fire roaring you could cut out one of the lamps, because the fire made that wonderful flickering light which will ruin your eyes if you try to read by it but which, I believe, was responsible for making a President of Honest Abe. You backed up to her and warmed the seat of your pants, with your boots still on, and then turned and baked a little cold out of your chapped, wrinkled hands. Only then did you sit down and haul off the Old Man's boots, with one of his feet seized between your legs and the other in your chest, and then he helped you prize your boots off the same way.

It's funny the things you remember, isn't it? I remember a pair of ankle slippers made out of sheepskin, with the curly wool inside. I would set 'em to toast by the fire as soon as I came through the door. When I popped my bare feet into 'em, they were scorching and felt like a hot bath, a cup of coffee, and a pony for Christmas. Then some hot water on my hands, to wash off the salt and the greasy fish and the dirt. Now I started out to do the supper.

The Old Man said that in deference to his advanced years he had to take a little drink of his nerve tonic, and the least a boy could do would be to lay the table and set up the supper. I liked that, too—the Old Man sitting sprawled in a rocker in front of the fire, his feet spread whopperjawed out toward the flames, puffing on his pipe and taking a little snort and talking kind of lazy about what all had happened that day. Shucks, getting supper wasn't any trouble at all.

You just started the coffee in the tin percolator and got the butter out of the food safe and sliced off a few rounds of bread and dug up the marmalade or the jelly. We had an iron grill that we slid into the fireplace as soon as she began to coal down into nice rosy embers, and it didn't take a minute to lay the halves of yesterday's bluefish or sea trout onto the grill. About the time the fish started to crumble and fall down through the grill I'd stick a skillet full of scrambled eggs over the fire, and in about two shakes dinner was served.

Full as ticks, we'd sit and talk over the second cup of coffee, and then the Old Man would bank the fire and blow out the lamp. We'd reel off to bed, dead from fatigue and food and fire.

These trips were only on week ends, of course, because there was that business about education, which meant I was bespoken five days a week. But from Friday afternoon until Monday morning early, when the Old Man dragged me out of bed before light in order to check my fingernails and cowlick for respectability, I was a mighty happy boy.

And it's funny, as I was saying earlier, but I can't remember the fish. All I remember very clear are Chris the Greek and the cussing lady in the hip boots and the Portygee with the earrings. And how the Old Man's face looked with the fire bright against it, making it cherry red on one side and shadowed black on the other, and how the wind sounded, thrashing on the stout gray shingles that kept us safe inside from storm. I haven't lit a fire from that day to this without seeing, and even smelling a little bit, the presence of beard and bourbon and tobacco and salt air and fish and fire that went to make up the Old Man. I guess that's why some people call me a firebug.

Bruisers of the Weed Beds

By Ben East

IN A FUTURE CHAPTER, I INTRODUCE CHARLIE ELLIOTT'S STORY, "Adventures In Solitude," with a reference to the strong lineup of regular *Outdoor Life* writers and columnists through the middle decades of the 1900s. Among those I mentioned, the name of Ben East stands out as a stellar player.

Not only was Ben East the guiding force behind the very distinguished *Outdoor Life* Conservation Award, he was, quite literally, the magazine's "designated hitter" for taking on some of *Outdoor Life's* key writing assignments. Many of the great stories of the outdoors, particularly in the areas of adventure and survival, were lived by people who were not proficient or experienced writers. Their tales eventually came to the public for reading under the very capable stewardship of the talented Ben East, under the "As Told By Ben East" byline appearing below the name of the actual person relating the story.

Ben was no stranger to the traditional type of outdoor story either. He was a son of the upper Midwest of cold lakes, brawling rivers, and the deep woods where getting lost and survival gear were taken seriously. From ice-out in the spring, to ice fishing in deep winter, Ben East was part of the scene and the action, and he wrote about it all as few others.

Ironically, this Ben East pike fishing story did not originally appear in *Outdoor Life*, but in *Field & Stream*. It was included in the wonderful (and now very hard to find!) anthology, *Outdoors Unlimited*, edited by J. Hammond Brown and sponsored by the Outdoor Writers Association of America. The book was published by A. S. Barnes in 1947.

There is something about pike that is captivating to most anglers, some enduring appeal the "glamour" fish like trout and salmon cannot replace. Perhaps it is their ferocity, the way they roam the wilderness lakes like wolves, part of a world of loons and ducks and deep-shadowed forests where winter comes early, stays long, and survival is truly of the fittest.

If you don't already know what makes the pike such a great fish, Ben East will provide a splendid beginning to your education.

———

There was an even yard of him in length, lean and stream-lined as a torpedo, and he weighed about 12 pounds. That's a lot of fish if it's put together right!

He took the red-and-silver wabbler at the edge of a patch of weeds, just beyond a waterlogged old birch-top a hundred feet from our boat. He smashed into it without hesitancy. The minute he saw it he had marked it for his own, and he wanted the world to know it. He hit the plug with everything in the book, and his emphatic smash telegraphed across a hundred feet of tight silk and five feet of arched steel and stabbed into my arm like a left to the chin.

We sparred for a minute, and I could feel the solid shock of his blows, one by one. Then, away out there by the birch-top, the water boiled in an angry swirl, and the rod bent like a bow. He was making for the weeds, and I knew it. I set my wrist and my will against him and turned him, caught him off balance and took ten yards of line away from him.

Then he stopped, threshing and fighting like a wild steer on a rope, and I gave part of the ten yards back. He detoured, and the silk cut a little wake through the water like a midget periscope. Feeling for the weeds once more, he went deep, sounding in a short, savage rush. Then he remembered the lair he had left, back there in the sunken birch, and tried for it, but the live steam was going out of him and I made him walk at heel again.

Grudging and sullen, he gave what line he had to, flared suddenly to the top and jumped, bent double like a living horseshoe and leaving an empty crater in the water where he came out, twisting and rolling to break the gut that had him fast. He smashed back and drove himself down toward the weeds again, but his punches had lost their power, and I held him and let the rod deal out its steady punishment.

A boat-length away he made his last-ditch stand, flailing in a welter of water. When I snubbed him up short, he streaked for the boat and went under it, but I dipped the rod tip to keep the line clear and led him back where I wanted him, foot by foot, until he rolled his belly up beside the boat, white as a flag of truce, and I knew I had him.

Muskalonge? No. Pike—great northern. A fish that packs brass knuckles on his jaws and a blackjack in his tail. Old Longnose, the bruiser of the weed beds. *Esox lucius*, the books call him. It ought to be Lucifer. There's a lot of hellfire and brimstone in his make-up.

Maybe you don't like him. Well, we'll have no quarrel on that score. It's every man's privilege to pick his friends and his favorites. But before you blast the bruiser wide open with a long burst of scorn and derision, let me ask you one honest question: have you fought him in good water, up in the country that gave him the name of "great northern"? Have you taken his measure, toe to toe in the center of the ring, in a way a game fish deserves to be tried?

Sure, he's no muskalonge. Nor Atlantic salmon, small-mouth bass or speckled trout. He's a pike, and no apologies are called for. The world is full of worse. His cousin, the muskie, is the big tiger. He's the little tiger, and guts aren't always measured by weight or by length.

Fishermen have known him for a long time, on both sides of the Atlantic, and mostly respected him wherever they came together. Old Izaak Walton is rated something of an authority, and he admired Longnose enough to devote an entire chapter to him. There's something in his make-up—in his lean and sinister shape, his gaping jaws, his endless hunger and murderous disposition—that has stirred the imagination of men as have few other fish. Somebody has said that more fantastic tales and plain lies have been told about the pike than about any other fish found in the fresh waters of the world, and the statement is likely true.

There was a pike somewhere in England, for example, that grew to be 19 feet long and weighed 350 pounds. Whoever started that rumor let his imagination bog down pretty badly on the weight. A pike 19 feet long would go better than a ton unless he had the general outlines of a python.

There were other pike that swallowed dogs, one that made away with an infant child. One bit a boy's hand off, and still another "seized the foot of a young woman while she held it naked in a pond." Let's hope it taught her a lesson.

English anglers and the folk who lived by English streams took the bruiser seriously in the old days. They had some reason, if it comes to that, for at his best he reaches a length of 4 feet and a weight of 40 pounds. That's big for a fresh-water fish, but it doesn't account by itself for all the weird, outlandish tales they told of him. It was his manners, not his size, that gave him his early reputation.

Incidentally, the pike of those English rivers is the same one that inhabits the weed beds of Wisconsin lakes. *Esox* is a globe wanderer, a circumpolar fish, equally at home in the north of Europe, the north of Asia and the north of this continent. They named him well here in America when they called him the great northern.

They might with equal reason have called him the weed pike, as his dwarf kinsman that rarely exceeds a foot in length is known as the grass pike. The weed beds are his hang-out. What a brier patch is to a cottontail, weeds are to old Longnose. They shelter and feed him, hide him from his foes and give him cover when he hunts. He is rarely found far from them.

In the warm-water lakes in the south of his range, the big-mouth bass lakes, look for rushes and weed beds, and you will find pike if they are present at all. In the rivers, weeds waving in the current like fresh-water kelp mark his home precinct. In the cold rocky lakes of the North you waste your time trolling for him above the weedless reefs or in the black deeps. Seek out a bay, moderately shallow, and scout for weed beds if you hope to keep a rendezvous with the bruiser.

Some of the greatest pike fishing that has come my way I've had in Lake Superior. Now, Superior is literally one mighty, overgrown spring, crystal-clear and sparkling cold. Old-timers who live by its shores will tell you that it never freezes over in winter and never thaws out in summer. Which is to say it has a year-round temperature of not far from 45 degrees. That's hardly pike water. Lake trout and whitefish and big speckled trout (the famed coasters of the Nipigon country and Batchawana Bay and points between) along the rock-paved shores, yes.

Longnose doesn't want his environment that cold. But there's a big island up in the northern bulge of the lake—Isle Royale, youngest National Park in the United States, dedicated in 1936 and opened four years later. Its rugged shoreline is indented with long, narrow harbors that wind back between the timbered ridges like low-walled fjords. At the inner end of those harbors sluggish little rivers come loafing out of the alders, on the last leg of their jaunt down from the ridges. Moose like to wallow in the black muck on the banks of those lily-fringed streams, and off their outlets there is warmish water and the harbors are grown up with weeds.

What do you find in those weed beds? Pike, of course—big sullen devils with tempers like a wildcat's and an appetite like a cannibal's. I've seen 'em in Brady Cove, on the north shore of the island, on a still evening when the water was as flat and unstirred as polished glass, hunting their prey in the weed tangles like a pack of vest-pocket sharks.

We drifted down the cove one July evening just after sundown, and in half an hour we counted twenty or thirty big pike within sight of our boat. The weeds are sparse in that bed. They come up from the bottom in long green strands like frayed ropes, and the clumps are two or three yards apart. The pike were moving slowly and lazily in the open lanes between the weed fronds, no more than a foot underwater, like lean dirigibles scouting low about a farmer's woodlot. In the dim green light they were a black, ugly and hungry-looking lot, and I was glad I didn't live down in that cold-blooded, pitiless world of theirs.

We had a couple of rods in the boat, and we ended the hunt for half a dozen of 'em. It was the oddest and easiest pike fishing I'd ever done. We cast to our fish as a trout fisherman casts to a rise.

We would spot a pike drifting along thirty or forty feet from the boat. We'd lay a plug four or five yards beyond him and a little ahead and twitch it back so that it crossed his course literally under his nose. We could see his sudden interest in the lure; see the strike and his frantic flurry as he felt the hooks and the pull of the line. We could watch every rush and turn he made, whether at the top or deep down among the weeds. It was the best ringside seat I've ever had on a fishing trip, until the light failed and dusk gathered.

No two of them took the plug in the same fashion. One went into it with a rush—jaws gaping, pouncing like a leopard, hitting with a wrenching smash, starved and savage, making dead sure the prey had no chance to dodge into the weeds and get away.

The next was in no hurry at all. He lay idle, watching while the bait swam into sight and weaved nearer. He waited as if suspicious of trickery or uncertain whether this flashing, silvery thing was on his diet list. Whatever the critter was, it had no chance, and he knew it. It was small and hurt, and too far from the bottom to take shelter. He was a pike—a greyhound of the weeds, long and slim and fashioned for speed. There was no need for haste. He slid forward a yard, paused briefly to watch the bait at closer range, moved again without effort. His long jaws opened almost lazily, and the plug was gone and there was sudden strain on the line.

I learned something that evening. I had lived all my life in pike country without knowing the great northern would strike in the dusk of late evening, even in the last twilight when the western sky was turning gray and ashen and the water was like black velvet.

Those pike fed long after it was too dark for us to see them moving above the weeds. We used a flashlight to unsnarl a back-lash before we took the last one, and it was full dark when we rowed back and tied up at Birch Island.

I caught my first pike when I was a kid about ten. He wasn't big—a little better than three pounds, but he looked big to me. I took him on a minnow—or, to be exact and truthful, on a fingerling bluegill about three inches long. The bluegill fooled around a worm I was using for grown-up members of his own family, and when I brought him in I transferred him to a bigger hook on another pole and dangled him over a weed bed while I went on with my worm fishing. I hadn't much hope, but the pike came along, and the rest just happened.

He was my first fish bigger than a rock bass or a half-pound bullhead, and he made me a pike fisherman for life. Using that kind of bait would be illegal today—undersized pan-fish in possession, the warden would say—but I still can't think of any better use for a small bluegill. The point is, I caught my first pike on a fish smaller than himself, and I've been taking 'em that way ever since.

The bruiser is a sucker for a minnow. He's a plug-ugly, a toughie, and he revels in the role. He likes live bait, and he wants it red-blooded. Let softer and better mannered fish have the caddis larvae and the flies, the crawfish and garden worms. He wants his food made in his own image, *Esox* does. He delights in picking a victim under his own weight class, assaulting it and sending scales drifting down through the water in a silver cloud. Show him another fish small enough to be swallowed, and his eyes brighten with the pure light of murder. It takes several tons of little fish, scattered through his voracious years, to turn out the finished product of twenty-five pounds of pike. All of which makes Longnose exceedingly vulnerable to a chub or shiner deftly impaled on a barbed hook and dangled in his home range on a silk thread.

Give him a minnow first if you would accomplish his downfall. If your taste does not run to live bait, give him something that resembles a minnow. A strip of pork rind is a fair substitute. So is a spoon or spinner or wabbler, or any of the countless patterns of wooden, plastic, rubber and metal minnows. As a matter of fact, any trolling or casting lure that is minnow-like in shape, size or action will take pike, some more frequently than others, of course.

But stay away from surface baits. The bruiser doesn't go for 'em. His dining room is deep down among the weeds, and he waits there and lets his meals come to him. Most of the time he shuns the top of the water, and the deeper your plug or wabbler runs the more deadly it will be on great northerns.

Esox seems partial to red in artificial baits. It goads him as it goads a bull, and so most pike fishermen incline to a dash of red on whatever lure they offer him—a red-headed plug, red feathers on a treble hook behind a spinner, red lining for a metal spoon, red and white stripes on a wabbling gadget. That last one is hard to beat, incidentally. Maybe he favors red because it's the color of blood.

On one of the bruiser's traits all fishermen are in accord: that's his appetite. His harshest critic will admit it's second to nothing in its class. There are times when fish won't feed and there's nothing you or anybody else can do about it. You may stand in the best pool on the most famous salmon river that empties into the Atlantic and lay your Black Dose down with consummate skill a hundred times at the head of a dark hole where you know not fewer than six great fish are lurking, and if they aren't rising you'll quit empty-handed in spite of all you can do!

A fish's will is his own, and when he's on a hunger strike no man can coax him out of it. That's as true of old Longnose as of any other fish—but his times of fasting are few and far-spaced. Most of his life he devotes to foraging, tireless and single-minded. On top of that, he's an opportunist. Even when the pangs of honest hunger are dulled, the lust to kill is on him and he is prone to gratify it if the chance offers.

There are times when all the pike in the lake quit striking, to be sure, but such times are rare and brief in their duration. If you are on good pike water with the right bait and fail to get action, rest your rod for an hour or so. The odds are good you'll not need to wait longer than that.

On another of the bruiser's traits all fishermen are not agreed—that is, his fighting heart.

There are those who will tell you he has no guts when the hooks are home and the blue chips are down. Up in Canada they call him the jack-fish and despise him as most fishermen despise the carp. They are honest enough in their opinion, too, but they malign old *Esox* for all of that.

He's no salmon, as I admitted earlier. He lacks the dash of a trout, the finesse and showmanship of a small-mouth bass. He hasn't the weight of a muskalonge and for that reason his performance isn't the knockdown-dragout affair which the musky stages. I know men who have taken both, and they argue that he's a fair match for the musky, pound for pound; but I've too little evidence to defend that.

But whatever his shortcomings, the bruiser is no quitter. He fights, and he does it in his own devilish way and by his own rules. Fair play has no place in his tactics. He slugs and gouges, puts his knee in your groin, hits below the belt and after the gong has rung. He's no gentleman and makes no false claims. He's a bully, and he battles like one because he knows no more likely way to save his own skin.

He has little taste for flashy sparring at the surface. Most of the time he stays deep and makes his punches count. Give him weeds, and he'll go down like a corkscrew and foul your line to gain the slack he needs for throwing the hooks. Give him rocks or logs, and he'll snag you if he has a tenth of a chance. If all else fails, he'll do his damnedest to saw through your leader with his awl-sharp teeth, and plenty of times he succeeds.

While the last hand is being played he'll take cover under the very boat he dreads and tangle you or smash your rod if he is able. And when he's licked and knows it, he'll lie doggo at the top, floating on his side, and then spend his last ounce of hate in a vicious lunge, coming at you as you reach for his gills, and slashing your hand if you're unwary or slow.

He's no trout, old Longnose isn't, but he's quite a fish for all that. Those who say he won't give a good account of himself at bayonet range have never tried him in proper water, or they deny the evidence.

In the northern midlands, where I know him, he plays one part that's out of character: he's a mortgage-lifter of some consequence. The vacation industry is big business in more than one state nowadays. Anything that brings outside visitors and outside money is important, and the weed-bed bruiser brings 'em in a big way.

One other role he fills outstandingly well. He livens the long, dull weeks of winter for a host of anglers in the snow belt. He's one of the big five on the ice fisherman's list. In Northern lakes and rivers the black bass virtually hibernates for the winter. He retires into sunken logs, crannies among rocks, holes beneath water-logged trees and stumps. His appetite as good as disappears, and as a result bass fishing, waning through the autumn, dies out about Thanksgiving in the North.

Trout, which spawn in the fall or very early spring, would not be available to the fisherman even if the law permitted, which it doesn't. So the ice angler falls back on pike and walleyes, perch and lake trout, and in recent years bluegills, to bridge the lagging days from December to April. Of the lot the pike ranks first in the affections of winter fishermen. But that doesn't win him any place in paradise with the average summer angler.

Ice-fishing is, to begin with, an odd sport. Those who follow it put it ahead of eating. Those who don't contend it should not be talked of in the same breath with honest fishing. Certainly it's no pastime for pantywaists, but for the outdoorsman willing to take a little discomfort with his fun it affords plenty of entertainment at a season when the wide open spaces are snowbound and fishing of any kind is a rare privilege. I'll admit that catching a pike on a hand-line on a wind-swept, frozen lake bears little resemblance to taking brown trout on a dry fly in the warm dusk of a May evening. But each has its time and place, and luckily all men do not seek the same things in angling.

The fisherman who wants to avoid the bulk of the hardships that go with winter fishing turns to an ice shanty. It's a small, dark, weatherproof shelter, heated with a stove no bigger than a three-gallon can, and in it the angler is as comfortable as in his own living room. The winter wind may sing its dreary song outside, but a fire of dry pine or cedar pops cheerfully in the tiny stove and all is snug and warm within.

The shanty is windowless, lighted only by the reflected pale-green light that shines up through a hole cut in the ice to match a hole of equal size in the floor. The warm darkness is in sharp contrast with the bright underwater world below. All that moves within the shanty-man's range of vision, to a depth of ten or twelve feet, is seen as clearly as in an aquarium tank. He waits in endless patience, ready with a short iron-shafted spear fastened to the shanty wall with a stout line, in the fashion of a harpoon. Down in the water a big chub or shiner, hooked on a lighter line, swims in slow circles above the dull-green moss and water weeds, serving as a decoy.

The minnow gives ample warning when a pike, or other fish big enough to be feared, is coming in. It shows sudden activity, swinging far out under the ice in an effort to escape danger as yet invisible to the spearman. Then, from the opposite side of the hole, an ugly long-jawed head slides into sight. *Esox* is coming to lunch. He lies idle for a few seconds just beyond the spear's range, watching the struggles of the crippled chub. Then he drifts ahead, gathering speed.

But the spear is moving down through the water now, unhurried and deadly, trailing a few silvery bubbles. A foot above the bruiser's back it checks for a split second. The spearman is making sure of the target. When he lunges, it is swift and hard, and the barbed tines go deep behind the ugly head. He lets go the spear instantly, and it sinks down and carries the impaled pike with it, holding him on the bottom with its weight.

There's a wild flurry for a minute, and a cloud of mud floats up. When the wounded fish subsides, the spear can be drawn up. The shantyman kicks open the door and backs out on the ice with his catch, and never sees the snow eddying across the white level of the lake, never feels the bite of the January wind.

So long as he keeps that same location a little handful of pike scales will shine bright on the lake bottom to remind him of his kill. Deride it or not, ice-fishing is far from a dull sport.

It all adds up this way: wherever and however I have taken *Esox* he has given me my money's worth, paid his own freight. He's even good on the platter. Not, of course, if he comes from warm, stagnant, mud-tainted water. Take him from a cold, clear lake if you want him for table fish, and let the skin go with the scales. After that, treat him as you would a trout.

"He is choicely good," Izaak Walton summed it up a long time ago. "Too good for any but anglers and honest men."

Who are you and who am I, my friend, to question the judgment of such a sage? Longnose has his faults, to be sure, but he has virtues as well, and he gets my vote any place and any day!

Roll Cast

By Neil Patterson

IN HIS BOOK *CHALKSTREAM CHRONICLE*, PUBLISHED BY LYONS AND BUR-
ford in 1995, Neil Patterson brings the experience of living beside an
English chalkstream—what we in America mostly call a "spring creek"—
into prose so vivid that it quite literally shares everything Patterson has
seen and felt during his idyllic streamside pursuit of happiness.

Chalkstreams. Spring creeks. England, Pennsylvania, Montana, and
other places. Cold, pure water pumping from within Mother Earth, 365
days a year at the same temperature. And trout. Trout that can be seen and
studied—and sometimes caught.

As much as I would like to, I knew that I will never have the opportunity to live on the banks of a chalkstream and take up the challenge
of learning what makes it tick on a year-round basis. I'll settle for my
occasional visits, and the opportunities to try to take up the challenge of
getting trout to strike my fly. In the meantime, Neil Patterson has given
me a great gift by sharing his thoughts of doing the very thing I cannot:
Patiently observing and fishing the river day by day.

From the moment I first picked up *Chalkstream Chronicle*, I was
hooked. Today, after rereading it several times (since only 1995), my faith
in the book as being destined to become an angling classic has never
wavered.

This excerpt from *Chalkstream Chronicle* is a wonderful fishing story
that is but a portion of the treasures that await the reader in the complete
book. Here a common fly fishing situation becomes a challenge calling
for seemingly unworldly abilities, but as usual in fly fishing there's always
someone ready to say, "Let me try for him."

As you will see, Patterson refers to sections of his stream with what he calls, "*Wind-In-the-Willows* eyes." He names various stretches and bridges of his home river in the same charming way Kenneth Grahame might have done.

—◦—

The Fast Shallows below the Red Gate are exactly as the name suggests. They're fast, and they're shallow, zipping down a slight gradient at a wild, bubbling, sparkling rate more akin to a rainfed stream, rather than a sedate chalkstream. But we don't complain—and neither do the trout lucky enough to live in one of the many gravel-bottomed soup bowls laid out on this fizzing dining-room table, waiting for an insect to drop in at lunch-time.

These shallows are only two hundred yards from the footbridge that marks the end of a length of thick water that flows in front of the end of the lawn at the Doctor's Cottage. As soon as this water has massaged the backs of the resident shoal of grayling on the ford behind the footbridge, it tumbles down the shallows to the only other island on the fishery, stopping for nothing and no one.

From there onwards, the river fans out wide, rolling deep and mysteriously for the last quarter of a mile, down to the Old Iron Bridge at the end of the fishery, and away. Both sides of the shallows are lined with hawthorn bushes. You can't fish them from the far bank. You can't even see the river through a dense curtain of hawthorn, alder and sloe bushes. On the nearside bank, things aren't much better. There are only two places where it's possible to part the bushes and slide a rod out into the daylight and make contact with this giggly stream that has never grown up.

But even when you've found a window to open, there's only room to cast to fish directly across from you. It's like fishing through a car window. For this reason, at this time of year, I climb into the bottom of the shallows and wade up it. This can take a morning, or more, to fish sensibly. And this is where Roll Cast and I set off to spend the first few hours of the season. Large dark olives will be making their first appearance at lunch-time if text books, like this one, are to be believed. But their show is no more than a quick, short strum on the banjo, as this book must be quick to point out. The hawthorn fly, on the other hand, as this book will reveal, is available to the trout all day long, at a shake of the wind's finger. And if there's no wind, I still have an option. I can always try and persuade Roll Cast to go to the head of the shallows and shake bushes.

To the flyfisherman, the hawthorn is an insect. To the trout on the shallows below the Red Gate, it's manna from heaven.

Hawthorn flies gather in, and over, flowering hawthorn bushes where they spend most of the time sucking at the buds and hovering in their hundreds. A restless, smoky cloud, at the mercy of the merest whim of a breeze. Born under decaying leaves in between the rotting floorboards of Wild Wood and the Ashes, the hawthorn is a land insect, not an aquatic one. But it's thanks to them that the season starts with a crash, a bang and a wallop, for the hawthorn fly is the King of Belly-floppers, bringing trout to the surface for the first time in the season.

On the back of the hand, the hawthorn looks like a large housefly. In the air, it looks like a biker in a black leather jacket trailing a long, black pony-tail. This pony-tail is a pair of hairy legs. One thing is for sure, when the wind drops or changes direction, the airborne hawthorn very speedily becomes waterborne—and trout bound. The hawthorn doesn't shy off giving a lively demonstration of why it has never won a medal at the Olympics. Wallowing around the surface on a big, shiny belly, what it loses in spectators at the Olympic Pool, it gains in crowds of winter-starved trout queuing up on the Red Gate Shallows to pounce on it.

I poked my head through a gap in the bushes. Roll Cast pointed to a thin-waisted male hawthorn head-butting my phoney artificial which is trailing on the end of my line in the wind. In one quarter, at least, my artificial has met with approval. For a hawthorn fly with only a couple of weeks to get it all together, this was no casual affair. A hawthorn can't be too fussy. Trout, however, can.

The hawthorn is perhaps the only fly I know that can put the fear of God into a trout when it first appears. I've often wondered why this should be. Maybe it's because the hawthorn is one of the first flies to bring trout to the surface and away from his subsurface supermarket. I think this has something to do with it. Unlike the large dark olive dun which the trout 'follows' to the surface in nymphal form, the hawthorn is delivered to him from above. Crunch, just like that. With the large dark olive, as with every other water-born insect, the introduction is a great deal more formal and above (or rather below) board. In its nymphal, or pupal form, the trout can investigate the potential food item's credentials as it tracks it in ascent. The trout finally makes its move when its prey is at its most vulnerable, when it is hatching out, trapped at the surface between stages of metamorphosis. When it is 'between insects'.

There's a school of thought that says that trout wouldn't feed on the surface if nymphs hadn't brought their stomachs up there to begin with.

Even so, hawthorns are fearsome creatures. There have been days when I have walked the river bank wishing I had been wearing a crash-helmet. A dense hatch of mayfly can give you the uneasy feeling that they're crawling all over you (which they probably are), but their soft buttery bodies and gauzy wings prevent you from thinking for one moment that you're at risk of injury. A female hawthorn on the rampage falling wide of her mate, however, can fracture your skull.

This early on in the season the hawthorns don't usually appear until there is a blink of sun. For the past three days, this hadn't been happening until near midday but I was still hopeful.

One of the Two Scarlets, a pair of identical twins who share a week-day rod, but exactly which one I have no idea, had been out yesterday fishing the upper Bywater near the Boss's cottage. Early on in the season, big fish make their way up in this direction from the Wetlands. High up in the smell valves of their nebs they carry the walnutty scent of escapee calf pellets from the stew ponds. There had been a gale the night before, and hawthorns had poured out of the bushes onto the river like Licorice Allsorts out of a split bag.

Neither of the Two Scarlets are big men, and the One Scarlet in question certainly wasn't any bigger than the other One Scarlet, which isn't surprising since both the Two Scarlets were exactly the same size. In fact, if there's a high wind on the river, we tighten the guide ropes of whichever of the Two Scarlets is on the river that day, and make sure the pegs are well hammered into the ground.

He'd seen a fish rising close under the far bank, in some dark cor-ner. He'd covered it with a Hawthorn and the fish had taken it without hesitation. After a long fight, the One Scarlet in question managed to get it within reach. A cock fish, it was a monster for the river weighing not that much more than the One Scarlet; five pounds, perhaps more. The fish was not happy. The story goes that when the One Scarlet got it on the bank, it leapt out of his arms, got up and started to slap him round the face with its tail.

To adopt the pinned-down hawthorn's inelegant posture, the artificial needs to lie with its body rubbing into the film. This is impossible to achieve without the hook hanging under the water—if you use normal tying methods. For this reason, along with my more conventional pattern, I always carry with me a version tied in the Funneldun tying-style. The trick I use to make sure my hawthorns land belly down, hook up on the surface is as simple as tying a normal Funneldun. I always carry a Hawthorn tied this way, for the day I don't will be the day I find a trout that has seen everything, has probably been hooked by everything, and still lives to tell the tale. And it's usually the biggest on the beat.

But sometimes the problem of getting a trout to take your fly has nothing to do with the pattern, upside down, inside out, Mini Mouse or King Kong. Instead, it has everything to do with being able to get the fly to the trout in the first place.

On a well-kept chalkstream—a chalkstream where the bankside vegetation is left well alone—the fish have places where they can lie unreachable, unmolested. Here, the fishing has an edge. Such enclaves where a trout can dig himself in, are available on the Red Gate Shallows, in spades.

But even if you climb in and wade, flyfishing these furiously fast shallows is no easier than if you stayed at home and fished in your bedroom. Hawthorn bushes hang on all sides like the screen round a four-poster bed. If you're a trout considering moving into the area, take my advice, stay clear if you suffer from claustrophobia. This is not a problem in the mind of one particular self-assured, round-shouldered specimen squeezed into a corner of a black run behind a submerged boulder where wisps of creamy fast water fizzed like soda. This was the position he held as we watched him lift to hawthorns showering down on top of him from a small area just above a sloe tree. Here a large group of hawthorns was attempting to bob on the spot, a high proportion of them ending up in the river and coming down the current at full-speed, as if riding an avalanche.

Every one of my fool-hardy attempts at casting at him had thrown my fly into the arms of the bushes, where any self-preserving natural should have stayed cowering to begin with. But the greatest problem wasn't the bushes in front of me, it was the impenetrable wall of grasping branches directly to my rear.

It was my partner's turn at the fish. I poked my head round a bush to watch him in action, perhaps even sneer. But with Roll Cast this was not to be, and I knew it. With a flick of the wrist, rod pointing in the direction of an area just above the trout, a length of line was thrown forward, Roll Cast's finger holding the line up against the cork handle, terminating slack. I heard someone putting the lid back on a plastic dustbin. It was the trout tipping the surface, crunching his way through hawthorns as if they were macadamia nut brittle ice cream.

The rod tilting to the side, Roll Cast raised the tip just as the fly moved down past the trout—on a line parallel to it, but ten foot short of it. As soon as the fly levelled with the trout's tail, Roll Cast raised the tip again smartly, the rod still tilting to the side. As the line and the fly slid towards us, his wrist began to brake slightly as the tip passed the vertical position.

As it moved back slowly, the bushes stretched out to claim the rod tip—but it had reached its most rearward position, and there it stopped. And with it, the line. The rod swung into a vertical position. With thumb on top of the rod handle, Roll Cast applied pressure to pull against the line lying idle in the water in front of him. With the thumb squeezing down into the cork and pointing at an area above the trout, he brought the rod tip forward swiftly, bending into the line. As the rod tip lowered, the line unrolled across the shallows. The fly continued, programmed to strike the black run. Held tight against the cork, the line straightened out and the leader stepped forward, ditching the hawthorn three feet up from the boulder.

The trout didn't wait for the Hawthorn to come; the trout came to the Hawthorn. It sucked the fly in through its mouth along with a creamy mixture of air and frothy water which it blew out through its gills, making sure the chewy Hawthorn remained to be crunched and swallowed without ceremony. But it never came to this.

Roll Cast tightened. The trout turned to the fast run of shallows for help, this was granted and the fish disappeared down river, not stopping until it was past the island and into open water, the Old Iron Bridge and freedom in sight.

Now you know how Roll Cast got his name.

Adventures in Solitude

By Charlie Elliott

THE NAMES OF SO MANY OUTSTANDING COLUMNISTS AND CONTRIBU-
tors have been associated with *Outdoor Life* magazine for so many years
that a list stands out like a veritable "Who's Who" of readability. For open-
ers, try Jack O'Connor, Ray Bergman, Ben East, Joe Brooks, and Charlie
Elliott. Any editor who could be dealt a hand like that in five-card draw
would have to say, "No cards for me. I'll play these."

Charlie Elliott, who passed away in the spring of 2000 at the age of
94, was the most unassuming man in the world to be packing around
the kind of talent that he brought to the typewriter every time he got
his fingers on the keys. A native Georgian, he was a son of the pinelands,
gallberry flats, and mossy swamps where such modesty often runs deep
and pure.

As a writer, Charlie produced so many great articles in *Outdoor Life*
that listing them would be impossible. Many of them are collected, and
sometimes expanded, in his numerous books, which include a book on
quail called *The Prince of Game Birds*, written while Charlie was head of the
Georgia Fish and Game Department. The book has an introduction by his
boss, the Governor, a former peanut farmer from a little town called Plains.

One of Charlie's books that I often go back to when I want to sit in
front of the fire and read a good story is *Gone Fishing*, published by Stack-
pole. "Adventures in Solitude" is from that particular collection.

Why people have a horror of getting lost, I'll never understand. It is one
of the most fascinating of all experiences in the woods. Some of the finest

moments I ever had on a fishing trip happened when I didn't have the slightest idea where I was, how I got there, or if I would ever get back to a trail or a dirt road.

The terror which seizes a man in the woods when he realizes he is lost, has cost many a life. I've known men to wander in circles, or even run through the woods, stumbling, tear off their clothes, or hurt themselves.

A real woodsman, and sometimes he gets just as completely lost as any tenderfoot, simply does not become panic stricken when he is turned around. He knows that he is not hopelessly lost, only confused, or he will accept the Indian's philosophical attitude toward being confused: "Indian not lost; Indian here. Wigwam lost."

One of the joys to which I look forward when I arrive at that time of life in which a pipe and an easy chair are more inviting than the jagged, windswept slope of a mountain, or the thunder of some lost cataract—if such a time ever comes—is a review of my amazing treks into the wilderness places of the earth. Many of them happened when I was turned around in big timber, or in some far swamp tangle. I shall fold my hands over an expanding belt line, plop my soft muscles across the plush of a favorite foot stool and watch blue pipe smoke curl, and remember the best trout stream I ever found while I was lost in the Bitter-root Mountains, or the grizzly that charged down the slope like an avalanche out of the face of the mountain itself. I intend to recall some of those breathless moments when the earth and sky seemed hung in suspense, but most of all I shall remember those times when the little red gods worked miracles that almost, but not quite, carried me into the realm of the super-natural.

Those are perhaps some of the most dramatic minutes I ever lived. They are rare and indelible in the life of any man who carries a rod or a gun.

I recall a night on Isle Royale, perched on the blue waters of Lake Superior. I was there at the time on a seemingly unconquerable forest fire, and fishing a little at unauthorized intervals. I had come off a fishing trip late in the afternoon and immediately taken the trail back into the woods. At ten o'clock, black scud drifted in and blanketed the heavens. Not even the faint glimmer of a star relieved the intense darkness. I moved slowly, cautiously, feeling along the trail with my feet, my hands up to push away the invisible spruce limbs that crowded into the narrow footpath.

I struck a match and looked at my watch. The yellow flare went out and left me wrapped again in inky blackness that was just short of a cold shiver.

"Let's go back," I suggested, "and get a fresh start in the morning."

"Eight hours"— Noel's voice cracked through the gloom—"may mean life or death."

He was two feet away and I could not see him. I heard him turn and move up the trail. I followed the soft pad of his footsteps on moss. Somewhere out in that wilderness two boys were lost. They had been unaccounted for when the fire crews came in at dusk. Whether they had stopped enroute to the landing, or whether they had failed to report to the assembly line at the tail end of the fire, we did not know. Out in a roadless, uninhabited land, they might now be lying face downward at the foot of a cliff.

The battle of Isle Royale forest fire was won. For three months, exhausted crews had slugged it out with blazing fir and birch. On hundreds of acres the humus had been burned away creating naked rock. Tamarack swamps, which had been green and rich with life, were desolate nightmares in cinders. Thirty five thousand acres, almost one fourth of the island, had gone up in smoke.

Now the fire was under control. Crews were mopping up by extinguishing the smokes in stump holes and smoldering snags. Soon after the discovery that two city bred firemen had failed to come in with their crew, Noel Wysong and I left the landing at Rock Harbour with only a flashlight. Miles away from where our boat was anchored in the rocky cove, the bulk of the flashlight had winked out. We were in complete darkness, stopping now and then to "hallo" at the top of our lungs. Each time the same whispers had come back to us—the hoot of an owl, the staccato bark of a coyote, or a moose crashing away into the brush.

One hour past midnight, we crossed a rocky promontory that jutted out into Lake Richie. The trail twisted off the ridge, down through a dense spruce forest to the lake shore, two hundred yards further on.

"One more call," Noel said, "and I'll be ready to give up for the night."

"Who is that?"

The startled voice came out of the air, so close that I stumbled backward, almost falling over a log.

"Who are *you?*" Noel asked, in unsteady tones.

"There are two of us." The voice came quaveringly back. "We got lost from the others."

I breathed a lungful of relief.

"You sound close enough to touch," Noel said. "Where are you?"

"We don't know," the ghostly voice replied, "but we're on the shore of a lake."

"It must be this lake," Noel muttered. "Voices carry long distances across water, and the lake at this point can't be more than a few hundred yards wide."

"Face the lake," he instructed, "and then come around the shore to your left. We'll meet you."

"OK." The voice seemed to have regained some of its confidence.

Noel turned up the trail and I followed, relief swelling inside me.

"How'd you fellows happen to get lost from the others?" I asked in normal tones.

There was no reply to my query. Noel stopped.

"Hello there," he called.

Silence filled up the space where his words had rung. I could hear him breathing hard in the darkness.

"Something wrong here," he said.

He blasted the silence at the top of his lungs. Somewhere out in the distance a coyote answered. We turned and walked back thirty yards to the spot where we had first heard the voices. Noel yelled again.

"What's the matter?" asked the voice, seemingly at my elbow.

"Didn't you hear us call a few seconds ago?" Noel answered the question with another question.

"No," the voice said.

"If you are on the lake shore—" Noel's words were slow and succinct—"stop and look this way." To me he instructed, "Strike a match."

I scratched at the sulphurous tip and it flared into flame, burning my finger.

"Can you see that?" I asked, out into the darkness.

"See what?" was the reply.

Noel exhaled sharply.

"Stay on the lake," he said to the voice, "and keep coming. We'll meet you."

We broke twigs from a tree, started a fire and spread a ragged copy of the Isle Royale map on the ground.

"If they were around this point," Noel indicated the promontory behind us, "they would have heard us before now. If they were across the lake, they could see our fire."

He put his finger on a body of water designated as Intermediate Lake that lay beyond a ridge almost two miles away.

"I don't know what the answer is," he said, "but they can't be anywhere else except there."

We ground the red coals of the fire under our heels into the damp earth and took the trail to the head of the lake. There we deserted the footpath, forced our way through a narrow swamp and climbed the ridge. At the top of the ridge Noel swung west toward the head of Intermediate Lake, and I stumbled downhill through the darkness in the opposite direction.

Noel's hunch was right. We caught the lost fire fighters at dawn. They were completely out of their heads, had deserted the lake shore and were plunging into a wasteland of swamps and rocky ridges, out of which they never would have returned alive.

The next afternoon Noel Wysong and I walked to the head of Lake Richie to puzzle out the weird adventure. This is what we found: A narrow swamp, not shown on the map, cut through the ridge and connected Richie and Intermediate Lakes. Exactly opposite the mouth of the swamp on Lake Richie we could talk with the lost fire fighters as though they were in the same ten square feet with us. When we moved a hundred feet away from the spot opposite the mouth of the swamp, we were in another world. Our own voices had crossed Lake Richie, followed the corridor swamp, crossed Intermediate Lake and come back to the boys lost there, from the opposite direction from where we stood. Instead of walking toward us, they were going away. Only Noel's quick thinking saved them from possible death in that mixed up land of swamps and cliffs and lost forests.

Usually, mysteries of the woods have some explanation. If we had not returned to puzzle out that one, I would have forever and eternally attributed it to the supernatural for lack of a more lucid explanation.

Two years ago I was on a fishing trip in the Okefenokee Swamp that has given me so many great moments of my life. I knew I was lost, but not hopelessly lost. Somewhere within twenty miles was dry land upon which a man could walk without sinking out of sight into bottomless mire. But pushing a boat through this jungle of brush was like trying to thread the eye of a needle with a two by four.

To the east lay the clean, open water run that was the main artery of traffic between Jones Island and Big Water Lake. It split the heart of the Okefenokee Swamp that lay humid and sweltering all around me.

I'd paddled away from the black water trail, into a maze of sloughs that had no beginning and no end. The emerald wall had gradually tightened against my boat, bottling me up like a frog in a green glass jug. I stopped to rest, my arms aching from paddle strain, and smoke a pipeful of tobacco.

The thread of water I had following in from Minnie Lake had vanished in a lane of grass and lily pads. Each sprig of aquatic vegetation dragged at the boat with gluey fingers. Beyond the bow the lane was rolled out like the close tufts of a reseda carpet, but I wasn't fooled for an instant. The moment I stepped out of the boat, I knew I'd wallow out of sight and vanish from the eyes of mortal man forever.

Lem Griffis, Okefenokee's famous guide, had planned to come along and fish the hidden lakes with me, but that morning he'd had a hurry call into Waycross—something to do with government land.

"I wanted to show you the big gator holes," he said, "around the head of Minnie Island. They haven't been fished in years. But I've got an uneasy feeling about letting you tackle them alone."

"Look," I said, "you remember the time I *walked* out of the Okefenokee? I can certainly get out in a boat."

He remembered it all right, and so will you when I tell you about that fishing adventure. He shrugged and sketched a crude map, but he had forgotten to tell me that the runs, or watery trails, were snarled together like a back-lashed fishing line, and that each one looked exactly like its twin.

For twenty years I had fished the easily accessible lakes of the chain leading into the heart of the swamp. There was a time when any lure dropped on the water brought a surging crash out of the depths and a bronzeback battle royal through the cypress knees and along the fringes of the lily pads.

Although public fishing in the lakes and runs was heavy, it remained good, since bass and bream were continuously funneled into them from three hundred thousand acres or more of the actual lake area. Any diligent, careful fisherman could lure some bass out of the lakes and alligator holes, but few knew the hidden waters off the beaten track, many of which were as primitive as the day the Big Boss hid them there.

The guides don't give out that information. It's dangerous for a man inexperienced in the treacheries of the swamp, to travel alone off the recognized water trails. I had learned that once before, the hard way. The cut over cypress forest is impenetrable in many places. The brush growing in water from four to ten feet deep, is so interwoven and intwined that walking, swimming or paddling a boat through it is physically impossible.

Scattered throughout the swamp are wide, deep holes of open water. These are kept clear by the alligators, which in the last few years have increased tremendously under government protection. Fish experts say that alligators feed on the sluggish fresh water creatures, such as turtles and terrapins and take only an occasional faster game fish. That must be right. I know that any alligator cave, when fished with long casts over the lilies and grass, will almost always yield one or two good bass.

I knocked out my pipe and pushed on into the narrowing grass trail. It drove like a wedge into the phalanx of brush. Every foot I gained was like driving a champagne cork back into the bottle. I was almost ready to give up and back out of the bottleneck when it opened into a run of clean, black water. The wall of brush spread out and I could paddle again. I was so relieved that when a deadly cottonmouth moccasin nearly dropped into the boat off a low hanging limb, I didn't see him in time to pull out of the way. After that I guided the boat more cautiously and a dozen turns of the trail brought me into the neck of a large run, bordered by a rim of lilies and studded at the edge with cypress knees. The little lake curved out of sight into the brush. Beyond the distant shore a group of pine trees thrust up their emerald crowns.

From long experience I knew this meant dry land. Water around its feet is death to a pine. Nevertheless, the presence of the pines set off an alarm in the back of my brain. According to Lem's crude map, if this was Minnie Island, it was on the wrong side of the little lake.

I forced myself to relax and look around. From all appearances this was virgin water, typical of many such nooks I had found in the Okefe-nokee in the years gone by. An eight foot alligator slid off the rim of the grass and slowly submerged into the dark depths, leaving a wake that rippled in the moss hanging at the water's edge. The wave disturbed a huge cottonmouth, which dropped from sight out of the low branches.

I laid my paddle where I could snatch it up and use it as a weapon, then clicked my flyrod together and soaked a leader over the stern. My choice out of the tackle box was a small flyrod frog with hairy legs. I tied him on and moved cautiously down the left shore of the hidden lake. For the first time the witchery of the place stole over me and I pushed aside all thoughts except those of being in a lost corner of the world, in a spot few eyes had seen. The moment was sufficient unto itself. I dropped the lure beside a clump of cypress knees and worked it slowly out. I put the second cast into a mirrored corner beside the partially submerged trunk of a tree. The ripples died and I twitched the frog once. The tiny waves curled out and vanished and I touched it again.

I had tensed my arm to retrieve the floating bit of wood and col-ored hair when the water erupted violently. Even though I was expecting action, I jumped as though Lem had prodded me with his heavy gig.

The bass exploded in a shower of drops and swept the surface of the lake for ten feet with his tail. I gave him line, took it in again and gave him more. The bite of the hook sent him into an aerial performance that would have done credit to a cold water smallmouth. Then he bored for the safety of the submerged trunk.

Holding on with every ounce of strain I thought the leader would stand, I turned him back into the middle of the pond. His fourth and final jump almost threw him in the boat. Then he gave up, exhausted, and I slid the net under him. He tipped my mental scales at a good six pounds, so I filed him on the stringer for future reference.

I waited until the lake had settled once more to its normal mirrored beauty. One cast to the edge of the lily pads brought another explosion. This was a small three pounder. He went into battle maneuvers that took him completely around the boat. I checked his bid for the safety of the lily patch and after a breathless five minutes snapped him on the stringer.

While the water calmed a second time, I examined my leader for frayed spots and tested the knot between the line and gut. I worked out the remainder of the flat, padded shore line and a narrow neck that jutted off the main lake. The shell of a mammoth cypress tree crowded the entrance to the neck. Its base was split by an inverted V that showed the black water in its bowels.

I luckily made a perfect cast into the opening of the V and left the frog there, almost out of sight, for a full minute, until it became a part of the dark surface. I flicked the rod tip to move the frog into the open, but the little lure didn't move toward me. It disappeared in a silver arc that boiled the surface inside the cypress hull like a bold spring.

The frog was no longer visible, so I set the hook, hard. Nothing happened except the rod held its quivering arc and the line vibrated like the E string on a violin.

For a moment I thought the fish, whatever it was, had wrapped my leader around the bottom of the cypress tree. Then the line began to move, with quiet stubbornness toward the middle of the lake. I had my choice of playing out line or breaking rod or leader, so I played out line.

The critter on the other end of the stiff-backed bamboo took nylon through the straining guides and kept taking it. For a moment a queer feeling welled through me that I had hooked the old boss alligator of the hole. With one hand I turned the boat and paddled after the line that plowed inexorably into deep water.

I had a sudden inspiration. There was another frog plug in my tackle box, so testing the strength of the leader, I set back on the rod with a jerk that would have broken the neck of a tarpon.

That did it! The barb bit deep. The flyline straightened suddenly and swept into a curve as the fish plowed out of the inky depths and hit the surface with a crash like a falling tree.

I threw down the paddle and caught the rod in two hands. The chunk of flesh done up in scales was the biggest I had seen since Vernon Phillips came up to his boat house triumphantly dragging a fourteen and half pounder behind his boat.

My blood pressure shot up a dozen points. I pumped him again and he waltzed across the water, shooting for the crop of lilies and the submerged trunk. I swung on as grimly as I dared, muttering a little prayer that my slender gut would hold, while wishing I had him on the right end of a sailfish rod.

He went down again into the center of the lake, hanging there as though he had anchored himself to the tip of the sunken tree. For three breathless minutes I was not able to budge him. Lem had once showed me how to move a big bass by jarring the rod butt with the heel of my hand. It worked. The finned giant turned loose, raced twice across the lake and came in, his struggles growing less frantic by the moment.

When he drifted to the surface, ten feet off the starboard, the hook had torn through his cheek and was hanging by a sliver of skin. Cautiously I held on with one hand and picked up the net. He was a record fish in anybody's division, and I didn't want to lose him.

Catching a glimpse of the net as I slipped it into the water, he made a final lunge. I tried to give him line, but it was too late. The wooden frog tore out of his jaw and whipped against my fishing hat. The mammoth sank slowly out of sight into the dark water.

For a long minute I watched the spot where he had disappeared. I laid my rod across the seat and dug for my pipe, spilling tobacco grains on the floor of the boat. With trembling fingers I stuck a match to the bowl, then turned the boat slowly and paddled to the upper end of the lake.

I knew there was no chance of finding my way out of the swamp before dark. I wasn't eager for night to trap me between the jungle fringes of the water trails with venom loaded moccasins hung on every other bush. Lem knew I was without supplies and would come looking for me within a day or two.

The sun was still more than an hour high when I pulled my boat up on the cypress knees and waded ashore in ankle deep water. The little island where the pine trees grew was some four feet above the surface of the lake. Here was partial security from the hidden dangers of the darkening swamp.

With my heavy hunting knife I cleared out brush around the pines and gathered heaping armloads of fire wood by breaking dead branches off the trees. From the low limbs I pulled a dozen loads of spanish moss.

Shadows had lengthened over the lake when I went back to the boat and pulled in my two fish on the string. The gator was floating a few yards out in the lake with only his eyes above the surface. If I left either bass tied to the boat, the gator or a turtle would get him before morning. If I hung him above the water, out of reach, he'd spoil.

The six pounder was too large for my meal, so I turned him back to his liquid home. I gutted and skinned the three pound bass and brought him back to the camp site with my tackle bag, in which I always carry salt and a can of hardtack.

I whittled a three pronged stick out of the brush, wrapped the fish on it with one of my gut leaders to keep the cooked meat from falling off and built a campfire there in the heart of the Okefenokee.

By the time I had broiled the bass steaks and put my teeth into the delicious meat and hardtack, the sun was gone and twilight had cast its purple shadows over the land of trembling earth.

There is no peace on earth like that of being alone in the deep wilderness, in the glow of a bright campfire. With my back against the giant pine, I sat out the last vestige of day and listened to the awakening night life of the drowned woods around me. From somewhere out in the swamp, I heard the distant call of a barred owl, blended with the soft treble of a raccoon padding along his run. Above the rising symphony of night, an alligator boomed and the strident cry of a heron answered. I might have been the first man or the last, alone in the universe at the dawn of the world, or at its end.

My pile of wood was almost gone when I curled up on the moss and went to sleep.

Cold gray daylight had invaded the swamp when I awoke. The damp wind moving through the trees had dewed the bushes at the water's edge. I built a fire on the warm ashes and baked out my moist clothing until the sun came up. Nibbling a piece of leathery biscuit for breakfast, I crawled into my boat just as the first flaming rays touched the tops of the gray cypress.

The surface of the lake was quiet, so I tied on a deep running bucktail and spinner, tipping the hook with a piece of pork rind. The first two casts got strikes from bluegill bream larger than my hand, but the hook was too large for their mouths. They dragged the streamer under, shook it once or twice and turned it loose. Then I caught a bream that weighed more than a pound. I released it and took off the spinner and bucktail, replacing it with a small broken-back plug that was really too heavy for my flyrod.

The selection was a choice one. The third cast brought a walloping strike that I missed, then a bronze-back snagged the plug and came out of the water in a twisting, slashing attack as he tried to disgorge the steel barb. He was in the five pound class, so I put him on the stringer.

I picked up another five pounder, then one that went almost four pounds before I worked back to the cypress tree with the inverted V. For twenty minutes I fished the spot carefully but the bite of my frog had evidently been too sharp and the old warrior wasn't rising to any bait I put in the water.

Reluctantly I left him there and turned down the lake to the maze of runs. By the time I had reached the end of the lake I had strung six bass that would read OK in anybody's book. So I took the rod apart and permitted myself a last, lingering look at my virgin lake. Then I plowed recklessly into the river of grass, hoping fervently that it would lead me to traveled water and Lem's camp.

There were some traces of my previous day's trip. Here and there a bush had been skinned by the heavy boat or a twig broken. The openings I had made in the grass had been closed again by the flowing water, which on this side of the swamp drained into the headwaters of the Suwanee River.

The discovery gave me sudden inspiration. There were innumerable runs, but those leading east and west were crossed by slow currents of water. All pliant vegetation leaned toward the south. By traveling with the current from left to right, I knew that eventually I should stumble into the narrow trail that would lead me to Minnie Lake.

I've known the Okefenokee for a long, long time. I have a profound respect for its temperament. And brother, it's loaded with temperament. One moment it lies in wait like a coiled moccasin. The next it strikes in sudden fury that rips the open prairies and whip-lashes the timber in wind and rain. But it is never more terrible than when it sprawls sinister and brooding by its very silence building tension and suspense.

At noon the wind died and the sun bored in. Not a leaf quivered. No birds sang or streaked across the unnaturally bright sky. The bream no longer plopped or swirled under the stillness of the trees. The splash of my paddle was too loud. I paused for a moment, wedged on a cypress knee, and strained my ears against the empty silence. With every creature in the drowned world around me so still, a sudden panic grabbed me amidships.

Sweating, swearing under my breath, I dug the blade of my paddle deep and tried to shove the craft off the knees. When it wouldn't budge, I plowed it around by awkward force and jammed my paddle against a sunken log, shoving until my arms struck bone against the shoulder blades, and until my muscles hurt.

The next few moments were so swift, so incredible, that they might have been something out of a nightmare. The boat broke loose with a grinding tear and flew backward as if it had been shot out of a torpedo tube. It crashed against the wall of brush that hemmed me in. Before I could regain my balance, I was struck behind the shoulder with something that I felt like the crack of a whip.

I was convinced that nothing but a rusty old cottonmouth could pack a wallop like that. I plunged out of the boat, just as another staggering blow hit me behind the ear. The bottom of the run was as grassy as a cow pasture. I don't know how long I stayed down. I remembered crawling under the water until I bumped into a lot of crooked stems. I wiggled into them and cautiously came up for air. With the back of my hand I slapped the water out of my eyes.

The stern of the bateau was covered with a swarm of storming hornets. I breathed relief so loud I thought they would hear and come gunning for me in the bush. My pounding pump throttled down to normal and I looked around. Open water glimmered beyond the brush wall.

Moving carefully, I slid through the branches. The lake looked like the one I had paddled away from only a few hours before, but then, all Okefenokee lakes are similar. But it was open and clear of the beastly brush. I dug my knife out of my soaked pocket to clear a path through which I could rescue my bateau from the raging horde, but the warlocks seemed determined to put me down. Just as I deposited an armload of limbs, I slipped on an underwater root. The knife flew out of my hand and I went down again, completely submerged in the oozy goo. I floundered for air, blowing moss and mud out of my head like a wounded porpoise.

"Greatjumpingmoses!"

Lem and Dan McMillan crouched in their boat about thirty feet away, their eyes run out on stems. I spluttered under my breath.

"In fifty years," Lem gasped, "I've seen some strange sights in this swamp, but this beats 'm all."

"We almost potted you fer an old black bear," Dan grinned.

Lem peeled off his clothes and helped me complete the tunnel through the brush. We maneuvered the boat gently from under the paper globe where the hornets lived and hauled it through the snags into the deep water of Minnie Lake.

"Other than that knot on your head," Lem asked, bluntly, "what luck did you have?"

I felt for the string of bass, but somewhere in the confusion, it had torn loose from its moorings and vanished into the murky water.

"None," I said, "I went to the wrong place."

Lem's gray eyes shot me through, so I described the lake with the pine trees at its head. He smirked.

"You were too far north. I remember that gator hole. Used t' trap coons in there."

I didn't tell him about the fish I had caught or the giant I had missed. I didn't want him beating around that water with his deadly rod. I wanted a second date with the old bronzeback myself, and the next time I wouldn't be lost when I was there.

Being lost in a swamp or a desert, or any flat surface of the earth, is much worse than having yourself turned around in mountains or hilly land. In the mountains you don't even need a sense of direction. You can find your way out of almost any mountain range in America by locating a stream and following it down hill. I'll admit that it's a little rugged sometimes, and that following a creek or river through some of the wilderness areas in North America is not exactly like strolling along the pier at Atlantic City.

There was the time I was lost in the Cabinet Mountains of Montana, with no compass, only a little food and a very strong urge to find my way out. I was forty miles from a road, trying to get from one watershed to another. The second night I spent out in the mountains, I had used my last match in building a fire. Clouds had blanketed the whole mountain chain, so thick that I couldn't see more than thirty feet in any direction around me. I didn't know which side of the ridge I was on. If I went down the wrong slope, it was fifty miles by stream to the nearest settlement. A road ran around the base of the mountain on the other side and I knew that it wasn't more than twelve or fifteen miles away.

I walked down hill until I found a thread of stream that I hoped would lead me out to the road. My hunting and fishing treks up and down the continent have carried me into some rough places, but that was about the roughest of them all. I crossed windfalls where the timber was criss-crossed and in many places piled twenty feet above the ground and shot through with bristling, second growth of spruce and fir. Sometimes I walked the logs for half a mile without putting a foot on the mossy earth.

The stiff spruce branches tore at my clothes and ripped slivers of meat out of my hide. In places where the creek poured through a gap in the ridge, I had to climb the hillside around sheer rock wall canyons.

Fortunately I was on the right side of the mountain. I climbed the road embankment just at dusk, a sorry sight with my clothes torn half off and my arms raw and bleeding from the stiff spruce branches. But I was alive and unharmed.

I don't have to wonder what would have happened if I had lost my head and traveled in circles around that mountain top. I know. It's happened to stronger and better men than I am.

But after a few experiences of being lost in the woods, I began to make a sort of game out of it. Now mind you, I don't get lost too much, because when I'm in unfamiliar territory, I always carry a compass in my pocket. But I began to wonder that if a man was caught far from a grocery store shelf full of canned goods, or a restaurant where he could slide his fanny on a stool and order ham and eggs, if it would be possible for him to live off the natural foods the Big Boss has so generously supplied to his mountains, plains and swamps.

I am thoroughly convinced that any fisherman, or any hunter, could find enough forage to keep him alive in almost any wooded area of North America, if he had the slightest knowledge about getting along in the wilderness.

Each Saturday morning, when I was a school kid in middle Georgia, I used to leave home at the crack of dawn and spend the day in the sedge fields or in the river swamps. I never carried a lunch with me. A piece of bread and a small bag of salt were my only supplies. I had fish hooks and lines and leads, and I always packed along my gun and a few shells.

Game was plentiful in those days, but not particularly more so than it is now, if you know where to look. I frequently flushed one or two covies of quail during the day, and I rarely failed to kill a number of doves. I could kick at a few brush piles and run out a rabbit when I wanted one, and I knew several swamps where the mallards always fed.

Even today I carry a fish hook and line tucked away in my pocket-book. It is a habit brought down from those carefree days when all the world moved along in a sort of adventurous charm and expectation.

It's small wonder that I wasn't poisoned a dozen times. I was eternally experimenting with new foods. I never went hungry. When one item was not available for the forest menu, I tried another.

I remember that someone once told me that fresh water periwinkles made delicious soup. I collected a double handful of the tiny gastropods and tried them. They were no doubt nourishing, but I am sure that earthworms would have been just as palatable.

The tiny salt water periwinkle, now, makes an excellent broth when the creatures are strained free of sand, boiled, the soup poured off and flavored with butter, salt, pepper, cream or milk. It's like a combination of oyster stew and clam chowder.

I remember another adventure with acorns. Somewhere I had read that acorns, pounded into meal, made good bread. I picked up a hatful of large white oak acorns, peeled them and scraped them against an old file I had brought along for the purpose.

After wearing the skin off my fingers and knuckles, I finally had sufficient acorn flour for a large, fat cake. I put in baking powder and salt and fried it in bacon grease. Wow!

No one had told me that the tannic acid had to be washed from the meal, and that it should be allowed to dry in the sun. The first bite convinced me that the Indians must have led a hard life. However, after I had worked hours to make that cake, I was determined not to waste it. The experience ruined an otherwise perfectly good Saturday.

On my trips into various wilderness places, I have tested all sorts and kinds of food. Some were delicious, others could hardly be called appetizing. But I did learn that nature has a way of producing green vegetables and other foods with low caloric content for her inhabitants in the spring and summer, and of supplying in autumn fat producing foods to carry them over the long, cold months.

Even the squirrels, that we think of as existing entirely on nuts from one season to the next, eat young shoots and buds in the spring.

I have tried unusual foods. In the Yukon territory a red-coated mountie once told me that the gray tundra moss that feeds much of the northland, would keep a man alive. I sampled it. The tender shoots have the taste of uncooked mushrooms.

On one trip down a southern river, we killed a large alligator. Upon skinning it, we found the meat of its tail to be as pretty and white as any meat I had ever seen. We cut off a small portion and fried it in our skillet. The meat was a bit coarse, but so delicious that we made a meal of alligator tail. Before you turn up your nose at that statement, try it.

Have you ever eaten boiled, fresh young cane leaves in the spring? No? Well, let me tell you that bamboo shoots are hard to beat. You pay a fancy price for them in chop suey.

There was a time when the tomato was known as the love apple and thought to be poisonous. The egg plant is no object of beauty.

I have often wondered if it would be possible for anyone to forget his inhibitions, take a gun and fish hook and support himself in the wilderness. Nature is so generous, I am sure that with the proper study and experimenting, he could go into the forests and fields and live with her in a bountiful manner.

I can think of a dozen foods which come out of the wilderness and for which we pay a high price on the market. Wild honey is one, and there are the young shoots of the old Pokeberry, from which we used to get the colored juice to paint our faces for the Indian war path—long ago. There are the young plants of lambs quarters, which are sold as delicacies. There are a hundred others which would support us from season to season.

For years I have stood and watched an old lady who comes to the lawn under my office window after a summer shower and gathers mushrooms. My wife buys them in cans. All of us should know a few of the tiny edible fungi—know enough to tell the difference between the poisonous ones with the cup at the base and those which are delicacies when cooked in butter or with a thick, juicy steak.

The meat of young crows is very good. Someone once shot a sparrow hawk and fed it to me at a dove supper. I think the joke was on him for giving up that choice morsel.

Once in a southern swamp, we collected two turtles which one of the party had seen in the open patch of water below our camp. We cleaned them, boiled them for a couple of hours, then added salt, pepper, rice, potatoes and cooked the mixture a little longer, I ate so much turtle stew that I probably would have married the next lady snapper that came crawling into camp.

Later we learned that a hermit, who lived near camp, had existed for years off the swamp, taking on all manner of foods, the substantial base of which was fish.

Fish taken out of the water and fried on the river bank are many times more delicious than those bought at the market. An oak fire, the smell of pine woods, the soft breeze—all seem to add flavor that cannot be obtained under a roof or within the four walls of a house.

Many southern residents live year after year on the shore of the Atlantic Ocean or the Gulf of Mexico with little or no money. There are shrimp, crabs, oysters, fish, sea birds, turtle eggs and a super abundance of foods with life giving vitamins.

Not long ago I was hunting with an urban friend. When we left in the morning, I informed him that if he saw a squirrel or rabbit, he must pop it quick and straight, since our only lunch would be what we killed for the pot. He looked at me a little dubiously before he nodded in agreement.

We separated and hunted alone all morning in the river swamp. I tried a dozen places I knew but could not find a single living creature which would supply us with lunch. I racked my brain to think of other wilderness foods we might secure if no other game were taken during the morning, and kept my eyes open as I hunted.

At noon I met my friend at the appointed place. He had killed a rabbit. I almost cheered.

"That'll be enough for lunch," I said.

He looked at the rabbit and then at me. He didn't have to say a word. I could almost sense what went on in his mind. Cook a rabbit without a pot or pan, without grease? Eat it without bread? He picked up his gun and wandered off into the woods while I built a fire and cleaned the rabbit at a nearby creek.

Lunch was almost ready when he returned. I had split the rabbit and put it on a spit. I had turned and turned it over the coals until the flesh had begun to take on a golden brown color and the aroma from it was beginning to make my intestinal cilias curl.

When the rabbit was brown to a turn, I ripped it off the spit and tore it in equal portions and handed half to my companion. We squatted on our heels there in the dank wilderness, gnawing meat from the bones, much as our ancestors must have done in the days before skillets and long handled forks and electric ranges.

After my friend had finished his meal, he wiped his hands and dug into his pocket for tobacco. He spoke somewhat apologetically.

"Say—that was good!"

If there was not a little wonderment in his voice at his own enthusiasm, then I'll never broil another rabbit over outdoor coals. It was his first real treat of primitive eating. An old woodsman told me once that buckeyes, which were so valuable to us as charms when we were boys, are edible when properly prepared. Raw, they are said to be poisonous. But Horace Kephart, as fine a woodsman who ever left a boot print in the trail, told me that they may be roasted, hulled, peeled of the outer skin, mashed and bleached. The remaining paste, he said, may be eaten baked or cold, and makes a tasty dish when a guy is hungry.

Acorn meal, handled with finesse, does make delectable cakes. In the fall, the south produces muscadines, persimmons, field maypops and in some sections, pawpaws, chinquapins, hickory nuts, walnuts and butter-nuts. I have seen children of the coastal plains in the south pick up seeds of the longleaf pine and eat them with relish. These are one of the main food sources of the southern quail and squirrel, and even of the deer and wild turkey in the fall. I have tried them. They have much the same flavor as the nuts of the western pinion pine.

There are a great many bulbous plants—wild cucumber, wild turnip and even the Indian turnip, which may be prepared in such a way that is edible and nourishing.

There is, however, one danger in experimenting with wilderness foods. Most of us are not expert enough to try any and every plant we find in the woods. I never intend to experiment to such a degree that searchers will find me drawn up in a knot somewhere, cold. I know too many foods which are good, and I do not have to risk my neck and other more delicate organs in testing the others. I think that no one should attempt to eat food found in the wilderness until he is certain what it is.

One of the most interesting trips I ever made in this connection was into the northwestern part of Montana, in the Coeur d'Alene mountains. The end of summer was near and the groves of willows and alders on the mountain slopes had donned a dress of riotous color.

Old Bill Sutphin, boss of the trail and road crews on District Three of the Cabinet National Forest, was with me. We had been asked to go into the back country that lay on top of the Cabinet-Coeur d'Alene divide and look over a section of trail which had been constructed during the past summer.

We estimated that our job would require only two days, but to be on the safe side, we carried a three day supply of food.

Even before we reached the beginning of the trail, the first cold rain and snows of autumn set in and we were forced to take refuge for two days in an old deserted homestead at the foot of the mountain.

Although we had eaten sparingly, when we were ready to set out on the inspection tour, our food supply was not sufficient to carry us to the end of the trail and back.

"Wal," mused Bill, plucking at the end of his handlebar mustache, "What d' ye say? Shall we try it?"

Somehow I have always had the feeling that Bill was merely asking that question just to see what my reaction would be. He was a capable woodsman. He had lived in the West for fifty years and as far as anyone knew, was one of the original settlers in the Plains valley.

"I'm beginning to feel a little tight around the middle now," I replied, "but if you're game, we'll take off."

Bill laughed.

"All right. We'll give it a bar'l."

We threw on our packs and set out up the bleak, windswept ridge. Neither of us knew whether the winter snow would catch us before we could get out again. The prospect of a good trip looked forlorn to me, and going without food for a couple of days did not especially appeal to the vicinity where my appetite lay. But I knew that I would never live it down if I reversed my decision.

For three long days we tramped over the trail, making notes and measurements, and when we arrived back at ranger headquarters a week later, my appetite was not nearly as demanding as I had thought it would be. Bill knew the woods. He knew how and where to secure food and he made use of that knowledge. We lived without killing one of the numerous deer we met along the trail.

"Waste of meat," was the old foreman's comment.

I think perhaps the thing that stands out on that trip was my introduction to the Richardson Grouse, which is known throughout the section as the Fool Hen. We were tramping along the trail one afternoon, looking for a campsite.

"Like to have fried chicken for supper?" Bill asked.

"Would you like a slug of fifty year old scotch?" I retorted.

Bill caught my arm and pulled me back. He pointed to two grouse in the narrow opening of a low tree, four or five feet from the trail. While I watched the birds, the grizzled woodsman stepped across the trail and cut a stick.

"Watch," he said.

He placed the stick on one bird's head. This may sound a bit incredible to one not acquainted with the fool hen, but the bird made no attempt to fly. It twisted its head, trying to get out from under the stick.

Bill rapped it sharply across the skull. The he killed the second bird. That night we ate fried grouse for supper, and it was so good that I resolved to repay it some time with the fifty year old liquid.

"I've been caught several times in the woods without food," Bill explained, "and these crazy birds are always easy to get."

He also told me that the porcupine was an animal that the woodsmen of the northern forests never kill unnecessarily. It is one animal that a starving man can take with a stick.

I have an idea that any real outdoorsman can live in the wilderness without civilized food almost indefinitely. There are few rural spots on the North American continent which do not support sufficient wildlife to keep a man alive. Usually there is no end to the variety and amount of food, and the knowledge of how and where it may be obtained and how it may be prepared, many times makes it possible for a lost man to live comfortably until he finds his way back to the pavement and electric lights.

Sachem River

By Roderick L. Haig-Brown

AT THE HEAD TABLE OF ANY GATHERING OF THE TRUE GREATS OF angling literature, one name tag will always reserve a chair for Roderick L. Haig-Brown.

Haig-Brown was born in England in 1908 but lived most of his life along the banks of his beloved Campbell River on Vancouver Island in British Columbia, the setting of many of his stories, essays, and books. He authored many books before he passed away in 1976, the most famous perhaps being *A River Never Sleeps*, first published in 1946. Some of his books, including *A River Never Sleeps*, have been reissued by Nick Lyons.

In his works, Haig-Brown's abilities as an angler are always understated in prose that focuses more on conveying the true sense of the angling challenge, the ever present doubts and frustrations about trying to find fish and make them strike. Regarded today as one of the true high priests of fly fishing, Haig-Brown was far from being a purist or fly-rod teetotaler. Although fly fishing was his favorite, he was a sensible angler who enjoyed the pursuit of all kinds of fish, from pike to salmon, and he was always at the ready to use the rods, lures, and tactics that would catch fish according to the conditions and situation.

From the first day Nick Lyons and I discussed publishing this anthology of great fishing stories, I knew a Haig-Brown story would be included. But which one? The choices are so vast. Finally, I let the voice of Haig-Brown himself make the decision for me. In the first paragraph of this story from *A River Never Sleeps*, Haig-Brown calls it "the best fishing story I know." Nothing could be more perfect for this book.

I have told this story before in different ways, but it is the best fishing story I know and it touches one of the loveliest rivers I know.

In the summer of 1927 I went up to the northern end of Vancouver Island to work for the Wood and English Logging Company on Nimpkish Lake. I had heard, before I went, that the Nimpkish River had a run of tyee salmon probably at least the equal of the Campbell River run, and I made up my mind that I was going to get some fishing out of it. In 1927 I was away at the head of the lake all through September and missed the run, but in 1928 I was ready for it, with a brand-new Murdoch spinning rod, a good line and plenty of spoons that were supposed to be of the right kind.

My knowledge of the fishing was wretchedly slight. The tyees ran in September—that seemed fairly definite. Someone, a few years earlier, had caught a sixty-seven-pounder by trolling with a hand line inside the river. But, so the boys in camp told me, it was the height of folly to expect to catch such fish on rod and line: in the first place, no such fancy gear could possibly deceive them into taking hold; and if by some obscure chance an especially foolish fish were to impale itself on the hook, no possible good could come of it; rod, reel, line and everything else would be irreparably smashed or else taken right away in the first run.

Fishing for trout in the river and waiting for ducks on the tide flats at the mouth of the river during the previous year, I had learned a little about the water; but I didn't really know where to start in. Not too far above tidewater, I thought; perhaps the first pool above. And that was where I went with my new rod and a big bright spoon on the last Sunday of August.

The pool I had chosen was very big, deep and fairly slow between high, steep banks. I found it difficult to fish and discouraging because I could not wade to cover it properly, and no fish showed to convince me that I was not wasting my time. As a matter of fact, I doubted if any were yet in the river, and my main purpose in coming down had been to size up the water before the fish came in rather than to catch fish. So in a little while I left the big pool and followed the river on down.

I came almost at once to a much more promising pool, one at the head of tidewater which I later named Lansdowne Pool. It was separated from the other pool by a wooded island and a short rapid. The main body of the river flowed on the east side of the island, under the bank that I was following, and stretching back from the pool on this side were several acres of cleared land with a primrose-yellow farmhouse set in a small orchard in the middle of them—something altogether unique in the Nimpkish watershed, but I knew the farm belonged to the Lansdowne family and I had met the two sons once or twice when I had been trout fishing up the river. I tried a few casts in the pool, but there was a deep eddy under my bank which made it difficult to reach the water properly, and I strongly suspected that the best lying place in the pool was under the steep rock bank on the far side. So once again, and very fortunately, I told myself, I was exploring rather than fishing and went on my way.

I had great hopes of the estuary of the river. I knew that at Campbell River the tyees were caught only in salt water and that, generally speaking, Pacific salmon were supposed to be impossible to catch once they had left salt water, though I knew also, from Cobb's *Pacific Salmon Fisheries*, that they were caught by anglers in the Willamette River. I supposed vaguely that my best hope might be to find some tidal pool where the fish rested before committing themselves to fresh water. On this Sunday of exploration the tide was fairly well in over the flats, and I could not follow the river channel as closely as I had hoped. But I could see that there was a short and narrow pool under the far bank some two hundred yards below Lansdowne Pool and a larger pool under a high-cut bank of blue clay a hundred yards down from that. Opposite this Blue Clay Pool was a small grassy islet, Sachem Island, then a shallow channel about forty yards wide, then a much more considerable island, the Indian Island, with several Indian smokehouses standing on it, separated from the bank I was following by a deep backwater.

A little below the Indian Island I met Ed Lansdowne. He was sixteen years old then and looked younger, dressed in a shirt and a pair of blue shorts, without shoes or stockings, his hair a tight cap of red curls above his sunburned face. I liked what I had seen of Ed up the river and I felt sure at once that he would prove a valuable conspirator in this salmon-fishing project. He was not talkative or much given to asking questions, but the new rod caught his admiring eye and I told him what I was looking for. He was doubtful, but not discouraging.

"There was a policeman used to come over from the Bay and troll in the river with a hand line. He caught a few. Pete and some other guys come once in a while, but they fish outside."

He pointed downstream to where the Fishing Island, a low triangular island with more fishing shacks and net racks, split the tide and held the river in its channel.

"Beyond the Fishing Island—between there and Green Island—you can see the fish finning out there when the run's in. You see them all the way up the river too, past Sachem Island and as far up as our place."

"Do they seem to lie much in the pool opposite your place?" I asked.

"Sure, they lie there pretty good. We see them jumping and rolling—you can hear them all night sometimes. But I don't think there's any in yet this year." He grinned. "Gee, I'd sure like to see you get one."

I told him I wanted to fish the pool the next Sunday. Did he think the fish would be in and could he get hold of a boat from somewhere? He thought that the fish would surely be in and he knew of a boat he could probably get. So we made it a date.

I was down at the side of the pool well ahead of the appointed time, in spite of a five-mile walk from camp, and Ed was soon with me. He had not been able to get a boat, but he had a raft, a heavy thing of logs with planks spiked across them, which would float when the tide came in and which he thought we could maneuver enough to cover at least some of the good water. The fish were in all right. A big one jumped soon after I arrived, and others jumped at intervals all through the morning while we waited for the tide. From time to time I waded out and tried to cast to where they were lying, but I had not yet learned to handle the big six-inch spoon very well and I knew I wasn't reaching them. So at last I sat down to wait with Ed and plan what we would do when the raft floated. Every five or ten minutes a fish jumped and the splash echoed back from the timbered hill opposite. They were huge fish, cleaner and brighter than I had dared hope, though some were bronze rather than silver; I tried to guess weights—thirty, I would say, forty-five. Then a great pig of a fish would come over in a short-bodied arc, and I would realize that if the last one had been forty-five this one must be seventy at least. And perhaps he was; the Nimpkish had yielded her ninety-pounders to the nets.

The tide came in at last, the raft floated and we pushed off. The surface of the pool was still and dark now, with only an easy current through it and a little ripple close under the foot of the rapids, which still ran white and strong and broken against the big boulders. I fished carefully and thoroughly and expectantly, working the big spoon very deep and slow; we covered the whole pool several times, but nothing touched the spoon. It wasn't easy to handle the heavy raft with only a paddle and pole over the deep water, but Ed did really well with it and worked at least as hard and enthusiastically as I did for a long while. We went up behind the island and found a deep still backwater fed by only a light riffle of water from the Canyon Pool, and once or twice we saw the shadows of big fish moving or lying near bottom. Ed, whose brother was a commercial troller, began to wonder if my spoon was working just right, and knowing little of how a spoon should work, I began to feel doubtful myself. Then Ed suggested that we might do better when the tide started to ebb, so we ran the raft back to the beach and waited. Ed went up to the house and came back with huckleberry wine and sandwiches.

"Do you really think we've got a chance to catch something?" he asked.

"Sure," I said, and I was sure. "The hand trollers catch fish, don't they? There's no difference in what we're doing."

"They mostly catch them out in the salt chuck."

"I know that. But there's no reason a fish should change so much just for coming up a mile or so on the tide. And anyway, they fish mostly in the salt chuck. You said so yourself."

The tide began to ebb at last, and we started to fish again. This time we took the raft straight across to the low rock face of the far bank and held there, for it seemed that we might have disturbed the pool too much by moving about in our first attempts. I worked the spoon through the water every way I knew, fast and slow, deep and shallow, steadily and in jerks, casting upstream and across and down. Still nothing took. I could see that Ed was getting a little restless and told him about a fisherman's faith in the last cast of the day—if you make enough of them, saying each time "just one more," you're sure to get something.

"You still think there's a chance?" Ed asked. "I don't."

"There's always a chance," I said. "I'm going to try it right through to dark. You stay with me, and if we get a fish, I'll send you up a Hardy trout rod from town next week."

So we kept fishing. I really had plenty of hope left in me. After all, I had fished the Frome with Greenhill every day for a solid week to catch my first Atlantic salmon and I knew something of how dour and moody nonfeeding fish can be. The tide was almost out of the pool now, and a hand troller came up, rowing right through the middle of it. That, I thought, wouldn't help any. I made a cast at a long angle upstream and fished it back to me deep down. I noticed that the sun was gone behind the hill and most of the pool was in shadow. Then the spoon came against something solid and heavy. I struck hard; the line ran out for fifteen or twenty yards, then went slack.

"That was it," I said. "But we'll get another."

We did. Two or three casts later I felt the spoon stop, brought the rod up and was into a fish that ran with wild strength straight up toward the rapids. I checked him as hard as I dared, because I had only sixty or seventy yards of line on the reel. There were about a dozen turns left on the reel when he came out in a beautiful jump not ten feet from the stern of the hand troller's boat.

"Let's get across," I said, "and finish him from the bank. He'll tangle in that guy's line if we don't."

Ed picked up the paddle and drove the raft across. I jumped overboard in three or four feet of water with the fish still on. But we had him. He ran again, several times, almost as strongly as the first time. Then he was swirling and fighting about twenty feet away, unable to tear loose from the strain I held on him, but still too strong to give up. I walked back onto dry land, drawing him in, then went forward again into the water, shortening line. He came close, and I reached for his tail, gripped it and carried him ashore. He was a perfect fish, silver and clean, certainly a spring salmon, but he was hooked just ahead of the dorsal fin and weighed only twenty-one pounds.

"What do you think happened?" Ed asked. "Do you think we just snagged him?"

"No," I said. "He came at it; I'm sure of that. We can't prove it though—not till we get another one."

"Tonight?"

"No, you've earned that trout rod now. Next Sunday."

Ed had a boat the next Sunday. We fished the pool for a while without touching anything, then went down the river to see what we could find. I wanted a thirty-pounder, to meet the British Columbia angler's traditional but arbitrary distinction between tyee and spring salmon, and I wanted him hooked fairly and squarely in the mouth, so that I'd have an answer for the boys in camp who still insisted that there was nothing new about snagging salmon—anyone could do that.

There was some tide in and the water was quite smooth. Below Sachem Island we saw the little arrowhead ripples of a school of fish swimming up the river, and I cast across them from the boat. A big fish turned and had the spoon. I had spliced an extra length of backing onto my line since the previous Sunday, but he had all the old line and backing and a good part of the new out before I could bring him up to break the surface. He didn't exactly jump when he did come up, but for twenty or thirty seconds he stayed right at the surface and thrashed the water white. Suddenly he turned and came hard back for the boat, getting himself some slack line, but I soon picked that up, and he seemed well hooked. For about twenty minutes he fought this way, running close to the surface, turning when I put heavy pressure on him, running again and jumping occasionally. He made one more short run, which I held easily, then I told Ed to head in for the island, where we could tail him—we still had no gaff. Something made him run again, strongly and fiercely for forty or fifty yards. That seemed to finish him. He lay on the surface with little movement. I tried to lead him back to the boat, and he began to roll.

"Quick," I told Ed, "row out to him. I think I can get him right where he is."

Then the spoon came away. The fish was still rolling in the surface, his belly showing white. Ed drove the boat toward him, and I crouched, ready to grab any part of him I could reach. But as we got there, he righted himself and all we saw was his big, pale, shadowy form swimming slowly down through the clear water.

"Gosh," I said, "forty-five pounds anyway. And that's leaning over backward to be fair."

"Yes," Ed said. "Hooked in the mouth too. I could see."

"Seeing like that's no proof though."

"There's no proof he was forty-five pounds either."

We got what we wanted the next Sunday, a thirty-two-pound fish, bright and clean, hooked in the mouth and killed after a good fight in the shallow water between Sachem Island and the Indian Island. That was the last fish we killed that season. I had to go up to work in the camp at the head of the lake, and by the time I got back to the river again, it was October and a high freshet had drawn all the big fish on upstream to their spawning in Woss Lake and the Kla-anche River. But at least we knew the game was worth trying; we had killed two fish, had narrowly missed getting a third, and had run several others, some of them in Lansdowne Pool. Next season, we promised ourselves, we would be really fishing, with proper equipment and at least some knowledge to start on.

It happened that September of 1929 found me with a broken elbow and a very slim bankbook after a bad summer of contract logging. As it turned out, that was a fairly convenient set of circumstances: I couldn't hire out on another job until the elbow was mended and I was within easy reach of the Nimpkish. The logical thing seemed to be to go there and combine business, pleasure and convalescence by catching what tyees I could and selling them.

The season started slowly. A few fish were in the river at the end of August, but Ed and I were busy cutting a winter's wood for Mrs. Lansdowne. When the wood was all split and piled in the woodshed, we began to fish. This year we were well off for boats. We had a small power boat, a good ten-foot dinghy and a canoe, so we could cover a lot of water in searching for fish. I caught the first tyee in Lansdowne Pool on September first, a fine fish of forty pounds, and after that we picked up fish fairly regularly all the way down the river from the pool and out in the salt water as well. There was a great run of big cohos in early September of that year, so we spent quite a lot of our time on them, using the little power boat to tow the dinghy and canoe over to Race Pass or wherever the fish were feeding. Pound for pound, the cohos outfought the big tyees, and fishing for them was certainly more remunerative than fishing for the tyees because they took so freely. But after the first few days I always stayed in or near the river; in spite of the quick-jumping fight of the cohos, there was something in the solid, heavy take of the tyees and the tremendous power of their first run that I could not resist. Besides that, there was the steady hope of a fifty- or sixty-pounder and all the attraction of fishing a river instead of salt water.

It is difficult to pick out the great days of that month of fishing—almost any day that one has the luck to kill a salmon of thirty or forty pounds is a great day. But there are some days and some fish that I remember more clearly than others. There was an evening at Sachem Island, with a flooding tide and sunset light smoothing the water until it seemed as still as a lake's surface on a windless evening. I had anchored the dinghy a little below the island and about forty yards over toward the right bank of the river. I could see schools of fish finning three or four hundred yards downstream, opposite the Fishing Island, and I knew that they would soon came up to pass me; so I waited, standing in the dinghy ready to cast. In a little while the first school came on, thirty or forty big fish, each one pushing his slender, arrowhead ripple ahead of him on the face of the still water. It was very quiet, and the crash of a great fish jumping somewhere up in the bend seemed to hang over the river long after its last echoes had died away. The fish were very close now, coming steadily but slowly. I swung the spoon back, then sent it out across them; it flew well for once, cutting the air with its edge, and dropped gently ten yards beyond the school and perhaps ten yards upstream of the leaders. I could see the outlines of the big bodies under the finning ripples and the tiny flashes of the spoon as I reeled it in, held only a few inches below the surface by a half-ounce lead. The leader of the school turned toward it and began to follow it, two or three feet behind the hook. I could see him clearly, and he was very big; and muscles tightened all through my arms, making my hands clumsy on the reel. A ripple moved, fast, from the near side of the school, and something hit with a jolt that dipped the rod hard down. I struck, and the still water was heaved by thirty or forty great smooth swirls as the school turned short away. The reel ran wildly, and I checked with all the strength of my fingers until my fish jumped twice about seventy yards away. He turned then and ran hard back for the boat, bored deep down, came out again in another jump, very high and very near the boat. Ten minutes later I gaffed a thirty-five-pounder.

Twice more the same thing happened. Once the fish threw the hook when he was halfway out on his first run; the other time I gaffed another thirty-pounder. The sky was still light, and I could see the colors of trees and grass; but it was almost dusk, and the surface of the water had that clear, dark shine that makes every movement of it seem oily and slow. Another school came up and another fish took. After my strike he was still for perhaps one full second, as fish often are, then he began to take out line, jumped in the first ten yards, jumped again a moment later and kept going. Something warned me to grab for the anchor line. The fish was still running. The anchor came free of the shallow and hung straight down in deep water. The river current and the start of the ebb carried the dinghy down, and the fish still ran, straight out for salt water. He jumped again, high and tumbling over, falling flat, ran a few yards and jumped again just as high. He was big and very silver, and I clamped down on the reel until he was towing the dinghy. Twice he checked, and I picked up on him until most of the line was back on the reel. But each time he ran again and jumped in his running with all the abandon of a coho and all the authority of his own forty-five-pound weight. I was outside the river mouth when he came alongside at last, completely played out so that I could slip the gaff under his gill cover and lift him into the dinghy. He was unlike any fish I had seen in the river before, beautifully clean and with a greenish sheen along his back, thick and deep as a good fish should be, yet gracefully shaped instead of hog fat as so many tyees are. No other tyee ever fought me that way.

I remember too a leaden-gray morning when the light made the water seem opaque and palely off-white. I was on the salt chuck below the river mouth, halfway down to the old breakwater, when a school showed near me, and I made a quick cast which immediately hooked a fish. He ran a few yards, and the spoon came back. I cast again, hooked another and fought him in frantic haste while the school kept showing near the boat. I killed him, a thirty-three-pounder, in six minutes and cast again as soon as he was in the boat. Another fish took, ran and sent the spoon back. Three times that happened, then I hooked and killed a thirty-nine-pounder. By the time he was in the boat, I had lost the school, but they, too, were bright, clean fish, newly arrived from the north and not yet rid of their salt-water ways.

At dusk salmon crowd into the river channel from all their near-by lying places. I was there one evening in late September, working the last stage of a long ebb tide. There were schools all around me in the narrow channel, and I had already touched several fish without hooking one of them. I made a careless cast that landed right in the middle of a school and saw the great swirls of frightened fish all around the spoon. I began to reel in disgustedly, holding the rod high to hurry the spoon. Thirty feet from the boat a fish took with a slash that broke water, jarring the rod almost to breaking. I saw a great, dark tail roll out in the swirl, let him take line and slipped the anchor. He made a heavy run, deep and strong. I made him work for line and brought him to the surface in a threshing break sixty or seventy yards away. He came in a little—or rather the tide and river drifted the boat up on him—but went away again and went down. He didn't sulk but swam strongly and heavily, and I couldn't lift him at all. Suddenly he came up fast, slashed the water with his great tail and went down again. I told myself that here was the sixty-pounder at last and I could afford to take things slowly, even if it was getting dark. When he came up near the boat, we were within a hundred yards of Green Island, drifting fast for the kelp bed. I reached for the gaff, but he was still swimming strongly three or four feet down in the water and ten or fifteen feet away from the boat. Nothing that I could do would bring him closer, and we drifted into the kelp bed that way. I thought it was all over then; the line would tangle on one of the heavy stems and give him his chance to tear away the hook. But he seemed afraid of the kelp. He turned deliberately away from two plants, tried to turn from a third and the movement let me lift him. On the surface he seemed helpless, floundering among the trailing ribbons while I floundered to bring the boat within gaffing reach. Three times I missed with the gaff, clumsily and inexcusably; then suddenly he was easy, and I had him, not sixty pounds, but forty-eight, a noble bronze color, so deep-bodied and hog-backed that for once I doubted the steelyards.

That was 1929. I missed the next two seasons, but in 1932 and 1933, Ed and I fished again. We were both of us wiser and better fishermen, and we fished carefully and thoroughly, keeping close records not only of every fish we killed but of every day we fished and every fish that moved to us at all. They were fine records, full of details of time and tide and light, of the condition of the fish, of the leads we used and the spoons, even of the angles of the casts that hooked fish—upstream, downstream or straight across. But we stored them in a house that burned down in 1934. There is less now to check my memory of those two seasons than the simple notes I kept of the earlier ones.

But we did learn certain things. We solved, in some measure, the difficulty of catching fish in Lansdowne Pool by finding that the best time in any day comes after the sun has gone behind the hill. Between that time and full darkness we were nearly always able to hook at least two fish. There were exceptions to this for which we could never properly account—September 2, 1932, was one of these. Ed went down to the pool at three-thirty in the afternoon. I followed him an hour later and found him fighting a thirty-five-pounder; he had another already in the canoe and had lost three others after short runs. Between that time and darkness we hooked and fought nine more big fish and lost at least as many more in the first or second run. The fish were almost the start of the run, and the pool was full of them. Time and again they took as the spoon hit the water. It was a No. 6 Superior, copper at first, changed to brass as the light failed, and fished with a ¾-ounce lead. At the head of the pool and just below the rapid there is a fast ripple three or four feet deep between the line of the main current and the light flow that comes in from the backwater behind the island. Holding the canoe in the backwater and dropping the spoon in the shallow ripple, we hooked fish after fish, and many times we saw the flash of their heavy bodies as they turned in striking. Ed hooked the biggest fish of the day, a forty-eight-pounder, in the main run. I knew somehow in the moment the fish took that he was heavier than the others and I drove the canoe hard to follow his run. He jumped once, still running, turned at the tail of the pool and started back. I had turned the canoe and was holding it well over toward the west bank, but he ran straight for the foot of the rapids, jumped there and swung over into the eddy.

"That's the end of him," I said. "He'll come back to us now."

He circled and did come back, and I put the gaff where I could reach it easily. Ed tried to lift him, but he swirled his great tail once near the surface, then ran again upstream through the strongest current. It was a moment before either of us realized what was happening; then Ed said, "He's going on, straight up for the Canyon Pool."

He jumped then, right among the rocks and the broken water, thirty or forty yards up in the rapid. Then he was quiet, and we couldn't see him or tell exactly where he was because the current held the line down. I pushed the canoe up along the west side of the river to the backwater, then swung out across the foot of the rapid and picked up the pole. Ed got his drowned line up out of the water, and we could see that the fish was at least fifty yards above us and still working slowly upstream.

"Heave the daylights out of him," I said. "It's about the only chance. Pick up your line fast when he comes down through."

Ed lifted with everything the rod had. The strain turned the fish across the current so that it caught the side of his body and threw him down, but as he came back, the line still ran out.

"Round a rock," I said and pushed the canoe in tight against the foot of the rapids.

Ed jumped out and started up, stumbling and slipping on the rocks but making time; he had to find which rock was holding the line and bring the rod round it. He was almost there when I saw the fish, hanging helplessly on his side, bounced by the current waves at the head of the pool. I picked up the gaff and began to edge the canoe toward him; then Ed was round the rock, and the fish was drifting down out of reach. Ed came back, half swimming, and piled into the canoe, and I gaffed the fish for him down at the tail of the pool again.

There were no other days in the pool like that one, but we caught fish often enough in the broad-daylight hours to keep us trying. And we caught fish down below, outside the river, in the channel by the Fishing Island, off Sachem Point, in daylight and dusk, on many different stages of tide. The biggest we killed weighed 52½ pounds, which is not really big for a tyee. We saw many jumping that were much larger and, perhaps once or twice, we hooked larger ones. There was one that I hooked below

Sachem Island in the first hour of a big ebb tide. He took deep down in twenty feet of water and made his first run lazily downstream. We followed him almost carelessly in the boat. Suddenly he turned into the stream and really ran, still deep, straight up the main channel. I saw the hundred-yard mark slip away on the line.

"Get after him, Ed," I said. "I can't stop him."

Ed pulled hard on the oars, but for several seconds the line was still going out; then the fish turned and came slowly downstream toward us. I held hard, trying to lift him, but he came back to the boat still two or three fathoms down. Rowing steadily, Ed was little more than holding place against tide and river. The line started out again fast, cutting the water toward the channel between Sachem Island and the Indian Island.

"He'll break this time, sure," I said. "There can't be more than five feet of water in there."

But he didn't break. He took a hundred and twenty yards plus whatever distance Ed's rowing moved the boat and came slowly back near bottom all the way.

"Gosh," I said, "if he doesn't show soon, I'll begin to think he's big."

"You aren't bearing down on him. You never let one get away with that much line before."

"I never had one wanted it so badly."

Then the third run started up the channel between the Indian Island and the bank. It went on and on, stronger and faster than either of the others, yet Ed was rowing up hard in the slack water behind the island. The hundred-yard mark flashed out again; then the reel stopped running. I knew he was off, but neither of us would believe it until we saw the spoon come back to us, wobbling its stupid flashes in the green water.

The Beginning of the Season

By John Waller Hills

Among the several classic chronicles of English chalkstream fishing, the one I find myself returning to most often for sheer enjoyable reading is John Waller Hills' *Summer on the Test*. One reason might be that Hills's book is not written in an "instructional" vein, but rather as a straightforward description of the fishing under varying conditions. When Hills takes us to the stream, our spirits fall and rise as his own. The river gives for a while, then it takes away, as hatches disappear and trout sulk. The pageant of the seasons, the off-again, on-again nature of the hatches, scroll through *Summer on the Test* like enchanting but mysterious dramas in which we view our leading player, Mr. Hills, with empathy and hope.

Summer on the Test was first published in a limited edition in 1924 and reprinted in a popular edition with new chapters in 1930. The book endures today as a classic of the first rank.

The Seasons, surely in these northern climes,
Laugh at their image drawn by modern Rhimes.
For spring oft shivers in the British Isle,
But warms, in British song, with Maia's smile.
                    The Anglers. By Dr. Thomas Scott. 1758.

The spring of 1924 was black and cold. By the beginning of April few flowers and leaves had succeeded in the hard struggle, and indeed I have known the north of Scotland more forward than was the Test valley.

Through the first half of the month we had bitter north winds, frequent hail and occasional snow. A miraculous change came just before Easter, and for four or five days from the 18th the conditions were like June. Then the fine weather broke, and there followed a series of gales, lasting till nearly the end of the month, culminating in a regular hurricane on the 27th. Now, it so happens that these conditions combine all the elements adverse to fly fishing. Extreme cold in early spring may bring up fly, but makes trout lethargic. Very hot weather means a poor hatch, and so do gales. Thus our three types of weather were all unpropitious; but of the three, the cold spell at the beginning was best, for at any rate there was fly, and without fly you are defeated, since even the accommodating trout of the Test cannot rise at nothing. Still, there were many occasions when fly was abundant but hardly a trout moved, and on the best days you did not have the chance of many fish, often only two or three; and you had to be lucky if you landed a brace of these, and they turned out to be over the limit of a pound and a half. In the hot weather the surroundings were delightful, but fly very scarce. And the days of gale were the worst of all.

I fished at Mottisfont on eight or nine days in April, somewhat unsuccessfully it is true, though I got some good trout. An exceptional number of bungles were made, and some very heavy fish were lost, one, which I shall always regret because he cannot have been less than three pounds, defeated me after a long fight in a manner which I cannot bear to recall. However, though rewards were small, the days were interesting. The rise was usually concentrated and short, the trout were particular about pattern, and fine gut had to be used. 26th April was a day typical of many. There was a wild wind from the south-east, heavy rain until one o'clock, and it was cold. But, when I started out, even under these unpromising conditions, I did not despair. At any rate, I said, the day was better than the one before. Then the wind had blown from the south-west, masses of inky black, rain-soaked clouds had scurried in succession across the sky, and there was that uncomfortable heavy feeling in the air beloved of our forefathers but which is the worst in the world for the floating fly. The present day was much better, for the air was nimble, and if it had a bite in it, why the large dark olive of spring is a lover of cold. Sure enough, at half-past twelve, summer time, the first olives appeared, and they were large and smoky grey, flickering delicately in the gale, tempting food for winter-starved stomachs. But, as usual, the fish paid no notice at first: so when it grew too cold to sit still any longer I walked up, eyes roaming over the water.

At last there was a movement under my bank; it might be a rat, but let us try my dark olive quill; its size was 0, and my gut 3x. The first cast was swept wide by the wind, but at the second there was a confident rise and a good fish careered down stream. The river was fairly clear of weed, the current ran full and strong, and after a merry fight I netted a fat fish, not two pounds in weight it is true, but well over the pound and a half limit. I walked up, and suddenly, without preparation, unexpected and wonderful as it always is, however often you see it, the real hatch started. Olives were coming down thick, in little bands of half a dozen or so, blown together by the wind, and trout were rising quietly and quickly and continuously, all up the river, three or four of them within reach, and good fish too. There is a quality of magic about these early spring rises. The river looks dead and lifeless, and this impression is heightened by the bare meadows and the leafless trees. The stream runs with a dull lead-like surface, which nothing disturbs and apparently nothing ever will disturb. You expect a rise and it does not come, and then suddenly, when you have given up expecting, trout start moving simultaneously as though the signal had been passed round. At one moment you see fly after fly sailing down untaken, and you think nothing will ever break the unbroken surface: at the next the river is alive with rings of rising fish. It has come to life, and the sturdy vital trout, which a moment ago were hidden so completely that you doubted their existence, have mysteriously reappeared. I crawled to the bank, knelt down and watched. There were five fish within reach, and I looked eagerly to see which was the best. This period of expectation, when fish are well on the feed, is one of unmixed happiness. When action begins, when you have to cast, you may put the trout down, or you may break, or make some other dreadful bungle: but in the stage of exciting anticipation, when you see that great trout are to be caught if you can catch them, any extravagant success is possible and your pleasure is unalloyed. However, I did not spend as long as it takes to write this in deciding, for near me, and above, a big fish was swallowing olive after olive, almost in perpetual motion.

I was rather too close to him, but the wild wind ruffled the water, and concealed my presence: I put my dark olive over him three or four times: I made certain he would take, but he did not, though he went on steadily eating natural fly. What is the meaning of that? Another fish was rising, opposite me, smaller but takeable, as was a third, higher up in the middle, and I could reach each without putting line over the first. I was not sure about the size of either, but I must know if my pattern is right. They both disregarded it. When it was certain that all had seen and neglected it (and as usual I kept it on too long) I reeled up and knotted on a medium, not dark, olive quill, a size smaller. The effect was immediate. I floated it over the first fish, he rose, but I think I struck too quickly. Anyway, I did not hook him, alas, for he was heavy. Next I tried the one under the opposite bank. He took at the first cast, and I pulled him downstream, out of the way, and netted him out. He also was not two pounds, but he was some ounces bigger than the first I had killed. Then I crawled back to my position: two or three fish were still rising, not perhaps so madly as at first, and I was perfectly certain they would not go on long. Quickly I picked out the best and, after considerable trouble with the wind, managed to get a fly to him. He took, made a gallant, hard run, but then came off: the wind was so strong and wild that it was impossible to keep the line taut, and I lost him, the best fish of the morning, without a doubt. Then all was over. The rise, the concentrated part of it, had lasted barely half an hour. I ended up with two trout, no great bag, but a brace that weigh not far from four pounds is something.

This indeed is the peculiarity of early spring rises, that they start and end suddenly. You are lucky to get a fish before they begin: when they end, you can go home. Whilst they are on, fish are not difficult, provided there is not too much fly: but you very rarely do well when your artificial has to be a member of a drove of naturals, for the competition is too severe. But, in these short April rises, you have no time for bungles or disasters or changes of fly: if you are to do well, your fly must be right to begin with. And this is not so simple as it sounds.

Hampshire was backward in April 1924. Not a kingcup was out, not a sign of white appeared on the dark twigs of the blackthorn, not a glint of green on the willows. And this is not favourable for sport, for my experience is that the earlier the season the better you do. If you were back from France in 1918, and keep a diary, turn up the month of April, and you will see that that spring was a full month earlier than the spring of 1924. It was a very good April. I got fish from the beginning, and I well remember two days towards the end, days which are symbolic of the conditions required for spring fishing. The 29th April was a hot, summer-like day, cloudless, with a light variable breeze. There was a bad hatch of olives, and a poor rise. With difficulty I got a brace of fish. The following day was the greatest contrast imaginable. There was a savage north-east wind, a heavy shower in the morning, the sky was overcast, and the air freezingly cold. I was on the Kennet, and went out at half-past ten, but nothing stirred till mid-day. Then I got three, one after another, in rapid succession: there were a few olives out, and fish took a blue quill, size 0. I had by then reached the top of the water, a broad, deep weir pool, with a rushing stream through the middle, and whirling eddies and backwaters at its head. In one of these, in a small, slow whirlpool, a big fish was lying low down, busy feeding on nymphs. I put on a greenwell's glory, wetted it, and after several casts managed to get it over him; he took, and rushed straight down to the tail of the pool. When I got down to him he rushed up, and I rather weakly allowed him to get into a patch of weed; but the water was shallow, I waded out, cleared my line, and the fish bolted into a second patch and from there into a third. I could wade out to that, and could see the fish lying in the weeds. Then I did a silly thing: instead of clearing the line or hand-lining him out, I tried to net him in the weeds. The result was that I missed him, he dashed out, and the hook came away. He was a fish between two and three pounds.

Chastened and pensive, I walked down to a sheltered spot to eat my sandwiches. As I had been playing the big fish, I had noticed more olives coming down, but now suddenly they appeared in droves, one of the largest hatches I have ever seen. A few fish rose, but only tentatively: I kept on my blue quill, and after considerable casting, for the trout were not taking one natural fly in twenty, I managed to kill two fish and returned an undersized one. After that not a fish moved, so I sat down to my sandwiches, watching the water. The weather was as inclement as ever, a raging north-east wind, and bitterly cold, but still olives sailed down in fleet after fleet. Caught by the northerly wind they were driven in packs into the southern bank, where they lay in all the little bays and curves of the shore, hardly floating with the current, and indeed often driven upstream by a more furious gust than usual. I expected every minute to see a quiet rise in one of these bays and a trout cruising about, picking the motionless fly off the water, but nothing happened. Three o'clock came, the wind grew colder and the fly thicker, but not a trout broke the surface and reluctantly I felt that it was hopeless, and there was nothing for it but to go home. Walking slowly back, watching the water intently, at last I saw what I had so long expected, a quiet rise and a good trout swimming around, swallowing fly after fly. He was on the lee shore, in the glass edge, in quite smooth water, cruising in an area of three or four square yards, making no more break than a minnow. Such fish are difficult, for you cannot always see where they are and make sure that your fly goes over them, and you are very likely to put the line across them, and then all is up. That particular fish I put down, but there was another small rise above. At the first cast I got hung up and lost my blue quill, which was a good thing, for it was too big, and I knotted on a Lock's fancy, size 00. No use, so I reeled up and tied on a hackle olive, 00, and this after many casts he took and I killed him. Then I rose and missed two more (you have to strike very slowly with these gentlemen), killed two, and rose and missed another. All this meant a lot of careful casting, and it was then six o'clock and the rise over. So I finished up with eight fish: a good day.

Now these two days were the opposite of each other; the first, fine and hot, produced hardly any fly and two fish, and the second, bitterly cold, showed an immense hatch and four brace of fine trout. Never, never believe that cold weather hinders fly. You will hear it, always and everywhere; but it is not only untrue but the reverse of truth. Except at the very beginning of April, you get more fly on a cold day than on a warm.

A good many Aprils have been spent after salmon, or after trout in northern waters, far from the Test. The great lesson which April trout fishing in these streams teaches you is never to despair. Fortune may suddenly change, and you never know what your bag will be till you have reeled up: and indeed I have actually done this and started for home, tired and dispirited, when I have been tempted back to the water, with the result that the basket which was light at five o'clock has been so full and heavy at six that my shoulder has ached agreeably under the weight. You get this on chalk streams, too, but not so often. You may get a fall of spinner as late as six o'clock or even seven. But on most days you are dependent on the hatch of duns, and this hardly ever starts later than three o'clock: in fact rarely as late, for from eleven to one is the usual time for it to begin. If I had to choose an hour in April, it would be between twelve and one. But though I have often wandered afar from Hampshire, I have many recollections of April in the south country as well as in the north. It is not one of the best of fishing months, but the Test valley shows then an individual beauty which is missed by those who do not start till May. Not many flowers are out, it is true, and the forest trees are still leafless: but there is a wash of green on the willows, the banks are tufted with primroses, and the kingcup makes broad patches of liquid gold over the meadows. This flower is a great favourite of mine, with its bowls of clear yellow and its dark glossy leaves. It has a bold, vigorous growth, typical of spring. It is at its best when it first flowers, for later on it gets ragged and straggly. Every day, also, the summer birds are arriving and one by one you can greet them all again. But the chief joys of April are anticipation and the sense that you are getting something for nothing. All the best of the year is in front of you, and you have not used it up yet. However bad your luck, nothing is wasted. The real season has not begun. And so, if you do get a good day, it is something additional and unexpected, something that was not in the programme, a pure gain, unlooked for and welcome: and if you get a bad one, there is no loss. It is this, and the delicious beginning of flower and leaf, which make April so enjoyable.

The Angler's Year may be divided into three stages. The first runs from the opening down to about the middle of May. It is marked by rises which begin and end suddenly: those of April are often quite short, but they lengthen gradually as May is reached. In the earlier part you depend chiefly on the daily hatch of duns, first of olives, later of iron blues as well, and later still of pale watery duns also. But do not neglect either spinners or nymphs. Always keep looking at the water to see if spinners are coming down. Try bulging fish with a rough olive, or your favourite nymph, or, what is best of all, an orange partridge. Look out for smuts, also, for they appear even on cold days. Above all, waste no time. You do not, either in April or in early May, find those casual risers which move at something all through the long June days. As the afternoons grow lighter, trout begin to eat spinners more and more, and there are signs of the evening rise start- ing, whereupon the first stage of the Angler's Year ends. Then on the lower Test comes the mayfly interlude: after that the second stage, with the typical long drawn out hatches of duns, beginning and ending in more indeterminate fashion than those of the first stage, the falls of spinners, the evening rise, smuts, and sedge fishing. This lasts till some date in mid- August, and after that comes the third stage of the Angler's Year, running until the end of the season.

Now, it will be obvious that both the fisherman's day and the flies he uses will be governed by these considerations. In early April most is done during the hatch, and since that hatch is short the one essential thing is that the angler should be at the right place at the right time and with the right fly. There is no room for the leisured experiments of June. But, as April runs towards May, and more especially during May itself, after the iron blue has appeared, you will do as much with the spinner as with the dun. The female iron blue spinner is a mighty favourite with trout. In fact in some years fish do not get really on to spinners until they have had a good meal off the spent iron blue. And, of course, nymphs will be taken right through the period. That great Test fly, the caperer, only appears at about its end, but you must always be on the watch for it. It is a marvel- lous good fly.

I consider the best early spring fly to be a blue upright, ribbed with gold wire, and you can use as big a hook as No. 0 on a wild April day. The dark olive quill, the gold ribbed hare's ear, or greenwell's glory all kill well. The variant, also an imitation of the dark olive, does not to my fancy do well till later. And you must never think that, though it is early April and blowing or raining or both, trout are not particular about pattern, for often they are. More and more, as years go on, do I use hackle flies. I have killed numberless trout on the hackle dark olive quill, but of late the blue upright has superseded it.

As May draws nearer, duns get smaller and lighter in colour, and your hook can be No. 00, or, if that is refused, 000. Your blue upright can be dressed without gold wire. If this is refused, my first change would be to a dressing which has a brown or ginger hackle, such as a ginger quill. Had I to choose one fly for the whole year, it would be a ginger quill. A tup will often be successful, especially on a hot, still day. And, for those who like it, the alder appears, but it is not a fly I often use. On the other hand, I use the welshman's button (the caperer of the Test) increasingly. It appears at the beginning of May, and both the winged and hackle dressings are very useful.

Imitations of spinners are exceeding hard to find, for most of those sold in the shops are worthless, whilst Halford's dressings, fairly good for olives and pale wateries, utterly fail to reproduce the glowing flame of the sherry spinner or the burning red of the female iron blue. However, this is to anticipate. No spinner, early in the season or late, equals Lunn's particular. In fact, I believe it to be the best fly in the world. It imitates admirably the spinner of the olive. And as soon as the iron blue has appeared, use the houghton ruby. It is a magnificent imitation of the female spinner. Mr. Skues, too, should be consulted, and so should a new book by Mr. Dunne, *Sunshine and the Dry Fly*.

In April and early May, you find the best fish in quick, rather deep, water of the main river. Not many are on the shallows as yet, or in still deeps, or in eddies, or in carriers. But as the weather grows warmer, they move into the thinner water. The first hatches of dark olives often bring up large and wary trout, and you may hook something unexpectedly heavy.

Thoughts in Coltsfoot Time

By Ernest Schwiebert

It seems hard for me to believe that nearly fifty years have passed since my colleague, Ernie Schwiebert, emerged as the *wunderkind* of fly fishing writers, with the publication of *Matching the Hatch* in 1955, while still an undergraduate at Ohio State.

Almost 20 books and a lot of fly hatches later, Ernie is still on the stream every chance he gets, and he still courts the muses of fishing with the skill and vigor of a young man. As this is being written, he has published magazine pieces on Saint Petersburg, the New Mexico years of Georgia O'Keeffe, the great castle hotels of Ireland, and the historic shrines of Ise Shima in Japan. But he is still reworking and polishing manuscripts on Alaska and its remarkable ecology, his exploration of little-known Atlantic salmon rivers in old Russia, a history of the famed Umpqua and its steelhead, and is preparing a definitive new edition of *Matching the Hatch*.

It has been my good fortune to call him a friend for thirty-odd years, and to have published many of his stories for the first time, in *Sports Afield* and *Outdoor Life*. I have witnessed his fishing skills firsthand, from the Langa in Iceland to the Brodheads in eastern Pennsylvania, and I can assure you that the man does infinitely more than "talk the talk," as the younger generation likes to say. Ernie also "walks the walk" with the best of them.

As an architect and planner with a doctorate from Princeton, and as an angler and a writer, Ernie has illuminated each of his personal interests with an inquiring mind and a relentless pursuit of understanding. If you are relatively new to fly fishing, perhaps you are not yet familiar with his works, including the definitive *Nymphs* and the towering 1854-page magnum opus called *Trout*. But his collections of stories, like the anthology from which this little tale of Michigan is taken—*Death of a Riverkeeper*—have the overtones of serious fiction and are wonderful reading. Such collections also include *Remembrances of Rivers Past*, *The Compleat Schwiebert*, and *A River for Christmas and Other Stories*. He also produced a superb travel book called *The Traveling Angler*, which was published by Doubleday in 1991.

Arnold Gingrich once observed that Ernie shares a genius for evocative detail. Gingrich is right, and Ernie's stories and books will not only make you a better angler, but they also have about them a sense of place I find irresistible. Sometimes an overpowering sense of nostalgia is found in his best prose.

The story I have elected to include describes his first memories of fishing with his father, on a tiny lake in Michigan, in the middle of the Great Depression. Ernie finally lost his father this year at the age of 104. He had published his last work of history in 1995, on his 100th birthday, and was still fishing for trout at ninety-three. "Thoughts in Coltsfoot Time" takes us back to southern Michigan, in those boyhood days that were the genesis of everything to come, days when Ernie's father was the one pounding away at the big typewriter, and the young angler was busily watching, learning, filing away potsherds of memory, and beginning to dream.

—✦—

Although the pretty yellow coltsfoot is not a species entirely native to our shores, its bright palette signals the last of Winter, and its flowering serves as a welcome harbinger of the coming spring.
                                                              —THOREAU

It is still raining softly this morning, after several days of false spring that started the coltsfoot blooming in the sheltered places. Deer are browsing through the oaks and beeches behind the house, their coats still the somber color of winter leaves, although the snow is finally gone. Grouse are drumming in the overgrown orchard, and it is almost time for fishing.

Coltsfoot is a spare, dandelionlike flower, and as with many other wildflowers, history tells us that coltsfoot is an alien species. It traveled across the Atlantic with our colonial forefathers, since its tiny leaves were dried and burned like incense to treat asthma and colds. Coltsfoot is found on sheltered slopes and in ravines that capture the late winter sun, although only a few blossoms are visible in their carpet of winter leaves. Its flowers signal the weakening of winter, in spite of the bitter April weather, and in my library in these Appalachian foothills, my thoughts are curiously filled with boyhood summers in Michigan.

My first memories of fishing are there, in a simple cedar-shingle cottage among the hardwoods and pines, fifty yards above a lake that shimmered in the August sun.

Lilypads filled its shallows, turning over lazily and drifting in a hot wind that smelled of orchards and cornfields farther south. Red-winged blackbirds called restlessly in the marsh. The lily pads were like the rowboats moored at the rickety dock, shifting and swinging in the wind, until their rubbery stems stretched and pulled them back like anchor lines. The hot wind rose and stirred each morning, offering little relief from the doldrums.

The boats were old and poorly maintained, with peeling paint and rusting oarlocks and eyebolts. Their wrinkled seams desperately needed fresh caulking. Moss-colored water surrounded a half-drowned bailing can in the rowboat that went with the cottage. The other boat was almost filled with water. Its wainscoat bottom rested on the mud, in the planking shadows of the pier. Its middle seat sheltered a small colony of tadpoles lurking in the tangles of its weathered anchor cord.

The hot wind finally dropped and died. Locusts began their harshly strident cadenzas in the trees, and the little lake became a tepid mirror at midday, its still surface marred only by the restless foraging of big dragonflies.

My mother was sleeping in the bedroom upstairs, with the window blinds drawn. Our family had rented the cottage for the entire month, and my father planned to complete a textbook he was writing, but fishing held a place in his schedule. The staccato rhythms of his typewriter on the screened porch began after breakfast, and continued after lunch when the work was coming well, and I dozed fitfully in the summer grass, thinking about the ice cream the farmer's wife made across the lake.

One morning when we went for eggs and milk, I watched the farmer's wife working with her tubs and cracked ice and salt in the springhouse. While she stopped to wipe her face, she let me wrestle with the crank of the ice-cream maker.

It was a summer of sweet corn and ripe watermelon and cherries, mixed with fishing for bluegills and yellow perch and bass. My memories are filled with peace and plenty. But it was also a summer of poverty and poor crops and fear, when wheat farmers were driven from family homesteads in the high plains country, and the terrible dust storms soon followed.

During those tragic years, my father and other college teachers were still employed, although their paychecks were thin. There were times when my father was the only man with work in our neighborhood. Small businesses and major corporations and banks were failing too, and factories and mills stood empty in heartbreak and silence. Many families in southern Michigan had lost their orchards and house mortgages and farms, but that boyhood summer beside a small lily-pad lake was strangely filled with riches.

Perhaps the simple rhythms of life sustained us through those Great Depression years, and bass fishing became part of our family rituals that summer.

My father usually awakened just before daylight, in the clamor of his big alarm clock. I could hear him wind it each night, through the thin walls of the cottage. My mother still lay sleeping under the quilts, and I could hear the bedsprings squeak as he reached for the alarm, and dressed in the darkness before descending the narrow backstairs to the kitchen. Cooking smells of scrambled eggs and tiny crumb-batter perch and sausages drifted up through the cottage, and in spite of his efforts to let us sleep, there was always the grating scrape of the skillet on the wood-burning stove, mixed with a muffled clatter of cups and tableware and plates. The rich aroma of coffee lingered long after he was gone.

Late August nights in Michigan are often cool.

Sometimes the tiny lake was shrouded in fog, and I heard him collect the wooden oars and tackle from the porch, before he disappeared into the mist. There was something of alchemy in such liturgies. It was delicious to lie there, partially awake under the patchwork quilting, listening to the familiar sounds of his morning rituals. Planking creaked as he reached the dock, the lures in his tackle box rattled as he placed it in the boat, and its padlock chain rattled as he stripped it through the eyebolt on the bowpiece. Oarlock rhythms marked his slow passage into open water.

His fishing was a mystery that I was still too small to share fully, but he sometimes took me out on short odysseys to explore its secrets, and on such mornings I waited restlessly through breakfast, wracked with delicious shivers of anticipation.

We caught nothing much, as I remember now, but I still savor the flashing handles of his bait casting reel, surrendering line as a lure arched out toward sheltering pockets in the lilies and pickerel weed and clodea. Once there was a wild splash that engulfed his red-and-white plug, but the bass was not hooked, and when the summer ended, it had been our only strike together. It was usually getting hot when we rowed back across the lake, and I sat happily in the boat, trailing my fingers in the cool water.

His textbook manuscript occupied the late mornings, as well as the hours after lunch, and the metallic rattle of his typewriter echoed across the lake. The work progressed well that summer, except for a brief disaster on the screen porch, when a sudden squall scattered his onionskin pages and carbons across the wet floorboards. Late in the afternoons, his interest in history began to wane, and as such academic preoccupations began to ebb, we often heard him start to sort through his fishing tackle.

It was time to clean and lubricate the prized Pfleuger reel, and its components lay collected in a saucer on the oilcloth table. Weedless spoons and tiny spinner blades and wobble plates were carefully polished. Hooks on his red-and-white striped spoons were sharpened. Pork frogs and fresh pork-rind strips were cut with his fishing knife on a cheeseboard, much to my mother's dismay, and stored in a pickle jar of briny water to keep them moist.

Supper was always early because of his fishing.

When the shadows of the red maples and oaks and elms began to lengthen across the boat-pier shallows, it was time to return to the lake. My father gathered his equipment and loaded the boat, stroked out through the lily-pad channel, and began to cast toward the weedy shoreline. He always worked clockwise around its periphery, finishing his twilight rituals just after dark. His fishing was a mixture of patient rites, and he seldom returned before nightfall.

I was never permitted to participate in these twilight expeditions, because my mother feared that I might fall overboard in the dark, with less likelihood of rescue. Sometimes it was completely dark when we finally heard his oar strokes, and I usually ran to meet him at the dock, waiting eagerly in the gloom while he fussed with the padlock and chain. Nocturnal returns usually signaled fish. It was always exciting when he reached down to lift a dripping stringer from the black water. There were usually two or three bass, and once we returned in triumph along the path to the cottage, while I proudly held the flashlight on a six-pound largemouth.

It remains a special summer in my mind, rich with memories of learning to dog paddle and fish for pumpkinseeds and perch, and sleeping on the porch, with crickets and katydids and whippoorwills working their magic in the darkness. Their nocturnal chorus seemed as exotic as jungle twilights in the headwaters of the Limpopo or Orinoco. It was a bucolic summer when my parents were both still young, and very much in love, and all the world seemed green. Mixed with such potsherds of memory is a brief encounter that took place during a weekly grocery trip into Baldwin.

Our route into town crossed a pretty trout stream, and my mother stopped the Oldsmobile just beyond the bridge—after a solitary fisherman had caught my eye.

The little river flowed swiftly, tumbling past the timber pilings of the bridge, and there were mayflies dancing in the morning sun. The riffling currents seemed alive over a pea-gravel bottom, where fallen cedar sweepers and deadfalls intercepted their flow, and the river danced and glittered over its bright cobble. The counterpoint of its music filled the moment, its lyric passages as sharply focused as memories of yesterday, after more than sixty years.

The trout stream was utterly unlike the lukewarm shallows of the lake, tumbling crystalline and cold from the springheads in its cedar swamp headwaters. Watercress thrived in the seepage places below the trusswork bridge, where the passage of the river was exposed briefly to the sun. The rest was hidden in its serpentine corridor of trees. Such ephemeral moments of illumination were quickly changing, in a collage of leafy sunlight and shadow. Such patterns seemed to brim with unspoken mysteries and life, collecting its kaleidoscope of foliage and sunlight in swiftly changing prisms, until their music seemed to sing of half-understood secrets.

The most pervasive memory of that summer remains the solitary trout fisherman working patiently upstream, with the swift shallows tumbling between his legs, while his silk fly line worked its amber magic in the brightness of an August morning.

It was the genesis of a lifelong odyssey in search of trout and salmon, a pilgrimage that began in Michigan, and has since carried me to the farflung corners of the world. There are many happy echoes of those travels, memories embracing rivers and river people, and the richly colored fish themselves. And with a cold rain misting through the skeletal black-trunked trees behind the house, such thoughts of fishing, and the butter-colored coltsfoot in the sheltered places, help to pass this wintry season of discontent.

The First Thousand-Pounder

By Zane Grey

To THE AVERAGE READER, THE NAME ZANE GREY CONJURES UP IMMEDI-
ate visions of shelves of western novels. Excellent and popular western
novels with romantic names like *Riders of the Purple Sage, Last of the
Plainsmen,* and *Heritage of the Desert,* to name only three of scores. But
among the hundreds of thousands of words Grey wrote his lifetime
(1872–1939), entire volumes were devoted to his deep passion for fishing.
Books like *Tales of Virgin Seas, Tales of Southern Rivers, Tales of Fresh Water
Fishing, Tales of Swordfish and Tuna.* Nine fishing books in all.

Zane Grey literally cut his angling teeth on bass and other fish in the
Delaware River and other nearby Pennsylvania and New Jersey streams
he fished as a youngster. He never lost his love for freshwater fishing
for bass, trout, and steelhead, but his eyes turned seaward eventually, and
the pursuit of big game fish in the briny became a veritable crusade. His
expeditions to the then-obscure corners of the globe in pursuit of marlin,
swordfish, sailfish, and sharks were backed by the considerable royalties
he earned from his western stories. Grey became an intrepid big game
fishing pioneer, searching for the big ones outside the reefs, in those distant years when there were no charter boats, guides, lodges, or even much
local knowledge about what was out there. The writer who wrote about
cowboys and pioneer trailblazers was a trailblazer himself when it came
to big game fishing. His books carry us along with him on those journeys
to meet the gladiators of the deep, to places like Tahiti and New Zealand,
fished by Grey long before most people even knew where they were.

George Reiger, today the Conservation Editor of *Field & Stream*
magazine and a Lyons Press author, prepared a splendid book on Zane

Grey called *Zane Grey: Outdoorsman* that was published by Prentice-Hall in 1972. Reiger presents many outstanding selections from Grey's fishing and outdoor adventure books, with introductions that form a wonderful biographical look at the man himself.

The very powerful story, "The First Thousand-Pounder," can stand on its own for sheer reading pleasure with anything ever written about big game fishing.

—⌣—

Time is probably more generous to an angler than to any other individual. The wind, the sun, the open air, the colors and smells, the loneliness of the sea or the solitude of the stream, work some kind of magic.

Morning disclosed dark, massed, broken clouds, red-edged and purple-centered, with curtains of rain falling over the mountains.

I took down a couple of new feather jigs—silver-headed with blue eyes—just for good luck. They worked. We caught five fine bonito in the lagoon, right off the point where my cottage stands. Jimmy[1] held up five fingers: "Five bonito. Good!" he declared, which voiced all our sentiments.

Cappy[2] had gone up the lagoon toward the second pass, and we tried to catch him, to give him a fresh bait. As usual, however, Cappy's natives were running the wheels off his launch, and we could not catch him. The second pass looked sort of white and rough to me. Cappy went out, however, through a smooth channel. Presently we saw a swell gather and rise to close the channel and mount to a great, curling white-crested wave which broke all the way across. Charley,[3] who had the wheel, grinned at me: "No good!" We turned inshore and made for the third pass, some miles on, and got through that wide one without risk. Afterward Cappy told me Areireia[4] knew exactly when to run through the second pass.

We headed out. A few black noddies skimmed the dark sea, and a few scattered bonito broke the surface. As usual—when we had them—we put out a big bonito on my big tackle and an ordinary one on the other. As my medium tackle holds one thousand yards of 39-thread line[5] it will seem interesting to anglers to speak of it as medium. The big outfit held fifteen hundred yards of line—one thousand of 39-thread and five hundred yards of 42[6] for backing; and this story will prove I needed it.

Off the east end there was a brightness of white and blue where the clouds broke, and in the west there were trade-wind clouds of gold and pearl, but for the most part a gray canopy overspread mountain and sea. All along the saw-toothed front of this range inshore the peaks were obscured and the canyons filled with down-dropping veils of rain.

What a relief from late days of sun and wind and wave! This was the kind of sea I loved to fish. The boat ran easily over a dark, low, lumpy swell. The air was cool, and as I did not have on any shirt, the fine mist felt pleasant to my skin. John[7] was at the wheel. Bob[8] sat up on top with Jimmy and Charley, learning to talk Tahitian. The teasers and heavy baits made a splashing, swishy sound that could be heard above the boil and gurgle of water from the propellers. We followed some low-skimming boobies for a while, and then headed for Captain M.'s boat, several miles farther out. A rain squall was obscuring the white tumbling reef and slowly moving toward us. Peter sat at my right, holding the line which had the larger bonito. He had both feet up on the gunwale. I noticed that the line on this reel was white and dry. I sat in the left chair, precisely as Peter, except that I had on two pairs of gloves with thumb-stalls in them. I have cut, burned, and skinned my hands too often on a hard strike to go without gloves. They are a nuisance to wear all day, when the rest of you, almost, is getting pleasantly caressed by sun and wind, but they are absolutely necessary to an angler who knows what he is doing.

Peter and I were discussing plans for our New Zealand trip next winter—boats, camp equipment, and what not. And although our gaze seldom strayed from the baits, the idea of raising a fish was the farthest from our minds.

Suddenly I heard a sounding, vicious thump of water. Peter's feet went up in the air.

"*Ge-zus!*" he bawled.

His reel screeched. Quick as thought I leaned over to press my gloved hand on the whizzing spool of line. Just in time to save the reel from overrunning!

Out where Peter's bait had been showed a whirling, closing hole in the boiling white-green water. I saw a wide purple mass shooting away so close under the surface as to make the water look shallow. Peter fell out of the chair at the same instant I leaped up to straddle his rod. I had the situation in hand. My mind worked swiftly. It was an incredible wonderful strike. The other boys piled back to the cockpit to help Peter get my other bait and the teasers in.

Before this was even started, the fish ran out two hundred yards of line, then turning to the right he tore off another hundred. All in a very few seconds! Then a white splash, high as a tree, shot up, out of which leaped the most magnificent of all the leaping fish I had ever seen.

"GIANT MARLIN!" screamed Peter. What had happened to me I did not know, but I was cold, keen, hard, tingling, motivated to think and do the right thing. This glorious fish made a leap of thirty feet at least, low and swift, which gave me time to gauge his enormous size and his species. Here at last on the end of my line was the great Tahitian swordfish! He looked monstrous. He was pale, shiny gray in color, with broad stripes of purple. When he hit the water he sent up a splash like the flying surf on the reef.

By the time he was down I had the drag on and was winding the reel. Out he blazed again, faster, higher, longer, whirling the bonito around his head.

"Hook didn't catch!" yelled Peter, wildly. "It's on this side. He'll throw it."

"No, Peter! He's fast," I replied. Still I kept working like a windmill in a cyclone to get up the slack. The monster had circled in these two leaps. Again he burst out, a plunging leap which took him under a wall of rippling white spray. Next instant such a terrific jerk as I had never sustained nearly unseated me. He was away on his run.

"Take the wheel, Peter," I ordered, and released the drag. "Water! Somebody pour water on this reel! ... *Quick!*"

The white line melted, smoked, burned off the reel. I smelled the scorching. It burned through my gloves. John was swift to plunge a bucket overboard and douse reel, rod, and me with water. That, too, saved us.

"After him, Pete!" I called, piercingly. The engines roared and the launch danced around to leap in the direction of the tight line.

"Full speed!" I added.

Then we had our race. It was thrilling in the extreme, and though brief it was far too long for me. Five hundred yards from us—over a third of a mile—he came up to pound and beat the water into a maelstrom.

"Slow up!" I sang out. We were bagging the line. Then I turned on the wheel-drag and began to pump and reel as never before in all my life. How precious that big spool—that big reel handle! They fairly ate up the line. We got back two hundred yards of the five hundred out before he was off again. This time, quick as I was, it took all my strength to release the drag, for when a weight is pulling hard it releases with extreme difficulty. No more risk like that!

He beat us in another race, shorter, at the end of which, when he showed like a plunging elephant, he had out four hundred and fifty yards of line.

"Too much—Peter!" I panted. "We must—get him closer—go to it!"

So we ran down upon him. I worked as before, desperately, holding on my nerve, and when I got three hundred yards back again on the reel, I was completely winded, and the hot sweat poured off my naked arms and breast.

"He's sounding . . . Get my shirt . . . Harness!"

Warily I let go with one hand and then with the other, as John and Jimmy helped me on with my shirt and then with the leather harness. With that hooked on to my reel and the great strain transferred to my shoulders, I felt that I might not be torn asunder.

"All set. Let's go," I said, grimly. But he had gone down, which gave me a chance to get back my breath. Not long, however, did he remain down. I felt and saw the line rising.

"Keep him on the starboard quarter, Peter. Run up on him now . . . Bob, your chance for pictures!"

I was quick to grasp that the swordfish kept coming to our left, and repeatedly on that run I had Peter swerve in the same direction, in order to keep the line out on the quarter. Once we were almost in danger. But I saw it. I got back all but one hundred yards of line. Close enough! He kept edging in ahead of us, and once we had to turn halfway to keep the stern toward him. But he quickly shot ahead again. He was fast, angry, heavy. How his tail pounded the leader! The short powerful strokes vibrated all over me.

"Port—port, Peter!" I yelled, and even then, so quick was the swordfish, I missed seeing two leaps directly in front of the boat as he curved ahead of us. But the uproar from Bob and the others was enough for me. As the launch sheered around, however, I saw the third of that series of leaps—and if anything could have loosed my chained emotion of the instant, that unbelievably swift and savage plunge would have done so. But no more dreaming! I was there to think and act.

By the same tactics the swordfish sped off a hundred yards of line and by the same we recovered them and drew close to see him leap again, only two hundred feet off our starboard, a little ahead, and of all the magnificent fish I have ever seen, he excelled. His power to leap was beyond credence. Captain M.'s big fish, that broke off two years before, did not move like this one. True, he was larger. Nevertheless, this swordfish was so huge that when he came out in dazzling swift flight, my crew went simply mad. This was the first time my natives had been flabbergasted. They were as excited, as carried away, as Bob and John. Peter, however, stuck at the wheel as if he were after a wounded whale which might any instant turn upon him. I did not need to warn Peter not to let that fish hit us. If he had he would have made splinters out of our launch. Many an anxious glance did I cast toward Cappy's boat, two or three miles distant. Why did he not come? The peril was too great for us to be alone at the mercy of that beautiful brute if he charged us either by accident or by design. But Captain could not locate us, owing to the misty atmosphere, and missed seeing this grand fish in action.

How sensitive I was to the strain on the line! A slight slackening directed all my facilities to ascertain the cause. The light on the moment was bad, and I had to peer closely to see the line. He had not slowed up, but he was curving back and to the left again.

"*Port, Peter—PORT!*" I commanded.

We sheered, but not enough. With the wheel hard over, one engine full speed ahead, the other in reverse, we wheeled like a top. But not swift enough for that Tahitian swordfish.

The line went under the bow.

"Reverse!" I called, sharply.

We pounded on the waves, slowly caught hold, slowed, started back. Then I ordered the clutches thrown out. It was a terrible moment and took all my will not to yield to blank panic.

When my line ceased to pay out I felt that it had been caught on the keel. I surrendered for an instant to agony. But no! That line was new, strong. The swordfish was slowing. I could yet avert catastrophe.

"Quick, Pete! Feels as if the line is caught," I cried, unhooking my harness from the reel.

Peter complied with my order. "Yes, by cripes! It's caught. Overboard, Jimmy! Jump in! Loose the line!"

The big Tahitian in a flash was out of his shirt and bending to dive.

"No!—Hold on, Jimmy!" I yelled. Only a moment before I had seen sharks milling about. "Grab him, John!"

They held Jimmy back, and in a second I plunged my rod over the side into the water, so suddenly that the weight of it and reel nearly carried me overboard.

"Hold me—or it's all—day!" I panted, and I thought that if my swordfish had fouled on keel or propellers I did not care if I did fall in.

"Let go my line, Peter," I said, making ready to extend the rod to the limit of my arms.

"I can feel him moving, sir," shouted Peter, excitedly. "By jingo! He's coming! . . . It's free! It wasn't caught!"

I felt such intense relief I could not recover my balance. They had to haul me back into the boat. I shook all over as one with the palsy, so violently that Peter had to help me get the rod in the rodsocket of the chair. An instant later came the strong electrifying pull on the line, the scream of the reel. Never such sweet music! He was away from the boat—on a tight line!

"Close shave, sir," said Peter, cheerily. "It was like when a whale turns. . . . We're all clear, and after him again."

The gray pall of rain bore down on us. I was hot and wet with sweat, and asked for a raincoat to keep me from being chilled. Enveloped in this, I went on with my absorbing toil. Blisters began to smart on my hands, especially one on the inside of the third finger of my right hand, certainly a queer place to raise one. But it bothered me, hampered me. Bob put on his rubber coat and, protecting his camera more than himself, sat out on the bow, waiting.

My swordfish, with short, swift runs took us five miles farther out, and then welcome to see, brought us back, all this while without leaping, though he broke water on the surface a number of times. He never sounded after that first dive. The bane of an angler is a sounding fish, and here in Tahitian waters, where there is no bottom, it spells catastrophe. The marlin slowed up and took to milling, a sure sign of a rattled fish. Then he rose again, and it happened to be when the rain had ceased. He made one high, frantic jump about two hundred yards ahead of us, and then threshed on the surface, sending the bloody spray high. All on board were quick to see that sign of weakening, of tragedy—blood.

Peter turned to say, coolly, "He's our meat, sir."

I did not allow any such idea to catch my consciousness. Peter's words, like those of Bob and John, and the happy jargon of the Tahitians, had no effect upon me whatever.

It rained half an hour longer, during which we repeated several phases of the fight, except slower on the part of the marlin. In all he leaped fifteen times clear of the water. I did not attempt to keep track of his threshings.

After the rain passed, I had them remove the rubber coat, which hampered me, and settled to a slower fight. About this time the natives again sighted sharks coming around the boat. I did not like this. Uncanny devils! They were the worst of these marvelous fishing waters. But Peter said: "They don't know what it's all about. They'll go away."

They did go away long enough to relieve me of dread, then they trooped back; lean, yellow-backed, white-finned wolves.

"We ought to have a rifle," I said. "Sharks won't stay to be shot at, whether hit or not."

It developed that my swordfish had leaped too often and run too swiftly to make an extremely long fight. I had expected a perceptible weakening and recognized it. So did Peter, who smiled gladly. Then I taxed myself to the utmost and spared nothing. In another hour, which seemed only a few minutes, I had him whipped and coming. I could lead him. The slow strokes of his tail took no more line. Then he quit wagging.

"Clear for action, Pete. Give John the wheel. . . . I see the end of the double line. . . . There!"

I heaved and wound. With the end of the double line over my reel I screwed the drag up tight. The finish was in sight. Suddenly I felt tugs and jerks at my fish.

"*Sharks!*" I yelled, hauling away for dear life.

Everybody leaned over the gunwale. I saw a wide shining mass, greenish silver, crossed by purple bars. It moved. It weaved. But I could drag it easily.

"*Mauu! Mauu!*" shrilled the natives.

"Heave!" shouted Peter, as he peered down.

In a few more hauls I brought the swivel of the leader out of the water.

"By God! They're on him!" roared Peter, hauling on the leader. "Get the lance, boat hook, gaffs—anything. Fight them off!"

Suddenly Peter let go the leader and jerking the big gaff from Jimmy, he lunged out. There was single enormous roar of water and a sheeted splash. I saw a blue tail so wide I thought I was crazy. It threw a six-foot yellow shark into the air!

"Rope him, Charley," yelled Peter. "Rest of you fight the tigers off."

I unhooked the harness and stood up to lean over the gunwale. The swordfish rolled on the surface, extending from forward of the cockpit to two yards or more beyond the end. His barred body was as large as that of an ox. And to it sharks were clinging, tearing the tail. Charley looped the great tail and that was a signal for the men to get into action.

One big shark had a hold just below the anal fin. How cruel, brutish, ferocious! Peter made a powerful stab at him. The big lance-head went clear through his neck. He gulped and sank. Peter stabbed another underneath, and still another. Jimmy was tearing at sharks with the long-handled gaff, and when he hooked one he was nearly hauled overboard. Charley threshed with his rope; John did valiant work with the boat hook, and Bob frightened me by his daring fury as he leaned far over to hack with a cleaver. Bob is lean and long and powerful. Also he was angry. Whack! He slashed a shark that let go and appeared to skip up into the air.

"On the nose, Bob. Split his nose! That's the weak spot on a shark," yelled Peter.

Next shot Bob cut deep into the round stub nose of this big black shark—the only one of that color I saw—and it had the effect of dynamite. More sharks appeared under Bob, and I was scared stiff.

"Take that! . . . And that!" sang out Bob, in a kind of fierce ecstasy. "You will try to eat our swordfish!—Dirty, stinking pups! . . . Aha! On your beak, huh! . . . Wow, Pete, that sure is the place!"

"Look out, Bob! For God's sake—look out!" I begged, frantically, after I saw a shark almost reach Bob's arm.

Peter swore at him. But there was no keeping Bob off those cannibals. Blood and water flew all over us. The smell of sharks in any case was not pleasant, and with them spouting blood, and my giant swordfish rolling in blood, the stench that arose was sickening. They appeared to come from all directions, especially from under the boat. Finally I had to get into the thick of it, and at that armed only with a gaff handle minus the gaff. I did hit one a stunning welt over the nose, making him let go. If we had all had lances like the one Peter was using so effectively we would have made short work of them. One jab from Peter either killed or disabled a shark. The crippled ones swam about belly up or lopsided, and stuck up their heads as if to get air. Of all the bloody messes I ever saw this was the worst.

"Makes me remember—the war!" panted Peter, grimly.

And it was Peter who whipped the flock of ravenous sharks off. Chuck! went the heavy lance, and that was the end of another. My heart apparently had ceased to function. To capture that glorious fish only to see it devoured before my eyes!

"Run ahead, Johnny, out of this bloody slaughter-hole, so we can see," called Peter.

John ran forward a few rods into clear water. A few sharks followed, one of them to his death. The others grew wary, and swam around and around.

"We got 'em licked!" said Peter. "Whoever saw the like of that? The bloody devils!"

Bob took the lance from Peter, and stuck the most venturesome of the remaining sharks. It appeared then that we had the situation in hand again. My swordfish was there still, his beautiful body bitten here and there, his tail almost severed, but not irreparably lacerated. All around the boat wounded sharks were lolling with fins out, sticking ugly heads up, to gulp and dive.

There came a letdown then and we exchanged the natural elation we felt. The next thing was to see what was to be done with the monster, now that we had him. I vowed we could do nothing but tow him to camp. But Peter made the attempt to lift him on the boat. All six of us, hauling on the ropes, could not get his back half out of the water. So we tied him fast and started campward.

Halfway in we spotted Cappy's boat. He headed for us, no doubt attracted by all the flags the boys had strung up. There was one, a red and blue flag that I had never flown. Jimmy tied this on his bamboo pole and tied that high on the mast. Cappy bore quickly down on us and ran alongside, he and all of his crew vastly excited.

"What is it? Lamming big broadbill?" he yelled.

My fish did resemble a broadbill in his long black beak, his wide-spread flukes, his purple color, shading so dark now that the broad bars showed indistinctly. Besides, he lay belly up.

"No, Cappy. He's a giant Tahitian striped marlin, one of the kind we've tried so hard to catch," I replied, happily.

"By gad! What a monster! . . . I'm glad, old man. My word, I'm glad! I didn't tell you, but I was discouraged. Now we're sitting on top of the world again."

"We've got him, Captain," said Peter, "and he's some fish. But the damn sharks nearly beat us."

"So I see. They are bad. I saw a number. . . . Have you got any fresh bonito?"

We threw our bait into his boat and headed for camp again. Cappy waved, a fine happy smile on his tanned face, and called: "He's a wolloper. I'm sure glad."

We ran for the nearest pass, necessarily fairly slow, with all that weight on our stern. The boat listed half a foot and tried to run in a circle. It was about one o'clock and the sky began to clear. Bob raved about what pictures he would take.

We were all wringing wet, and some of us as bloody as wet. I removed my soaked clothes and gave myself a brisk rub. I could not stand erect, and my hands hurt—pangs I endured gratefully.

We arrived at the dock about three o'clock, to find all our camp folk and a hundred natives assembled to greet us. Up and down had sped the news of the flags waving.

I went ashore and waited impatiently to see the marlin hauled out on the sand. It took a dozen men, all wading, to drag him in. And when they at last got him under the tripod, I approached, knowing I was to have a shock and prepared for it.

But at that he surprised me in several ways. His color had grown darker and the bars showed only palely. Still they were there and helped to identify him as one of the striped species.[9] He was bigger than I had ever hoped for. And his body was long and round. This roundness appeared to be an extraordinary feature for a marlin spearfish. His bill was three feet long, not slender and rapier-like, as in the ordinary marlin, or short and bludgeon-like, as in the black marlin. It was about the same size all the way from tip to where it swelled into his snout, and slightly flattened on top—a superb and remarkable weapon. Singularly, he had a small head, only a foot or more from where his beak broadened to his eye, which, however, was as large as that of a broadbill swordfish. He had a straight under maxillary. The pectoral fins were large, wide, like wings, and dark in color. The fin-like appendages under and back of his lower jaw were only about six inches long and quite slender. In other spearfish these are long, and in sailfish sometimes exceed two feet and more. His body, for eight feet, was as symmetrical and round as that of a good big stallion. He carried this roundness back to his anal fin, and there further accuracy was impossible because the sharks had eaten most of the flesh from these fins to his tail. On one side, too, they had torn out enough meat to fill a bushel basket. His tail was the most splendid of all the fish tails I have ever observed. It was a perfect bent bow, slender, curved, dark purple in color, finely ribbed, and expressive of the tremendous speed and strength the fish had exhibited.

This tail had a spread of five feet, two inches. His length was fourteen feet, two inches. His girth was six feet, nine inches. And his weight, as he was, 1,040 pounds.

Every drop of blood had been drained from his body, and this with at least 200 pounds of flesh the sharks took would have fetched his true and natural weight to 1,250 pounds. But I thought it best to have the record stand at the actual weight, without allowance for what he had lost. Nevertheless, despite my satisfaction and elation, as I looked up at his appalling shape, I could not help but remember the giant marlin Captain had lost in 1928, which we estimated at twenty-two or twenty-three feet, or the twenty-foot one I had raised at Tautira, or the twenty-eight foot one the natives had seen repeatedly alongside their canoes. And I thought of the prodigious leaps and astounding fleetness of this one I had caught. "My heaven!" I breathed. "What would a bigger one do?"

Notes

1 A six-foot, four-inch Tahitian, who, according to Romer, was the most expert of any of ZG's crew at handling the heavy cane poles used in bonito fishing.
2 Captain Laurie Mitchell.
3 Another Tahitian crewman.
4 Mitchell's guide.
5 117-pound test.
6 126-pound test.
7 John Loef was a California auto mechanic who asked Zane Grey what it was like to go fishing. One day ZG took him along and eventually trained him into one of his best boatmen.
8 Bob Carney, a photographer and ZG's son-in-law.
9 Zane Grey called his catch the giant Tahitian striped marlin; marine scientists have more recently identified the fish as a huge Pacific blue marlin..

Bright Rivers

By Nick Lyons

I HAD THE GREAT PLEASURE OF PUBLISHING NICK LYONS'S STORIES IN
Sports Afield before I had ever clapped eyes on the man. Getting to know
Nick personally was a bonus I never expected back in the early seventies
when I purchased "The Legacy" and made it a cornerstone piece in one of
the issues launching my six-year editorship of the magazine.

A lot of water has flowed down the trout rivers since then, and a lot of
prose has flowed by Nick's old Royal standard typewriter, which he clings
to like a man holding a lifebuoy, flaunting the electronic whiz-bang writing aids of today. I can say quite honestly that every Nick Lyons article
and book has always pleased me immensely with its sheer readability. The
talent I saw in the work of Nick Lyons in the first manuscript of his I ever
read has been manifested time and time again in the enormous body of
work he has produced, which includes everything from criticism in the
New York Times to essays in *Fly Fisherman* magazine. Everything from
describing the sheer utter heartbreak of being a rejected writer to describing the temporary heartbreak of fishing a rejected dry fly.

The Nick Lyons story is excerpted from the first section of the book
Bright Rivers, published by Lippincott in 1977. Here, my friends, is what
fishing is all about—especially a long-awaited fishing trip to someplace
very special. The journey begins in downtown New York, "where the game
for the big green is played," as Nick describes the setting. But ahead lie
Bright Rivers, and all that they promise.

Downtown, where the game for the big green is played, I go to a meeting that lasts eight hours. After the first ten minutes, I feel the tightening in my chest. I begin to doodle; I scribble out a meaningless note and pass it to someone I know across the table, because I've seen executives in the movies do that. I look for the windows, but they're hidden behind heavy, brocaded draperies so that the air conditioning will take—anyway, we're in the back of the hotel so even if the windows were open, I'd only see the backs of other buildings. Everyone is talking with pomp and edge; I jot down Evelyn Waugh's observation, "that neurosis people mistake for energy." I drink two glasses of ice water. I speak like a good boy, when spoken to.

Suddenly I begin to sweat. I've been in this windowless room for fifteen years. I have been a juggler, flinging my several lives high and carelessly into the air, never catching them, barely feeling one as it touches my hand. Nine to five I am here; then a salt stick on the subway and five hours in the classroom; then I am the fastest ghostwriter in the East, becoming a lawyer one week, an expert on Greece the next, then an adopted girl searching for the blood link. When there is time, after midnight, I write high-toned scholarship—on Chrétien de Troyes and Thomas Nashe and William Ellery Channing and Saint Augustine—and shaggy-fish stories; or I prepare a lecture on "The Generosity of Whitman." A smorgasbord, my life. Five hours of sleep and back at 'em again, the ghost who is not what he seems, back at meetings like this one, dreaming.

I say my piece in front of all these important men as enthusiastically as I can. These are the rules of the game. Part of what I say—a few words—has to do with rivers. From my words I catch their briefest warbling sound, like the faint rush of wind among the leaves, or a rushing faucet, and when I sit down, there in the back of the hotel, with the windows covered by heavy drapes and the smoke from cigars (mine among them) thick around our heads, as strategies unfold and campaigns thicken, I see a glimpse of them, inside. Deep within me they uncoil.

Rivers.

Bright green live rivers.

The coil and swoop of them, their bright dancing riffles and their flat dimpled pools at dusk. Their changes and undulations, each different flowing inch of them. Their physics and morphology and entomology and soul. The willows and alders along their banks. A particular rock the size of an igloo. Layers of serrated slate from which rhododendron plumes like an Inca headdress, against which the current rushes, eddies. The quick turn of a yellow-bellied trout in the lip of the current. Five trout, in loose formation, in a pellucid backwater where I cannot get at them. A world. Many worlds.

> ... oft, in lonely rooms, and 'mid the din
> Of towns and cities ...

as Wordsworth said in "Tintern Abbey," about a nature he felt but never really saw,

> ... I have owed to them
> In hours of weariness, sensations sweet,
> Felt in the blood, and felt along the heart....

Yes, I owe rivers that. And more. They are something wild, untamed—like that Montana eagle riding a thermal on extended wings, high above the Absaroka mountain pasture flecked with purple lupine. And like the creatures in them: quick trout with laws we can learn, sometimes, somewhat.

I do not want the qualities of my soul unlocked only by this tense, cold, gray, noisy, gaudy, grabby place—full of energy and neurosis and art and antiart and getting and spending—in which that business part of my life, at this time in my life, must of necessity be lived. I have other needs as well. I have other parts of my soul.

Nothing in this world so enlivens my spirit and emotions as the rivers I know. They are necessities. In their clear, swift or slow, generous or coy waters, I regain my powers; I find again those parts of myself that have been lost in cities. Stillness. Patience. Green thoughts. Open eyes. Attachment. High drama. Earthiness. Wit. The Huck Finn I once was. Gentleness. "The life of things." They are my perne within the whirling gyre.

Just knowing they are there, and that their hatches will come again and again according to the great natural laws, is some consolation to carry with me on the subways and into the gray offices and out onto upper Broadway at night.

Rivers have been brought to me by my somewhat unintelligible love of fishing. From the little Catskill creek in which I gigged my first trout to the majestic rivers of the West—the Madison, the Yellowstone, the Big Hole, the Snake—fishing has been the hook. And in the pursuit of trout I have found much larger fish.

"Must you actually *fish* to enjoy rivers?" my friend the Scholar asks.

It is difficult to explain but, yes, the fish make every bit of difference. They anchor and focus my eye, rivet my ear.

And could this not be done by a trained patient lover of nature who did not carry a rod?

Perhaps it could. But fishing is *my* hinge, the "oiléd ward" that opens a few of the mysteries for me. It is so for all kinds of fishermen, I suspect, but especially so for fly-fishermen, who live closest to the seamless web of life in rivers. That shadow I am pursuing beneath the amber water is a hieroglyphic: I read its position, watch its relationship to a thousand other shadows, observe its steadiness and purpose. That shadow is a great glyph, connected to the darting swallow overhead; to that dancing cream caddis fly near the patch of alders; to the little cased caddis larva on the stream-bed; to the shell of the hatched stone fly on the rock; to the contours of the river, the velocity of the flow, the chemical composition and tempera-ture of the water; to certain vegetable life called plankton that I cannot see; to the mill nine miles upstream and the reservoir into which the river flows—and, oh, a thousand other factors, fleeting and solid and telling as that shadow. Fishing makes me a student of all this—and a hunter.

Which couldn't be appreciated unless you fish?

Which mean more to me because I do. Fishing makes rivers my cor-rective lens; I see differently. Not only does the bird taking the mayfly sig-nify a hatch, not only does the flash of color at the break of the riffle signify a fish feeding, but my powers uncoil inside me and I must determine which insect is hatching and what feeding pattern the trout has established. Then I must properly equip myself and properly approach the fish and properly present my imitation. I am engaged in a hunt that is more than a hunt, for the objects of the hunt are mostly to be found within myself, in the nature of my response and action. I am on a Parsifalian quest. I must be scientist, technician, athlete, perhaps even a queer sort of poet.

The Scholar smiles wanly and says, "It all sounds like rank hedonism. And some cultism. With some mumbo jumbo thrown in."

Yes, I am out to pleasure myself, though sometimes after I've been chewed by no-see-ums until I'm pocked like a leper you wouldn't think that. There is a physical testing: the long hours at early morning, in bright sun, or at dusk; casting until your arm is like lead and your legs, from wading against the stiff current, are numb. That is part of the quest: to cleanse through exertion.

And the cultism and mumbo jumbo?

Some of trout fishing has become that, perhaps always was that. It is a separate little world, cunningly contrived, with certain codes and rules and icons. It is not a religion, though some believers make it such, and it is less than an art. But it has qualities of each. It touches heart and head; it demands and builds flexibility and imagination; it is not easy. I come to rivers like an initiate to holy springs. If I cannot draw from them an enduring catechism or from their impulses even very much about "moral evil and of good," they still confer upon me the beneficence of the only deity I have been able to find. And when the little world becomes too cunningly contrived? Wit helps.

My friend the Scholar says he is not a puritan or a moralist but that it seems to him it would be more satisfying to make something that would last—a book, a poem, a cabinet, a wooden bowl—than merely to fish well. He quotes Cézanne, from a letter, after a day of fishing: "All this is easier than painting but it does not lead far."

Not hardly. Not very far at all. Except that this may be precisely where I want it to lead. Let the world lead far—as one should frame it to do; let art last long and lead far and to form. Let a few other human activities lead far, though most of them lead us up a tree or up the asshole of the world. Let fly-fishing be temporary and fleeting and inconsequential. I do not mind.

Enough. Enough.

Too much theory and this pleasant respite from the north Broadway renaissance and gray offices will become an extravagant end that leads too far. Fishing is nothing if not a pastime; it would be hell if I did it all the time.

Beyond the dreams and the theories, there are the days when a close friend will pick me up at dawn on my deserted city block and we will make the long drive together, talking, connected, uncoiling, until we reach our river for the day. It is a simple adventure we are undertaking; it is a break from the beetle-dull routine, a new start, an awakening of the senses, a pilgrimage.

Flooded with memories and expectations, we take out our rods, suit up in waders and vest, special fish hats and nets, arrange flies and leaders, and take to the woods. Each article of equipment, each bit of gear in our ritualistic uniform, is part of the act. The skunk cabbage is thrusting up, lush and green-purple out of the moist brown mulch of last year's leaves; we flush a white-tailed deer that bounds off boldly; we see the pale-green buds pressing out of the birch branches. "Spring has come again," says Rilke. "The earth is like a little child who knows poems by heart—many, so many." We wonder whether the Hendricksons will or will not hatch at midday. We have our hopes.

With rivers as with good friends, you always feel better for a few hours in their presence; you always want to review your dialogue, years later, with a particular pool or riffle or bend, and to live back through layers of experience. We have been to this river before and together. We have much to relive.

Then we are on the river. It is still there. So much is perishable, impermanent, dispensable today, so much is gobbled up by industry and housing and the wanton surge of people, we half thought it might be gone, like that river we used to fish in Dutchess County, now bludgeoned by tract homes and industrial plants and trailers, now littered and warm and dead. Trout are yardsticks; they are an early warning system like the canary in the mine—when they go, what will happen to the rest of the planet, to the quality of life?

Yes, this river is still there, still alive, still pregnant with possibility.

"There's a swirl," I say, pointing.

"I saw one upstream, too."

"A few flies are coming off, see?"

"Yes, we're going to make a day of it."

My pulse quickens, the long gray city winter vanishes. In a moment we separate and belong to the river and to its mysteries, to its smooth glides and pinched bends, to the myriad sweet problems that call forth total concentration, that obviate philosophy.

Yes, these are Hendricksons, *Ephemerella subvaria,* and the hatch, on schedule, is just beginning. I am by profession neither an angler nor a scientist but there's always more pleasure in knowing than in not knowing. I take the lower pool and spot four good trout, poised high in the clear, flat water, waiting for the duns to hatch in the riffles and float down. By tilting my head close to the surface, I can see them, like little sailboats, drifting down. Two, three, there's another. Not many yet. A couple of birds are working, dipping and darting; against the light sky above the treeline I pick out one mayfly, watch it flutter, watch a swallow swoop, hesitate, and take it. What looks so pastoral is violent; it is, only on a smaller, more civilized scale, a horde of bluefish slashing a bunker school to bits, leaving blood and fin and head everywhere, to be picked up by the ravenous sea birds. The bites are cleaner here: the birds and trout take a whole creature in one mouthful.

Then back to the river. There are circles below me; the fish are feeding steadily. Shall I fish above or below them? They are so still, so firmly established in an irregular row across the channel in that clear flat water, that I elect the road less traveled and decide to fish down to them on a slack line—this way I won't have to cast over their backs.

It is delicate work, but I know that this year I have an excellent imitation of the natural fly, that my 5X leader is light enough, and that I've done just enough slack-line downstream casting to manage. Fishing is cumulative, though you don't learn all of it, ever.

I position myself carefully on the bank—it would be fatal to wade above such fish—strip about forty feet of line from my reel, and false cast twice.

My rod jerks backward. I've hung my fly in that low brush.

The interruption of the music, like the needle hitting a scratch on a recording of the Brandenburg Concerto, irritates madly but is not final.

When I return, the fish are still feeding, more steadily now, even rhythmically.

My cast lands well above the fish, and my fly floats without drag a few feet short of their feeding station before the line tightens; a little V forms behind the fly and it goes under.

I retrieve the fly slowly, unwilling to ruffle the surface until there are no more than ten feet of line still in the water, then cast again. The fly floats freely and I hold my breath. This time it will go far enough. It's two feet upstream of the first fish; I'm still holding my breath; the snake in the line unwinds and begins to straighten, slowly, then faster; I lean forward to give it another foot, another few inches; I watch the fish move slightly, turn toward the fly, inspect it, nose up to it, and then the fly drags and the fish turns away.

A deep breath.

Two more casts: one that quarters the river too amply and causes the fly to drag within two feet; another that floats properly but gets there a second after the trout has taken a natural. Then a good cast, a good float, and the fish pivots and takes, feels the hook, jumps twice, and burrows across and upstream. It's thirteen inches and not strong enough to cause much mischief; anyway, after the strike, after I have successfully gulled this creature from another element, linked my brain to its brain, I am less interested. After a few minutes I have the fish near my bank, lean down and twitch the hook free, and it is gone, vigorously—sleek and spotted and still quick.

When I've taken the slime off the fly and air-dried it, I notice that most of the fish have left their stations; only one fish is working in the pool now, across the main current, in a little backwater. It will require a different approach, a different strategy. I take fully five minutes to work my way downstream along the bank, into the water, and across to the other side, moving slowly so as not to disturb the life of the river. I am only its guest. The fish is still working when I get there.

I am directly below the trout now and can see only the periodic circles about forty feet above me. I don't want to put the fly line over it, and I know its actual feeding position in the water will be at least several feet above the mark of the rise form, which is floating downstream and is the final mark of his deliberate inspection ritual. I elect to cast into the edge of the main current above the fish and hope the fly will catch an eddying current and come down into the trout's position. The cast is good. Squinting, I watch the fly float down, then free of, the fast center current and my fly line hug the nearly dead water. There is an electric moment when the circle forms. My arm shoots up. The fish has taken the fly solidly and feels like a good one. It does not jump but bores into its little pool, then into the current; then it gets below me. I slip, recover, and begin to edge downstream, the fish stripping line from the reel now, boiling at the surface twice, then coming upstream quickly while I raise the rod high and haul in line to keep the fish from slipping the hook.

A little later I release the fish from the net, turning it out—a beautiful seventeen-inch brown.

I take two more fish, smaller ones, in the riffle below the pool, then head upstream again to where the first fish were feeding, approaching the spot from below. The hatch has peaked and is tapering now; the late-afternoon chill of late April has set in and I feel it for the first time. One fish is still feeding but I cannot, in six or seven casts, raise it, and finally it stops.

I breathe deeply and take out a pipe. There may be a spinner fall in another hour but I am exhausted. The river is placid, calm now. No fish are rising. The drama is over; the actors have retired to the wings. I have been caught for two hours in an intensely sensual music, and I want to stop, perhaps for the day—to smoke the pipe now, watch that squirrel in the oak, look for deer tracks and chipmunk holes. The city has become a bad dream, a B movie I once saw that violates my imagination by returning at odd moments. Most of the world would be bored by these past two hours. Most of the world? Most of the world is polluting the rivers, making the worse appear the better cause, peacocking, grating on each other's ears, gouging, putting their fingers on others' souls or their hands in the wrong pockets, scheming, honking, pretending, politicking, small-talking, criticizing.

"Is that *all* you find?" I hear the Scholar ask me.

"Nope. But there's a damned lot of it."

"You're a misanthrope, a hater of cities," he says. "You claim to love gentleness but . . ."

I don't especially want to answer his questions now so I look back at the river. We invented the non sequitur for just such moments.

Yes, we have made a day of it. Two, three hours sandwiched in. Little enough. But deep. And durable. And more than a day's worth. We've earned memories—full and textured—that live now in our very marrow-bones, that make us more alive. Our thoughts will be greener, our judgments perhaps sharper, our eyes a bit brighter. We live day to day with little change in our perceptions, but I never go to a river that I do not see newly and freshly, that I do not learn, that I do not find a story.

On the way home I still feel the tug of the river against my thighs, and in my mind's eye I can see that largest rising trout, the neat circle when it took a natural, the quick dramatic spurt—electric through my whole body—when it took my fly and I felt its force. And I wondered why I had not raised that last fish.

It was not the ultimate river, the ultimate afternoon; it was not so exquisite as a Keatsian moment frozen and anguished because it would not last. There will be others—never equal, always discretely, sharply different. A thousand such moments. Days when, against all expectation, the river is dead; days when it is generous beyond dreams.

A luxury? A mere vacation?

No, those rivers are more. They are my Pilgrim Creek and Walden Pond, however briefly. Those rivers and their bounty—bright and wild— touch me and through me touch every person whom I meet. They are a metaphor for life. In their movement, in their varied glides, runs, and pools, in their inevitable progress toward the sea, they contain many of the secrets we seek to understand about ourselves, our purposes. The late Roderick Haig-Brown said, "Were it not for the strong, quick life of rivers, for their sparkle in the sunshine, for the cold grayness of them under rain and the feel of them about my legs as I set my feet hard down on rocks or sand or gravel, I should fish less often." Amen. When such rivers die, as so many have, so too dies an irretrievable part of the soul of each of the thousands of anglers who in their waters find deep, enduring life.

September 18

By W. D. Wetherell

FOR MANY FLY ROD TROUTERS, AN ALTERNATIVE "RESOURCE" TO TROUT mania is readily at hand. And they are taking advantage of it, even though they continue to maintain an abiding affection for the fickle mistress that is trout fishing. One such angler is W. D. Wetherell, a card-carrying trout addict of the first rank who enthusiastically uncases his fly rod in the presence of another premier gamefish, the smallmouth bass.

America's and Canada's smallmouth bass fishing resource is a mother lode of pure angling gold currently being mined by a relative few prospectors who know a good thing when they find it. In rivers and lakes from New Brunswick to Tennessee, smallmouth bass in bountiful numbers are ready, willing, and able to put a bend back into your fly rod. You like numbers? Okay, we're talking 20-fish days, 30-fish days—what the hell, 50-fish days!—on some of the best rivers. Sure, you might get skunked, too! That's fishing. But we're talking mostly about getting plenty of action with wild, unstocked fish in beautiful reaches of water, without crowds of other anglers spoiling your fun.

This is all happening in rivers like the Connecticut, the Delaware, the Susquehanna, and the Potomac to name a mere few of the largest. But it is also happening on small streams and creeks, and countless hundreds of smallmouth-fertile lakes. In Maine alone, smallmouth fishing to dream about is waiting on rivers, lakes, and ponds where you may not encounter another angler. Sure they love fishing Down East, but the fish they worship are trout and salmon.

Ever hook a smallmouth in a river you were beating to a froth in hopes of a trout? For a few moments, you thought you had on a 17-inch brown trout, didn't you? I know. I've been there, done that, myself.

W. D. Wetherell is a familiar and stellar name in the Nick Lyons stable of writers. His most recent book, *One River More*, from which this selection was taken, ranks with the finest books of fishing prose of all time, in my opinion. I really mean it. Wetherell has always been good, but in *One River More* he has produced a book that is destined to become a classic. Trust me on this: Not to read *One River More* is to truly let a big one get away!

——～～——

Perfect conditions. The sailor asks that the wind blow from just the right quarter, at just the right speed; the kayaker that the river level be propitious, neither too high nor too low; the mountaineer that the weather fronts behave themselves; the photographer, that the light be soft; the hunter, that the biological rhythm that animates the game he seeks has them fully on the move ... and yet the fly fisher is fussier than any of these, because when he wishes for a perfect day he speaks of all these things combined, wind, water, weather, light, and instinct, so a perfect day for fishing is perhaps the rarest, most precious circumstance in any of the outdoor sports.

How rare? There's a day I look forward to all year long, yet only get perhaps one season out of five, so fussy are its requirements. It needs to be a day in the second or third week of September, when the Connecticut that runs past my home has been scoured by a long summer's flowage, so it shines brighter than it does at any other time of year, with a good three or four feet more of transparent depth. You need a frost in the early part of the week—the water must have noticeably, but not drastically cooled. It can't be past the equinox, since the storms we get then muddy things up. The wind must be from the south—from the north, you may as well stay at home. Most important of all, it must be a day when it's significantly warmer than it has been, so it feels like midsummer has been returned to you on a golden platter, with apologies for that trick of frost.

Get all these things without exception and it means the best small-mouth fishing of the year, a day when their biological clock is so exuberantly on it's as if you're fishing a solid river of bassiness, the water having by this perfect stirring of variables taken on striped bars and golden flesh and chevroned fins and glistening scales and extravagant muscle. It's something I anticipate all summer long, deliberately avoiding all engagements or appointments so I can be here at the right moment . . . and then spend September keeping track of all the various factors, trying not to get my hopes up but getting them up anyway, feeling good when that first early frost comes, feeling even better when it's followed by warmer weather, rooting for the wind to stay in the south, all but applying body English to the atmosphere, trying to bend and shape the elements to my purpose, if only for a single day.

When I woke up yesterday morning I thought I had the combination I was looking for. We'd had our frost earlier in the week, the northwest wind had swung around to the south, and there was a nostalgic stillness in the air that harkened back toward August. A heavy fog was fine with me, since one of the other ingredients in this kind of perfection is the slow warming of the shallows where the bass roam, and you get this when there's enough moisture in the air to act as a gentle scrim. By eleven, conditions would be just right, giving me time to work on my novel and thereby achieve that other cornerstone of perfection: going out to the river with a conscience that's clear.

I suppose there was some self-congratulation in my attitude—that I was clever enough not only to recognize perfection when it came, but to keep my calendar open for its arrival—and thus enough pride that it was goeth-ing for a falleth-ing. I had the canoe up on the car, had my rod stowed, my poppers packed, a lunch ready . . . I was heading back to the house for my hat, feeling the kind of happy urgency that transforms a middle-aged man into a ten-year-old kid . . . when there was a hard, sudden tap on my shoulder, the kind that fate often likes to deliver aurally, in this case as the frantic yipping of an aging retriever who had chosen that moment to impale herself on a rusty strand of barbed wire out on the far end of our stone wall.

At thirteen, Cider is as lively as a puppy and a bit nearsighted—a bad combination when it comes to stumbling into barbed wire. She'd cut herself badly on the back of the leg, and it was obvious it was going to take stitches to close the wound. This was the kind of thing I hadn't figured into my calculations, and made me realize that my criteria for perfection, though stringent enough, were nowhere near adequate, since they hadn't taken into consideration the chances of life becoming snared in the various entanglements that seem spontaneously improvised just to ruin your day.

Our vet lives twenty miles north. Cider did fine once I got her on the back seat; her expression was a combination of guilt and embarrassment, in the usual way of goldens, and every now and then to comfort her I had to twist my head around and say something reassuring. I was vexed, of course—more than vexed. Impatient, pissed, furious. The further I drove—the greater the distance I was putting between me and the day I had planned—the angrier I became, to the point where in order not to go flying off the road altogether I had to get a moral hold on myself, start figuring out what was going on.

Part of this was easy—the normal vexation anyone feels when their plans go awry. This was multiplied (let's say doubled) by the fact that it came at a particularly bad, or rather good time: the perfect day I'd been waiting for all season. This is something any fly fisher will understand, something so intrinsically part of the game it's hardly worth mentioning, but after this things became a bit murkier, more personal, and it was a while before I figured them out.

My reasoning went something like this . . .

Normally I'm the luckiest of fishermen, someone who can go fishing almost any time he wants. To suddenly have this taken away from me—to discover my charmed fishing life was mortal after all, and could be lost not to a major catastrophe, but a minor one—was a hard thing to swallow, though not without its value as a kind of therapeutic lesson, a reminder of just how remarkably lucky I am most of the time. Okay, I could understand this, reason was doing its job. But not being able to go fishing, even in this one slight instance, was making me overreact in a way that went far beyond this, and I finally realized it was because it made me remember a time when I couldn't go fishing at all—the long years I was stuck in the suburbs, someone who only dreamed of fishing, but for reasons too complicated and difficult to go into here, hardly ever went out. This only changed in my thirties when I broke away from that life, moved north to the country and was, quite literally, reborn.

Thinking in these terms, it's easy to see what was at stake: even a small threat to the kind of life I'd established inflamed the old scar tissue, burned as something I had to smother immediately with all the emotion I was capable of mustering—not a small vexation in an otherwise fine day, but a threat to my very existence.

And further. Fishing, right from the start, was an expression of the rebellious half of my nature, the anti-establishment part of me, the kid who went fishing when the rest of his generation stormed ROTC buildings or did drugs—the passion in me that is partly a finger jabbed toward the conforming philistine materialistic culture I've so thoroughly despised, actively when younger, latently today. Give my new life even one small check and the old emotion comes flooding back, the fury that used to possess me in my twenties when I realized the life I imagined was passing me by.

Poor Cider! There she was bearing stoically something that must have caused considerable pain, and there her master was gripping the steering wheel like he wanted to throttle anything and everything he could get his hands around, never mind the aching dog. But I got her to the vet without ramming into anyone. I held her as Dr. Wheeler examined her, helped where I could when he sewed her up, carried her back out and laid her gently on the back seat—and like a pet-ambulance driver, raced her back home in record time.

One o'clock—only two hours lost. I got Cider settled in the mud room, drove down River Road to the dirt launching area owned by the Nature Conservancy, loaded up the canoe with my fly rod and poppers, shoved myself off into the river. The sun had it shining in that penny brightness I had reckoned on; below the canoe, as I pried it out toward the wooded island that's my favorite spot, I could see small bass swimming over the sandy bottom, with the kind of heads-up alertness, eagerness, and hunger you see in June during spawning and then not again until a fall day like this one.

The river here is only slightly wider than where I fish for trout, and yet there's enough breadth now that it seems a much weightier proposition, something that doesn't rush and dance but sweeps and proceeds. With the breeze from the south, the surface had those little crisp folds that come at such short intervals they make the canoe seem like it's on a moving ramp, and in no time at all I was drifting past the weedbed at the island's upper edge, attached to a smallmouth that had taken the Olive Zonker I'd been trolling out the stern.

I caught six bass on the first seven casts—*that's* what I mean by perfection—and with every one I felt myself relax even more. Perfection? Though from long experience I recognize the conditions that prompt this, I'm still confused as to what exactly is going on, at least as far as the bass are concerned. Yes, the water has cooled off, and their metabolism must welcome this. Yes, the water is clearer, and those crayfish become an easier target for them in the shallows. But how do they know the wind is from the south and why does this please them? How do they sense the relatively low barometric pressure, since by rising or falling a few inches in the river they can make it anything they want? How do they sense winter is coming, by what mechanism or instinct? More specifically, how come they sense winter so strongly on the most summer-like days? It's reasonable to expect a feeding binge from a creature who is faced with seven months when it hardly eats at all, but why is the frenzy so closely tied to such fussy factors? Fishing magazines have always made a great deal over this feeding binge, so it's become an article of faith to most fishermen, but myself, I've rarely seen it, find fish in autumn to be at their moodiest, with this one specific exception: on the right day in September the smallmouth on the Connecticut River go absolutely wild.

As I came around the tip of the island my lee disappeared and the breeze pushed the canoe over toward the Vermont shore. This was fine with me—the bass line up there along boulders dumped down the bank when the railroad was built well over a hundred and fifty years ago. There are old telegraph wires, too, strung on sunken poles that dip right into the river, making it seem as if this whole vanished infrastructure, trains and telegraph both, have as their only function a soggy communication with sunken ghosts.

As I drifted, I cast—in autumn you can sometimes pick up a sunbathing bass right in the middle of the river—and cast standing up. This is against all the canoeing rules, of course, but I've been using this Old Town for so many years it's become an easy and comfortable position, and there's something daring and stately about it I enjoy, like riding a surfboard towed by dolphins.

Along the bank the wild honeysuckle had turned brown; a bittern, staying just ahead of me, blended perfectly with the color, and it took the crisp rattle of leaves for me to pick him up again twenty yards downstream. Where the bank steepened into a sandy cliff I pulled the canoe in and waded the last ten feet to shore. It's a good place to relax, since the bank slopes back like a chaise lounge; as I drank my tea, ate my sandwich, my neck was tickled by sand rolling down from the holes left by nesting swallows at the top of the bank.

I was in no hurry to go back out—if anything, the perfect day was turning out to be a little too warm, and so not quite perfect after all. A temperature of seventy-three makes the bass remember winter is coming and gets them feeding; a temperature of seventy-six makes them think it's August again and turns them perversely sluggish. I knew it was almost certainly the last day of bass fishing for the season. The forecast called for it to turn sharply colder, and already I could see coral-tinged thunderheads moving across the mountains to the north.

I caught more fish after lunch, though they didn't come quite so fast. On days like this one the smallmouth want a bullet-nosed popper, the slider kind with rubber legs, and they want it fished without any motion other than what the current does to those dangling legs. Casting these can be tricky. You need a mix of force and finesse to do it properly; force in ramming it sidearm under the overhanging white pine that line the shore; finesse (applied at just the last moment) in making sure the popper enters the thin window you're aiming for, the nine or ten inches between the top of the water and the bottom of the trees.

It's funny about trout and bass. As much as I love the former, I never experience anything even remotely close to a fellow feeling for them, and most of my interest revolves around finding them and getting them to strike. With smallmouth it's different. I have a very strong fellow feeling for them, and it comes primarily during the fight. Have I ever written about the glories of a smallmouth's fight? No fish, neither largemouth nor rainbow nor striper nor salmon, punches as hard as a full-bodied small-mouth. The explosive strike followed by those wild unpredictable first seconds when the fish sometimes jumps (maybe a tailwalk, maybe the classic cartwheel, maybe a wild vault back toward the bank) and sometimes dives, then the frantic second pull, followed immediately by the first seriously deep plunge, getting into your backing it dives so deep, coming back up again entirely on its own and jumping again at a distance, then plunging again *if* it's still on, plunging a third time, still reserving enough strength to jump one last time close to the canoe, and even at the very end, just when you reach down for him, retaining enough pugnacity it can flail at your hand and get away.

What is the fellow feeling in all this, the connection that makes me know exactly what the bass is experiencing? I wouldn't have known what to link it to, not until that little episode with Cider, that frantic overreaction on my part when it became likely I wouldn't be able to go fishing. Why look further? The bass fights with frantic and uncompromising purpose, and I share a portion of that frantic quality myself, at least when it comes to the passion with which I approach my time out on the water. Yes, I want a gentle, relaxed sport, one that involves myself, the river, the fish in a sometimes complicated, sometimes simple symbiosis, but how fiercely I want this, want this still. Bass and fisherman tug on opposite ends of the line, and yet on a ninety-nine and nine-tenths perfect September afternoon like this one, they end up striving toward the same kind of rebellious freedom, racing to see who gets there first.

Midstream

By Le Anne Schreiber

FOR ALMOST ALL ANGLERS, THERE COMES A TIME IN LIFE—EARLY OR late—when the moments you spend fishing your favorite water will be tempered by reflections of loss, a loved one ill or already departed. For Le Anne Schreiber that time came when she was living beside a wonderful little trout stream in the rural regions of New York's Hudson River Valley and experiencing the joys of new fishing skills and appreciation. At that time she learned that her mother had pancreatic cancer.

Schreiber began writing a journal of her mother's illness that eventually became a book published by Viking in 1990, *Midstream: The Story of A Mother's Death and a Daughter's Renewal.* This excerpt from that book is but a portion of the moving and engaging chronicle Le Anne Schreiber wrote about love and loss.

Le Anne Schreiber wrote on foreign affairs at *Time* magazine until 1976 when she covered the Olympics and switched to sports journalism. Later she became Editor of *WomenSports* and after that was Editor of the *New York Times* Sports Section, until moving to the *New York Times Book Review* as Deputy Editor.

Glenco Mills, N.Y. ◆ *Tuesday, April 16, 1985*
I am beginning to notice different things now. The softness of Midnight's fur, the pale green of his eyes and how the blackness opens from a vertical slit in his pupil to a full roundness in fright, overwhelming the inquiring green. The pinkness that edges a brook trout's fins, the signal that something alive is nestled among the stones at the bottom of the stream.

The grayish-green of their bodies blends so completely with the color of the stones that until I see the strip of slightly undulating white, I cannot discern the possibility of their sudden, startling flight.

I wonder now what creatures see. When I watch birds feeding through the red grid of my kitchen window, do they see me? They must, because they see Midnight at the pantry door and take off in skittish flight, cardinals first and chickadees last. But do they see my colors? form? movement?

I am struck for the first time by the miracle of perennials—dry, dead sticks putting forth buds or making way for new growth from the old roots. The dried remains of last year's flowers are still on their stalks while new plants spring up between their legs, seeking a share of light and air. In my borrowed garden, I clear away the old growth to make room for the new. But down the road, in Bruno's untended garden, the old stalks remain and new shoots find their way among them anyway. Maybe mine is an American impulse and Bruno, a French vintner's son, knows something I don't.

It has taken me, daughter of a farmer's daughter, forty years to discover these things, and belated as I am, I choose the slow way of learning, just observing what happens each day and guessing at what tomorrow will bring. I have no desire to go to books that might explain these things to me, how flowers grow, how trout make their way through the seasons, natural and legal.

Friday, April 19

I have been listening to fitful rolls of thunder for the past half hour. The sky is dark and the air still, but just when it seems about to storm, the sun bursts through the clouds and it's a sunny spring afternoon again. Just now, the sky turned gray-green and I hear the first faint drops, slow and tentative.

The thunder brought me home from the stream where, again, I fished without catching anything. It makes little difference to me whether I get a bite. I am still learning my rod and reel. Last Friday, I took the old reel apart to learn its secrets, then I put a new reel on the rod and filled it with line, discovering every tangle trial and error can produce. It's a task that requires four hands, and I had to make do with two and a pair of knees.

After several days of casting, I have become comfortable, even intimate with my rod, but I still discover something new about it every day. Yesterday, by accident, I cast farther than I ever had before, and then I realized it was the way I snapped my wrist that produced the effect. Before the cast, I had been whipping my arm slower or faster, in a longer or shorter arc, to control the distance, but now I see it is in the wrist, not the arm and shoulder, that distance is determined.

Discovering this, I realized I had known it all along; it was familiar but forgotten knowledge, something I had read or, more likely, been told by my father in childhood. Now I have learned it in a way I will not forget, on my own wrist.

Today, some instinct told me to pull the rod backward at the end of a cast, and suddenly I had solved the problem of slack that snarled my line when I started to reel it in. Discovering this, I again remembered that I had known it; the motion was one I'd seen my father make hundreds of times, but I never realized it had a purpose. I thought it was one of those poses that belong to men, like standing with hands on hips, head bowed, after exertion. I thought the rod-jerking motion intrinsic to men, not to fishing, just as I once thought the hands-on-hips posture belonged to men, not to deep breathing.

There was a time when certain actions, performed by me, made me feel both exhilarated and confused. Exhilarated because I knew I was trespassing where no girls were allowed, and it was dangerous, exciting. Confused, because it made me wonder if I was a true girl if such actions came unbeckoned to my body. Once, when I was standing, head bowed, hands on hips, after a long run in a touch football game, my college boyfriend said, "I hate to see you standing like that." I became self-conscious, and for the rest of the game tried to avoid that stance, but my body wouldn't cooperate, and then I realized it was because bodies, any bodies, want to do that when they need to catch a deep breath.

Thursday, April 25
Today I bought a "sportsman's tool" at Ames—a pocket-size wrench, pliers, wire cutter in one. I'm using it to cut two of the three hooks off all my

lures, so that when I catch an undersized fish, I can return it to the stream undamaged.

Tuesday, an hour before sunset, I went to the part of the stream that runs directly behind the house and waded my way upstream to a stretch of fast-flowing water that has several deep, eddying pools in it. I planned to start fishing above the fast water and work my way downstream, making a few casts into each of the pools.

At the first pool, I hooked a six-inch brook trout. When I tried to release the fish, I saw it had swallowed the lure, two hooks embedded up and down its throat. I tugged the line, and the trout flapped in my hand, rolling its eyes in panic. I put it back in the water, hoping against reason the fish might free itself by thrashing. A minute later, I hauled it back onto the rocks and tried to work the lure free with my hands, but it was clear the only way to remove the lure was by jerking the line so hard it would tear the fish apart.

I put it back in the water again, took it out again. Each time I returned the fish to the stream, it seemed more listless, and its flesh, a glistening greenish-black when first caught, was becoming an eerie, phosphorescent silver. I talked to the fish as if it were Midnight. "Oh, honey, I'm so sorry. It'll be all right. Just let me help." I cursed myself for going fishing without a knife to cut the line. At one point I decided to put the fish out of its misery, but the only way to kill it was by smashing it with a rock, and I couldn't bring myself to do that. Finally I yanked the line between my two hands and it broke, leaving the lure embedded in the trout's throat. I returned him to the stream alive, but I know he can't survive.

Wading back home as the sun set, feeling miserable, depressed and guilty, I vowed never to fish again. But gradually, as the water swirling around my knees turned from gold to lavender and then to dark purple, I began to persuade myself that I could still spend my days in the stream, I could still fish if I did it in some way that guaranteed I would be able to release what I caught. So this morning I tried to remove two of the three hooks from my lures with scissors and a hammer. I tried cutting the hooks off, bending them straight, nothing worked. Finally, I called my father in Minnesota to ask him how to fish without maiming the catch, and he told me about the "sportsman's tool." He suggested I try fly fishing with the rod he left behind on his visit last fall.

As soon as I mentioned I was having problems with three-hook lures, I could tell he understood. His voice became quiet and steady, full of inflectionless concern, as he described the tool and what it could do. He was talking to me the way I had talked to the fish. "It'll be all right, honey. Just do as I say and it'll be all right. . . ."

Sunday, May 5
Last night I dreamt that Mom and I were driving in an open-topped jeep on a country road at night. We were driving through a wooded area on a narrow road that went up and down hills, round curves and over bridges, a road like many of those I drive around here.

In the dream Mom was driving and I kept telling her to be careful, because she didn't seem to see that both shoulders of the road were lined with deer. She was driving fast and I was afraid we would hit one of them. I didn't think we were in danger; my concern was for the deer.

As we approached a small bridge, my attention was fixed on the shadowy forms and red eyes caught in the glare of our headlights, when all of sudden, a black bear lunged out of the woods. Before I could scream, he leapt through the car, grabbed Mom's head in his jaws and landed with her in the stream under the bridge.

Terrified and in shock, I stopped the jeep and ran back to the bridge. The bear had the back of Mom's head in his jaws and was holding her face down in the water. I felt her terror, her utter helplessness in the face of being drowned or mauled or both. I knew that even if the bear released her for a moment, she wouldn't be able to escape because she doesn't know how to swim.

Her submerged body was motionless in the bear's grip but I could tell she was pleading with me to save her. I tried to think of ways to get the bear away from her so she could breathe, but everything I could think of seemed more dangerous than doing nothing. If I threw stones at the bear, he might get angry and clamp his jaws tighter around her head rather than release her. If I jumped into the water to reach her, he would probably kill me as well as her.

I knew that each second I delayed brought her closer to drowning. I didn't know which was worse—doing something that would probably result in my dying with her or letting her drown thinking I hadn't even tried to help. The conflict between wanting to save myself and not wanting to abandon her was overwhelming, and I awoke with the most intense feeling of terror and pity I have ever felt in my life, waking or sleeping.

Going back to sleep was unthinkable. I got up and went down to the kitchen. A feeling of hopelessness, of sickening personal failure, stayed with me for hours. I have never before had a dream in which my mother's life was in danger. . . .

Edina, Minn.
Wednesday, September 4
Last night, after learning Mom's tumor was malignant, I began packing for an indefinite stay in Minnesota. "I want my daughter," Mom said, planting a new phrase deep in my heart. I promised her I would be there by noon today and booked a 10:00 a.m. flight out of Newark. I packed and worried into the middle of the night, then set the alarm for 6:00 a.m., allowing enough time for the two-hour drive to the airport. When I awoke at 8:00 a.m. and realized I would miss the plane, bolts of lightning traveled through my veins. I booked a later flight, called Mom, lied and drove the Taconic Parkway at the speed of my heartbeat, ready to defy any state trooper who dared to come between me and my guilt.

On the plane, I kept thinking of something that has worried me since my brother Mike's first call last Tuesday. I have never been able to stand the sight of Mom in pain. I respond to it bodily. If she burns her hand on the iron, I wince. If she coughs, my chest heaves. Once, when we were shopping together in downtown Evanston, Mom tripped on a crack in the sidewalk and smashed headfirst into the pavement. My whole body started tingling, and when I saw the fright in her eyes, I almost fainted. The right half of her face looked broken, caved in, and I lied when she asked me if there was a mirror in the shoe store where we waited for an ambulance. I remember the effort I made to keep looking at her, as if there was nothing wrong, as if her beauty was intact.

I have witnessed only a few, rare accidents, spaced over decades of her healthy life. I have never had to repress, or even think about, my body's impulsive identification with hers. How will I react now that the threats to her are so much more extreme? What help will I be, what comfort can I give, if I am simply the mirror of her suffering? I wonder if all daughters feel this. Do we all have to go through a second weaning?

On the drive from the airport Mike and Dad told me more about the treatment the medical center is recommending for Mom. The first step is surgery, not to remove the tumor but to expose it directly to the highest possible dose of electron-beam radiation. As soon as she recovers from surgery, she will receive daily radiation treatments, delivered externally, for five weeks. She will also need a nerve block to control pain, because even if the tumor is rendered inactive by the radiation, it will still be there as a fibrous mass exerting pressure on nerves close to her spinal column. When Mom asked if any other follow-up treatment would be necessary, the oncologist said, "No, just routine checkups every six months for the first two years." Dad says "first two years" were the sweetest words he ever heard. . . .

Rochester, Minn.
Thursday, September 19
We left the hospital this morning with a few days' supply of codeine and a round of cheery good-byes from the nurses. The farewells seemed inadequate, perhaps inevitably so. From the moment Mom was admitted to the hospital, these nurses became the most important people in the world. She depended on them initially for comfort, and ultimately for survival; in the first post-operative days, when her body literally could not function without them, we demanded that their concern for her be as profound as her dependence on them. We expected compassion as our due and we got it. Not until we were leaving did I realize how much we had asked of the nurses, and how much they had given. And yet, at parting, there was no time to acknowledge that extreme experience had been shared. There were, as always, new patients, new urgencies, new families demanding to be treated as the most important people in the world. And so we exchanged those inadequate, cheery good-byes. They pretended

that Mom is all better now, which she isn't, and we pretended that their's was simply a job well done, which it wasn't. My respect for good nurses is boundless.

Doctors are another matter. No doctor even came by to discuss what special care Mom might need at home, and no prescriptions had been authorized. We would have left without even an aspirin if I hadn't insisted upon something for the pain that still burns in Mom's back.

Before leaving the hospital, Mom took codeine to help her through the two-hour drive home. As she sat in a wheelchair on the pavement outside the hospital entrance, Dad lowered the front passenger seat of his Renault into a reclining position, and we placed pillows against the seat to support Mom's distressed lower back. We used an overnight case as a footstool, hoping raised legs would put less strain on her still-healing incision. The move from wheelchair to car caused a few loud groans, but once Mom was settled, with a pillow clutched against her abdomen and blankets up to her ears, she was comfortable enough to take notice of the rain clouds that stretched from Rochester to Minneapolis. . . .

Glenco Mills, N.Y.
Thursday, October 10
I just returned from the fish hole, where I sat for hours on my double-trunked log peering into clear water. I saw a large fish emerge head first from under the carpet of fallen leaves that covers the stream bed. He looked like he was giving birth to himself, wiggling his way out of the earth full grown. I also saw a molting crayfish scuttle across the bottom and take cover under a maple leaf.

Two small fish, about four inches long, seemed to be playing with each other. They are, I suppose, too young to mate but their movements reminded me of the lizards I watched mating on the patio in Italy this summer. One fish would swim up to the side of another, and when he was exactly parallel to the other fish, sideswipe him. The sideswipe would knock them apart, and both fish quickly circled back for another collision. It looked very like the soccer drill in which two players stand side by side, jump into the air and butt shoulders. The butting would be repeated four or five times in quick succession, until one of the fish gave up and darted away. A couple minutes later, they would repeat the cycle.

At other times the two fish seemed to sniff each other's tails, like dogs do, or stroke one another with a slow swish of delicate tail, like cats. A larger fish flipped on its side and seemed to scratch itself against the leaves on the bottom of the stream. It was almost as if the presence of leaves in their world made the fish behave like land creatures for a day. Every other time I spied on them from my perch on the fallen sycamore, they swam without touching each other.

Tuesday, October 15
Mom had her first radiation treatment today. She said it was "scary." She must lie absolutely still on a hard, narrow slab, which is then raised several feet in the air. She is not scared of falling. What frightens her is the sound of technicians literally running for cover as she is being lofted toward the source of radiation. She will take this ride five days a week for the next five weeks. . . .

Tuesday, April 1
Yesterday, I decided to try out my new hip boots in preparation for the opening of trout season today. The boots are heavy, and you strap them on with canvas knee braces inside the boot as well as by straps extending from the top of the boot to belt loops. This keeps them securely on my legs, but it also means I'll have two fifty-pound weights strapped to my body if they should fill with water.

With boots on, I lumbered through the yard and down the path to the stream behind the house. Last spring the path led to a rocky strip of beach from which you could enter the stream in ankle-deep water. But now the stream is so swollen with melted snow that the beach is an island separated from the bank by several feet of fast-flowing water. I stepped in, and although the water only reached mid-calf, I had a hard time keeping my balance. Even in the ankle-deep water on the other side of the island, it was hard to keep my footing. Whenever I raised a boot off the stream-bed, the rushing water carried it a foot downstream. It felt like moon walking, except that I knew gravity would reassert itself if I slipped.

Walking upstream was impossible, and the only way to make safe progress downstream was to slide my foot along the rocky bottom until it found the next firm footing. In knee-deep water, the force of the stream pounding against my legs was so great that I had to struggle to remain standing. One slight slip would have sent me on a long, bumpy, boot-bound ride downstream to safer, shallower waters or to fatally deep ones.

That prospect didn't appeal, so I slogged my way back to the bank wondering why trout-fishing deaths were not a seasonal epidemic. It had taken all my strength and attention to stay upright, and I wasn't fishing. How would it be with a fishing rod in hand, and my concentration focused on the hunt?

On the local television news tonight, they said dangerously high water had kept a lot of fishermen out of the streams. Personally, I needn't have worried. There were no fish to distract me from boot management today. I started at the fish hole, using one of Dad's homemade nymphs on my fly rod, but without the sycamore trunk spanning the stream and slowing the water, the fish hole is less of a pool. It's become a stretch of water too fast-flowing and turbulent for fish to laze about in. After several dozen casts produced only a fingerling, I moved downstream to the bridge, where I had no better luck. Since there is no insect life on the stream yet for my flies to imitate, I didn't really expect any smart fish to strike, but I hoped for an ignorant stocked trout or two....

Friday, April 18

Following Zack and Merc's advice, I tried fishing in the pools at the base of the dam behind the Kimberly-Clark Mill today. It didn't seem a very romantic spot to fish, but I figured if it's good enough for trout, it's good enough for me. I walked across the employee parking lot with fly rod in hand and clambered down the steep bank on a path worn through poison ivy to an outcropping of rock about fifteen feet wide and thirty feet long. The roar of the Roe/Jan plunging over the dam drowned out the hum of the mill's generators, but the frothing spray of the waterfall also made it difficult to cast into the side pools that were my targets. I nearly hooked myself several times when the force of the spray whiplashed the line back in my face. Finally I discovered that a low side-arm cast brought the fly to rest on the pool instead of me. Even there the water swirled so fast that the fly was instantly sucked into a vortex and then spit up into the air yards away in imitation of no creature in its right mind. My only hope was that the trout in these pools were too dizzy to be discriminating.

Pulling the line in to make my fifth cast, I found a stunned eleven-inch brown trout in my possession. The tug of the currents against my line was so great I hadn't even known he was taking a ride on my hook. It wasn't brilliant gamesmanship on my part, but still it was a respectable-size fish and I decided to keep him around for a while, in case I caught another and had enough to offer the friend I'd invited for dinner. Instead of threading him onto a stringer, I cleverly put him in one of the water-filled crevices on outcropping of rock from which I was casting. Nature's minnow bucket, I thought, from which I could return him unharmed to the stream or take him home.

A few minutes later I hooked another trout, this time knowingly, and I let it play the line in sportsmanlike fashion. When I landed him, I gently carried his ten inches to the crevice where I had left the first fish, thinking my evening's menu was settled. But the first fish was gone. I shrugged and returned the second fish to the stream, figuring my odds against catching a third fish in the same spot were impossibly high.

I resumed casting just to pass the time and began to wonder how that first fish managed to escape from the crevice. I set my rod down and returned to look for clues. On hands and knees I peered into the still water and saw a suspicious bulge in the silt at the bottom of the crevice. I reached into the water with my right hand and a cloud of mud exploded around my fingers. When the mud settled I saw my trout shuttling back and forth across the three-foot length of the crevice. Every time I grabbed, he dove straight to the bottom and stirred up a mud storm that left me in zero visibility. The water was only a foot deep, but that trout knew how to work every cubic inch of it.

I was so intent on our battle of wills that I failed to notice an audience had gathered. A dozen mill workers on coffee break had taken positions on a catwalk spanning the Roe/Jan about twenty-five yards downstream from me. The noise of the falls prevented me from hearing what they said as they gestured in my direction, but I could imagine the gist of it, and I knew I didn't have the protection of anonymity, because one of the men on the catwalk was Clara's husband, who no doubt informed the others I was the lady who bought his mother-in-law's house.

I waved and smiled, hoping they might arrive at a reasonable explanation for my behavior, then I returned to my task, which was, in fact, to save the fish. Personally, I couldn't have care less if he lived out the rest of his life in that crevice, but I feared it would be a short, unhappy life unless I rigged up an aerator and brought him food every day. The problem was the trout still thought of me as his enemy and I knew there was no way of talking him out of it.

Bare-handed lunging clearly didn't work. I considered tying on my tastiest fly and flicking it daintily into the crevice, but it was too late in the game for that. I looked about me for a solution and spotted a plastic carton, the kind that might once have contained a half-pound of coleslaw, littering the bank. I fetched it, rinsed it in the stream and hovered above the crevice awaiting my moment.

When the trout paused to rest at the narrow end of the crevice, I plunged and scooped up his tail. He wriggled free, but before he could slap the bottom, I scooped again and caught him head first in the carton. Grabbing his tail with my free hand, I carried him, half-in/half-out of the carton, to the pool, where, in my haste to free him before he flapped out of my grip into another crevice, I slipped on the wet rocks and slid into the water with him. An adrenaline rush of fear shot through me before my feet hit a ledge of rock and I found myself standing waist deep in the coldest water that ever lapped my thighs.

I climbed back onto the outcropping and thanked the powers that be at Kimberly-Clark for the brevity of their coffee breaks. On the short drive home, I passed Zack and Merc, who asked me if I had tried the pools by the mill yet. I said yes, I had just caught two twelve-inch brown trout there, and thanked them for the tip. They asked why I was shivering, but since they could see me only from the chest up, I left them wondering. . . .

Edina, Minn.
Friday, April 25

I hate Mom's doctors. When I arrived in Edina this morning, I found her thinner, frailer and in greater pain that at any time since her operation. Last week she went to the pain clinic expecting to discover an array of alternatives to drugs for the back pain her oncologist says is not caused by cancer; what she was offered was another nerve block, and she was so desperate for relief that she let them perform the procedure the next morning.

Now she is at home, taking mind-fogging doses of codeine to blunt the same intense burning pain the first nerve block caused. Her weight is down to 105 again, she has very little appetite and barely enough strength to walk from one room to the next. She is surprised by her misfortune and sure, as always, that she'll "feel better tomorrow." She doesn't remember that it took six weeks to recover from the side effects of this "cure-all," and nobody at the medical center reminded her.

I understand why most of the doctors cannot spend any more time or emotion on their patients than they do. They are specialists trained to intervene at moments of crisis, to cut, to radiate, to alter chemistry, then move on to the next patient. But why is there no place in this elaborate medical system for sustained care of the human being who continues to feel the effects of the doctor's knives and beams and chemicals? Why must medicine feel so much like a hit-and-run accident? . . .

Ancram, N.Y.
Sunday, July 27

I am having trouble explaining trout fishing to my city friends. They think it either idleness or blood lust, and can't imagine why I spend so much time in its pursuit. When they visit, I equip them for the stream, but they are bored within twenty minutes and look at me very strangely when I return home hours after they've resorted to more fail-safe diversions, like porch sitting, book in hand.

They don't feel the fascination of a stream, but then, neither did I before I began fishing. Oh, I was dazzled by the flow and sparkle, but that can be taken in at first glance, and unless you're in the mood to be hypnotized, it's not enough to hold one's attention for long. I only began to see things when I tried to think like a trout. The game of hide-and-seek we play is so stacked in the trout's favor that I must be as alert and wily as my inferior senses allow just to catch sight of him. When I approach the stream, I must step softly or he will pick up the vibration of my footfalls on the bank, sent express from my boots through the water to him. On sunny days, I must notice where shadows fall, so I can hide my own among those cast by the trees, or he will know a large, ungainly creature has darkened his shimmering world.

Before entering the stream, I sit on the bank for a while to see what insects are swarming above the water. I turn over rocks in the streambed to see who's living there. I am not a strict imitationist, but if I can't approximate the size and shape, color and movement of something above, below or on the surface of the water, I might as well surrender my hopes for the day. I have tried expressionist flies, but they work only on expressionist fish, like bass, who will leap for any gaudy bauble when they're in the mood. Trout have more refined tastes.

Even a finicky trout must eat, though, and he can't expend more energy getting food than the food supplies, or he will waste away to nothing; he must find some quiet spot and let the food come to him. This knowledge is my only edge, so once in the stream, I scan the surface of the water for variations in its flow. I look for large boulders above and below the surface, for fallen logs and indentations in the bank, anything that interrupts the flow of the stream, creating pockets of still water on its downstream side where a trout can rest without struggling against the current. I approach such places with great stealth, staying in the shadows when possible, inching my boots along the slippery, moss-covered rocks of the streambed, checking in all directions for overhanging branches that might snag my fly before it reaches its target. Wind permitting, I try to cast my fly just upstream from where I suspect the trout will be so my tempting morsel will float right past him.

If my fly lands on the water more indelicately than a gnat would, the older, wiser, larger trout will let it pass and I'll never know what I've missed. There are no second chances with an experienced trout; the merest suspicion of a predator in the vicinity and he will not risk revealing his hideout by taking any insect, hand-tied or God-made, for hours. I might trick a six-inch native trout or even a ten-inch stocked trout, a newcomer to the stream raised in the sheltering walls of a hatchery, but to catch a veteran trout, twelve inches or more, I must be perfect, and I seldom am. I may move soundlessly through the water for twenty yards, stirring not a ripple as I approach a likely spot, and then stumble just as I'm about to cast, sending a tidal wave of warning to even the most innocent stockie. Or my wrist may betray me and shoot the line out so fast it slaps the surface of the water or lands in a spiraling jumble, as if I'd cast the web as well as the fly.

When I'm fishing well, my concentration is so intensely focused on the surface of the stream that I enter a kind of trance, from which I emerge startled by some sudden sound or change in light. I'll look up, as if just awakened from a dream, and see a great blue heron taking flight at my approach, the tips of his spindly legs lagging three feet behind his crested head, curled claws still skimming the surface of the water. One hazy afternoon, I looked up, reentered time and felt a sudden searing stab of fear. Day had departed unnoticed by me, and the last rays of the setting sun shot horizontally through the woods toward me like the beams of a motorcycle gang waiting in silent ambush.

Often, on clear days, I'll see a cardinal fly across the stream ahead of me, a streak of red against blue sky for an instant before he's lost again in the green world of the other bank. Every time, I think of the passage from Venerable Bede about the flight of the sparrow through the mead hall. Bede likened the sparrow's flight from door to door to the brevity of man's life on earth. I too am reminded of mortality, but, midstream on a sunlit day, I have no complaint. If the cardinal's flight from bank to bank were less fleeting, it would also be less glorious. Midstream, it seems all right to die; sickness is the sin....

Saturday, November 8
Last night I dreamt that Dad and I were in a cemetery where Mom was buried. There was no plot to the dream, just a climate, strange to say, of contentedness. The cemetery was green and leafy and it seemed a fine place to be. Dad and I were smiling. There was a vivid sense of Mom's

presence there, and of her contentment with her new home. In fact, the mood was almost what it would be if one of us were showing the other two the new house we had bought and everyone was pleased with the choice. In this case, the new home was hers, a dream reversal of my frustrated wish to show her mine.

Montevarchi, Italy
June 1987

I have my answer, at least for now. I don't find the living presence of my mother in memory, in photographs or anecdotes; I find her instead in moonlight and breezes. On August nights, I pretend shooting stars are signals sent from her to me. I am not talking about belief but the experience of consolation. Certain, unexpected sights or sensations console me the way the feel of familiar beads passing through thumb and forefinger might console someone else. I am thankful that my discovery of death coincided with my discovery of a new setting, thankful that death found me midstream, where the play of light on water makes me feel blessed.

Fishing Streamers and Bucktails for Trout

By Joe Brooks

IN MY YEARS OF ASSOCIATION WITH OUTDOOR MAGAZINE AND BOOK publishing, including stints at the helms of *Sports Afield* and *Outdoor Life*, I can't remember an angler and writer whose name among his peers was held in the esteem of the late Joe Brooks. I personally did not have the opportunity to meet or fish with Joe Brooks, but those who did told me he was a companion and man whose picture could have been used alongside the word "gentleman" in the dictionary. Not only was he a skilled angler, Joe Brooks was tirelessly devoted to teaching the attributes of sportsmanship and conservation to young and old alike, wherever he went.

In his articles and books, one encounters example after example of Joe Brooks sharing what he has observed and learned with selfless and non-didactic ease. To Joe Brooks, every angling challenge was an angling opportunity.

There are many images of Joe Brooks that come to mind as I think about the pictures of him I have seen, and sometimes published, over the years. But my favorite section of all his prose comes from the *Complete Book of Fly Fishing*, when Brooks describes why he loved to fish big streamers for big trout. A high point in the piece takes place on Joe's beloved Yellowstone River, where he's trying for a big one late one last afternoon with winter coming on and the road back east beckoning.

───

If you want to catch lunker trout, use big streamer flies. When a trout reaches 2½ to 3 pounds, he has done with midges, freshwater shrimp and other small fry. He wants to gulp down something big enough to make his stomach sac press against his sides. Occasionally a 4-pounder will take a size 10 hairwing and once in a while he might even go for a size 18 or 20. But generally speaking, trout that big don't play for peanuts. They want the works.

Streamers bring out the yen for meat in these big boys and with the right presentation and retrieve an angler can get strikes from hook-jawed old busters that weigh in up in the heavyweight division. They are so hungry for substantial food that even if their stomachs are stuffed tighter than a Pennsylvania food locker the day after deer season, they still will grab another minnow that they can't even swallow and will swim around with the tail sticking out of their mouths, waiting for the swallowed part to dissolve so they can handle the rest. And believe it or not, those big-eyed aquatic so-and-sos, with that remnant of a partly digested meal still protruding from their throats, will hit a streamer. When I opened up one 4½-pound lunker last year, what did I find? Two field mice each about 5 inches long, two minnows each about 4 inches long, and one 5-inch min-now with its tail just showing in the trout's throat. Here was this jasper making like the filling of a knockwurst and he wants a bucktail, yet!

In streamer fishing the handling of the retrieve means defeat or suc-cess. You must make the lure imitate the actions of the natural food upon which the trout feed, so that they go for it totally unsuspecting. Streamer fishing calls for rod tip work and line manipulation that will make the fly out there act like a minnow. It should be retrieved in short jerks to make it look like a minnow darting erratically around the pool, or in longer strips to ape a more leisurely swim. A lure that is allowed to sink and is then played very slowly can be made to look like a minnow nosing the bottom for food and an extra-fast top-water retrieve makes the artificial dash across the surface, faking a natural minnow that is rushing along the top, trying to escape some great, toothy-mawed 5-pounder.

The angler should try all types of bringbacks until he discovers just which one will do the best job that day. I usually start with the cast across the current, mend the line, then let the fly float downstream broadside and without any motion. When it reaches the end of the float and starts to swim my way, I impart 6-inch jerks to it, then when it has finally swung in directly below me, I bring it back my way slowly and evenly for about

3 feet, then pick it up for the next cast. You can expect a thudding hit at any stage of that play.

Another effective cast and retrieve is upstream and across, bringing the fly back in 2-foot-long jerks, fast, right to the rod tip. Often a fish will follow such a retrieve and hit it just as the angler is about to pick it up for the next cast. And sometimes in a low clear stream it is a good move to cast directly upstream. This cast requires the same care and stealth in approach as does dry-fly fishing, but often such a throw and a slowly retrieved, sparsely tied bucktail will take trout when all other methods fail.

One of the fish-teasin'est ways of all is to figure where a fish should be lying in the current, cast the fly to that spot and instead of bringing it back all the way, just retrieve it a foot or two, then let it float downstream again, retrieve it a foot or so again, and repeat the whole procedure. It takes patience, but it's usually worth the effort in bringing hits that won't seem to come by other methods just then.

That retrieve paid heavy dividends one day when I fished the East Branch of the Antietam River with Bob Wishard of Waynesboro, Pennsylvania. The stream meandered through lush meadows, and at the bends the current had cut under the banks, making deep holes and swell hiding places for trout. At such a bend a brush pile provided shelter for fish. I watched Bob work a yellow and brown streamer in and out of one of those spooky-looking spots, giving it action that made it perform for all the world like a small minnow lying there just above the log jam and darting upstream, then dropping back, waiting for food to come to it in the current. Bob teased a trout so much with that retrieve that at last it zoomed up from out of that black hole and hit the fly so hard he was carried into the air by the force of his rush. As soon as he fell in again, he jumped and landed on top of the brush, snapped the leader and lay there on a big log, flapping, and finally slipped back into the water.

Bob's face was white.

"With all that water around, he has to jump on that bunch of logs!" he grumbled. "That trout weighed 3 pounds at least."

Later we both took a couple of good fish in the same way, by assuming that there was a lunker under every log pile, and teasing them out with a streamer.

During the spring when the streams are high and roily, and after rains during the summer, streamers are fairly commonly used by Eastern anglers, but few of them are used at any other time. Yet even when the water has dropped and is clear and a hundred anglers are walking along the banks of a 30-foot-wide Eastern river, a wide-awake trouter can get hits with a streamer. In clear water, a sparsely tied bucktail on a number 10 or even a 12 hook is very effective when used with a leader tapered down to a 5X tippet. These thinly clad numbers tied with wings of black and white, brown and white, blue and white, and brown and yellow, will do a swell job of making lazy trout hit.

In discolored water, on the other hand, all yellow, all brown or all black seem to show up best. Once on Beaver Creek in Maryland, the water turned so brown following a heavy downpour that we were ready to quit fishing.

"Sometimes I've caught trout in very muddy water with this fly," said Bill Snyder, holding up a brown hackle.

"Not in water this muddy," I said.

Bill tossed his fly midway out in the pool. A fish shot up through that muddy mess and took the fly like he had seen it through gin-clear water. Bill was so surprised he struck too hard and left the fly in the trout's mouth. But he had proved his point. I grubbed into my streamer box and brought out an all-yellow number, tied it on and was in business at the first hole upstream. A 14-incher roared up and knocked that yellow Sally silly. In the next hour we landed nine fish.

After that I took three dark colors and held them in the water, then took a couple of other flies with neutral colors and held them beside the dark ones. The yellow, brown and black showed up five times more plainly.

To fish streamers the angler needs a bigger rod than is used for dry-fly fishing but it is not necessary to go into the heavy equipment that some fishermen seem to think. Using a small streamer in a low, clear stream, an 8-foot rod weighing 4 ounces, with a DT-5-F line and a 10-foot leader tapered down to as low as 4X will do a workmanlike job. The tippet may be upped to 3X or 2X depending on the size of fish you are getting hits from. Sometimes when the line is being stripped, a big trout will sock the streamer, and the combined pressure of the pull and the hit will break the leader. So with a light leader you stand the chance of losing a few fish, but you will get more strikes, too.

The larger streamers are difficult to cast on a small rod and with a long, fine leader, and in order to throw them effectively, an 8½-foot rod weighing as much as 4¾ ounces is needed, and should be fitted with a WF-7-F line. The 10-foot leader should start off with a heavy butt section and then fade down to a 4X tipped (*see* TACKLE). Just before and right at dark, an even heavier leader is all right as in the evening light the trout don't seem to be scared by the larger tippet diameter.

Hook sizes in streamers should range from 12 all the way down to 1/0. Many times it is the size of the fly rather than the color that seems to make the difference between hits and no hits, so the streamer fisherman should carry a large assortment of both colors and sizes. Some day it will pay off heavily.

Out West, trout fishermen have always favored big wet flies and wooly worms, and with these they catch plenty of big trout. Yet if these same fellows would use streamers, I believe they would find the size of their fish increasing.

I well remember the day I introduced a Montana fishing pal to streamers. Len Kinkie had fished dries, and wets and nymphs, but the big black ghost I presented to him scared him.

"What is it?" he said. "Trimming for a gal's hat?"

"Trimming for a trout," I assured him.

It was just before dark. Len went up to the fast water at the top of the 300-foot pool while I worked down toward the tail. I was busily casting when I heard a shout. My head snapped around in time to see Len walking towards the shore, rod held high. Out in the current a great trout jumped clear and threw the hook.

"That was the biggest trout I've ever hooked," Len told me later. "He was 10 pounds. I know now what you mean about streamers."

Speaking of big streamers and big fish always makes me think of a certain pool on the Yellowstone River. If I'm within a couple of hundred miles of it, regardless of time or inconvenience, I'll head for it pronto. From that pool I've taken enough big trout—and put most of them back—that if they were laid end to end they would reach from Denver to the Rio Grande.

The last time I waded out into that pool was 4:00 p.m. on October 19, my last day of fishing before heading east. As always, I was expecting to sink my barbs into a 16- or 17-pounder.

Since I was sure there would be some big fish working there just before dark, I tied on a 2X tippet. I started at the head of the pool, dropping a size 1/0 white marabou 20 feet out in the fast water and letting it float a bit before bringing it back in fast, foot-long jerks. I lengthened the second throw 2 feet. And the next one another 2 feet. When I had 50 feet of line out, I floated it through and waded down to about where it had swung across on that last cast. Then I started the series of casts again. That way I was covering all of the holding water.

The first cast on the next series brought a strike when the marabou was only 20 feet away. That rainy hit almost on top and threw water 3 feet high when he took. Then he hung there for a second, heavy, and then my rod tip snapped back and the flyless leader shot high in the air. He had broken me off on the hit.

I tested the leader and put on another marabou. I started the series of casts from where I was. This time it took three casts and then again I almost jumped out of my waders when a hook-beaked beezer poked his nose out and clapped his mandibles at me. He missed the fly but he didn't miss giving me the cold chills. He looked bigger than the other.

I rested him for three or four minutes only, and then sent the fly over the spot where he had been and once again a fish had it, and once again the tip bowed down and stayed there a minute and then flaunted another flyless leader in my face.

I burned then! I was sure that every one of those fish went over 5 pounds. I put on a 1X tippet, cast again and once more got the same treatment. And that one took my last marabou.

I cut off the 1X, leaving just the heavier part of the tapered leader, and tied on a yellow and brown streamer. On the first cast a big baby out there took, rolled on the leader, and once again I was fit to be tied. The sun was away down, peeping over the top of the Gallatins, shadows already across the river, and back of me I heard a deer bleat.

This time I cut that 12-foot leader in half. I must have been up to at least 8-pound test after all that clipping.

While I was tying on a muddler, a fish rose 30 feet in front of me. I cast and he was waiting there with his mouth wide open. I didn't have time to strike because he started off so fast. He slashed across the fast water, then ran down with it for 30 feet and came out in a going-away jump. All I could see was a dark blob down there and as I dropped the rod tip he fell back in and went away again, fast.

He did everything a trout should do to get off. But somehow I gradually started to gain on him. He came upstream and I reeled fast to keep him coming, to get fly line back on the reel. When I got him close, he jumped right in front of me and threw water in my face and then went off again in a slashing drive across current, and then swirled on top and started to shake his head back and forth.

At that nasty maneuver I gave line in a hurry. Then he hung there in the current and I couldn't make him bat an eye. It was a draw for a couple of minutes and then I fooled him. I suddenly gave him slack and he slipped down with the current, and while he was wondering what happened, I tightened up and pulled him off balance and got him coming my way. He tried to get his head again but I held him and skidded him sideways now, in close, and up on top and into the net. He weighed 3¼ pounds, a nice fish to end the season.

As I waded ashore with him, I heard the sound of a riser out there in the current back of me. It made a noise like the thud of a rock falling on frozen ground. I wanted to go back but it was too dark.

"I'll get you next year," I said aloud. "I'll start fishing right here and I'll use a size 1/0 muddler, or maybe a white marabou."

Because I know it's big flies those big lunkers want.

A recent streamer-type fly that has had great success is the Big Hole demon, first tied in 1964 by rancher Nick Naranchi, of Twin Bridges, Montana. This fine fly looks something like a low-water wooly worm, and it brings lots of hits from big trout. It is fished across current and allowed to drift free for several feet, then a slow jerk is given to make it look alive and make it swim across the current in an enticing manner. However, most strikes come when the demon is floating still.

Dan Bailey ties two versions of the pattern, one with black and badger body, one with black and furnace body. Both are good. I use them on hook sizes 2, 4, 6, and down to number 10. Like all good patterns, this one was soon carried far and wide, to scenes far from the Big Hole River, for which the fly was named. Bebe Anchorena fished Montana the summer of 1965, and he took a couple of dozen Big Hole demons back to Argentina with him, and there he and Charles Radziwill cashed in with them, landing sea trout to 10 pounds.

There are many long-known streamers and bucktails that are temporarily forgotten because of the success of some new fly. Last year I broke out one such, the Bailey bi-fly, and fished it with such success that I won't forget it again. It can be used either wet or dry, but I have the best luck when I fish it as a streamer.

In general, trout fishing must be done with great quiet, and therefore the popping bug is seldom considered a good trout fly. Yet even big brown trout, smartest and scariest of them all, like a big popper, properly administered in the right place.

Two winters ago, while fishing the Chimehuin River in Argentina, I was taking a string of 6-, 8- and 10-pound fish on large streamers, enjoying the best trout fishing I've ever had in my life. But I knew there were bigger ones there. Bebe Anchorena and Jorge Donovan of Buenos Aires, who were fishing with me, had told me about the heft of some of those trout.

"Every year," said Jorge, "someone catches brown trout up to 25 pounds here in this river."

"Last year a friend of mine caught a 26-pounder," said Bebe. "He was plug casting with a spoon."

Suddenly I thought of popping bugs. I wondered. And I tried. I got out a big popper, one with a total length of 5 inches, from eye of the hook to end of tail.

It was a rough day. The water on the lake above was whitecapped and dark clouds blotted out the mountains and raced over the low hills. It was a rough day to tie into a rough fish, and that was what I wanted to do. Here in the river the water was bouncing with 6-inch waves, and I thought how perfect a spot this was to use a big bug, because it had the bulk a big brownie would like and the waves would not allow too loud a pop, to maybe scare off a suspicious fish.

I cast that big popping bug across current 70 feet, bringing the rod tip almost down to the water so the wind wouldn't blow the bug off course. I let it drift for maybe 10 feet, then retrieved it slowly, in foot-long pulls, trying to make the bug skip softly along. Suddenly I saw a big brown shape out there standing on its head. The rod tip went down violently and the reel began to sing and I was into a big trout. He went 8½ pounds.

I didn't see the next one because he hit in the middle of an incoming wave that still wore a frothy top. But I felt the strike more than the other one. It was a sort of double hit, as if he turned and missed and then took a second try. Or maybe he was hooked the first time, then turned fast and yanked his head around as he did. Anyway, I had all I could handle for the next ten minutes weathering his first frantic fight. Then it turned into a slug fest and it was fifteen minutes before I slipped him ashore, a good quarter of a mile downstream. He was a 10-pounder.

"Give me one of those poppers," said Jorge, who had been going right along with me.

"Me, too," said Bebe.

I handed a popper to each of them, and they left on the run for the next pool.

I had only brought three poppers with me, not expecting to use poppers on trout, so that left me with only the one I had been using. I decided to save it for some special occasion when I thought there might be an extra-big fish around. That occasion came only a couple of days later. I had fished down river for a good half mile without a hit. Then I came to a pool that was so fishy looking that there just had to be a big trout in there.

Out came that big popper. On the third cast I saw a great fish in back of the bug, his cavernous mouth open. I saw him bring his upper mandible down. I struck. Three quarters of an hour later I landed that baby, an 18½-pound brown trout that was 35 inches long and had a girth of 22 inches. A few days later I took a 15-pounder on the same bug.

Those were the two biggest fish of the trip. Popping bugs? You bet!

Striped Bass and Southern Solitude

By Ellington White

BACK IN THE 1960S AND '70S, SPORTS ILLUSTRATED MAGAZINE WAS A REG-
ular reading stop for me because from time to time they ran superb pieces
on fishing, and sometimes hunting. Duncan Barnes, who went on to edit
Field & Stream for many years, was a *SI* staff writer, as was Bob Jones,
author of several novels and nonfiction books on outdoor sports. Varsity
SI contributors included writers like Tom McGuane and Bill Humphrey.

A story in the October 10, 1966, edition of *SI* by a writer I did not
know, Ellington White, really held me hard. I was so taken by "Striped
Bass and Southern Solitude" that I kept a clipping of the piece for many
years. I eventually showed it to Nick Lyons, who thought so much of the
story that he included it in his wonderful anthology, *Fisherman's Bounty*,
published in 1970 by Crown.

Over the many years since I first read the story, my feelings about
"Striped Bass and Southern Solitude" have never changed, and I am
delighted that we can include it here. Once you begin reading it, you will
understand why *Sports Illustrated*, Nick, and I were all so captivated.

━━◦━━

The best way to fish is alone. The best time to fish is the fall. Believing
these simple truths to be self-evident, I set out alone each fall to fish the
rivers and creeks that flow out of Virginia into the Chesapeake Bay. It is
a good time of year all around. Everybody else in the world is watching a
football game. Leaves cover the roadside beer cans, and the traffic is light.
Whenever a car appears pulling a boat, I know it is bound for the city, not

the sea, for the water skiers have beached their skis and skin divers have taken up bowling. Praise the fall.

In truth, fishermen should do as fish do in the summer—lie low. We should give the beaches to the sunbathers and admit that during this idle season, when the great fiber-glass fleet rules the waterways, the thing to do is haul in our lines and run for cover. Of course, we will never do this. We aren't as smart as fish. We persist in thinking that the summer is big enough for all of us—fishermen, skin divers, water skiers, the whole she-bang. What a delusion.

But now it is the fall, and I am driving east on Route 33. Pine trees crowd the shoulders, and the morning sun is hot. In the Tidewater, summer and fall merge with each other so quietly that for a few weeks you need a calendar to tell where you are. Straddling two seasons, one foot in each, you feel both seasons at once.

At West Point, under a cloud of pulpmill smoke, I cross the Pamunkey and Mattaponi rivers, tributaries of the York River, which enters the bay just north of the James. All of these rivers belong to the fall in my mind, the James especially, where I once saw the fall arrive.

I had taken a boat up the river to fish for bass in the mouth of a small creek near Presque Isle Swamp, about twelve miles below Richmond. Here the James takes its time, dawdling along between odorous mud flats, mesmerizing fish and fishermen alike. It just about put me to sleep that day, I recall. After several hours I had had enough, and started back, half paddling, half drifting down the river on the outgoing tide, drowsing among the slumberous sounds of wallowing carp and turtles dropping off logs.

It was a warm day in early October. Most of the clothing I had started out in lay heaped in the bottom of the boat. I was glad the tide and I were going the same way. Farther down the river a handful of gulls was circling a row of stakes that had once supported fish-nets. The shoreline slid past, marshy and still. I drifted by a small bay and across a gravel bar. By this time the gulls were wheeling overhead. The fog lifted just enough for me to catch the glimmerings of an idea, something about gulls following stripers. . . . Oh, nonsense, I thought. Nevertheless, there was the rod resting against the middle seat. All I had to do was pick it up. Why not? I cast into the shore. It was an idle cast and went farther than I had intended it to, landing among a drift of leaves and pine needles. The surface plug bobbed a few times. The leaves bulged and then blew open. It was an astonishing moment. I had often driven hundreds of miles chasing stripers up and down the eastern seaboard, and here I had *drifted* into a school of them. Later I visualized our paths as two crooked lines, wobbling all over the river, and somehow miraculously bisecting under a flock of gulls. In ten minutes it was all over. We had drifted apart, and without a motor I had no way of following them. It didn't matter, though. I had four of them, all about six pounds, flopping on top of my clothes.

I don't know of any fish that gives as much pleasure to as many fishermen as the ubiquitous striper. He may not be as dazzling as a bonefish or as much a roughneck as a snook, but he covers more ground than these fish do and so comes into contact with more people. There is nothing provincial about him, either. He can get along in fresh water just as well as he can in salt water, river water as well as ocean water, shallow water or deep water—it's all the same to him. People fish for him in boats, on banks, in the surf or by wading. They use trolling rods, boat rods, casting rods, spinning rods, fly rods and every kind of bait made—wood, plastic, feathered and live. And he survives them all. Praise the striper, I thought, looking at my four, the most democratic fish that swims.

By the time I reached the landing, the temperature had dropped sharply. A chill wind swept across the river. I climbed back into my clothes and walked home smelling of fish. That was six years ago. The sweater is still with me, as is the scent. Maybe nobody else can smell it, after tons of mothballs and innumerable dry cleanings, but I was putting the sweater in the car this morning, prior to setting off down Route 33, and caught a whiff of it again, every bit as strong as that day I passed through a school of stripers.

Stutts Creek, my destination, is one of many tidal creeks found along the Virginia side of the Chesapeake Bay. Itself a branch of the bay, it sprouts still other branches and ends up looking on a map like a tree that has fallen into the bay's marshy fringes. Once a waterway for crabbers and oystermen, it has become in recent years something of a playground as well, conveying many more svelte Chris-Crafts than lumbering workboats. But like playgrounds everywhere, it is crowded in the summer and all but empty during the winter.

When I fish Stutts Creek I always stay with a man who was raised on it, Norris Richardson, who runs Pine Hall, an inn for fishermen and exhausted city dwellers who drive down on the weekends from Richmond. Pine Hall is a large white house overlooking the creek from a summit of green grass. Norris runs the place as though he were not really trying to, and as a result it is one of the best-run places I know of. You have the comfortable feeling that everyone is there to relax, even the help. Norris is a small, distracted man with an inexhaustible supply of country stories, little pastoral romances about coons and possums and what happened to old Uncle So-and-so when a pail of crabs turned over in his kitchen. Listen to enough of these tales and you forget all about Vietnam and overpopulation. I always like to hear one or two before setting off up the creek. They are like steppingstones to another world.

Stutts Creek enters the bay between two islands lying just off the mainland. One of these, Gwynn Island, is a well-known vacation spot, but the other, Rigby Island, is little more than an exposed sandbar. There is a channel between the islands, but elsewhere the water is shallow and marshy.

Stripers seem to regard the bay as a school they have to complete before graduating into the Atlantic Ocean. The school lasts four years. A few dropouts may tackle the ocean sooner than that, but the majority are content to wait until graduation day. Then they are ready to join the big ocean community on the outside. At least, this is what a tagging program instigated by the Atlantic States Marine Fisheries Commission indicates. The young striper just out of school tends to stay pretty close to home for the first year or so, but as his size increases so does his boldness, and off he goes to prowl the New England coast 700 miles away. In the fall he frequently returns, packing weights of twenty and thirty pounds. It is a curious fact that stripers reach the bay about the same time that alumni are arriving in Charlottesville, Virginia, to watch Mr. Jefferson's eleven take another licking, but if you think that homecoming is worth watching you ought to see what happens when the Old Boys get together in the bay. It's an alumni secretary's dream. Gulls throw up tents all over the place, covering the big feeds, and the campus becomes one huge thrashing contest. Before long the racket reaches the shore, and here comes a fleet of fishermen pounding out to join in the fun.

It's great sport if you like that sort of thing, and most striper fishermen do, but not caring for homecomings myself, in Charlottesville or the bay, I cut the motor and drift into the shallows behind Rigby Island. It's quieter there. You can hear the tide running through the grass. I toss out the anchor, rig up a rod, stuff my pockets with flies, climb into a pair of boots and wade off in search of a few first-graders.

Cold nights have distilled the water. Croakers, spot, crabs, nettles—all of summer's impedimenta—have been frozen out, and the once-green marsh is now the color of bronze. A line of pine trees stands on the far shore; nearer, dead limbs mark an oyster bed. Where the bay has breached Rigby Island slightly left of center, the tide crosses a sandbar and then spreads out over the marsh, dividing it into a number of small grassy clumps. The water is a hard, glinty, blue.

I have never yet caught a fish on a first cast, nor have I ever made a first cast without thinking I would catch a fish. My heart pounds, my hands shake. I tie on a white streamer, wet it with saliva so that it will sink fast, and drop it at the edge of the marsh. It crosses the tide on a series of swift jerks and returns to my feet untouched. I pick it up and cast again. By the fifteenth cast my hands are steady and my heart has resumed its normal tempo. Now begins the long haul.

Stripers like moving water, and when the tide is slack so are they. I walk along casting. Hours pass. I switch to a popping bug and try that until the marsh is brimful of water and a gold chain leads across it to where the sun is settling into a thicket of trees. Lights appear on shore. Gulls are coming in to roost on the channel markers. Soon it will be dark. I want a fish to whack the popper right out of the water, and I hold onto this hope as long as there is light. Then, when there is no more light, I return to Pine Hall.

So begins the first of many fall weekends on Stutts Creek. As the days shorten, my clothes increase. Sweaters pile up. By December I look like a woolen balloon with legs. Norris Richardson's dogs jump aside when they see me coming. Some mornings dawn fair, others overcast and wet.

The best mornings are those when frost covers the ground and a brittle stillness films the creek. Coming up, the sun looks like a forest fire. The worst mornings come out of Canada on a northwest wind that wants to shred you alive, and you need more than sweaters to keep warm. Some fishermen use insulated underwear, some carry bottles, some turn on the furnace words of the English language. I resort to fantasy myself. As soon as numbness reaches the top of my waders, I wrap myself in the vision of a big striper who has gotten tired of homecoming and returned to the shallows of his youth. I see him passing through the inlet just as I am rounding the marsh directly in front of him. There was a time when he would not enter the shallows without company, but now that he has grown up the rewards of fellowship have diminished and he finds that the marsh is something of a relief after the tumult of the bay. So here he is enjoying the freedom of being alone, and here I am doing the same—smothered in wool, walking toward him. I see him nudge the grass. His tail lifts a cloud of sand, then carries him into the mouth of a small feeder creek. (In actual fact, there is such a creek, though it lies closer to Pine Hall than it does in my fantasy. I never pass it without thinking what a wonderful place it would be to catch a striper—smooth sandy bottom, tufts of grass choking the mouth, a line of pine trees to break the wind.) Once he is in the creek, however, the striper finds that the water is not as deep as it appeared to be on the outside and he starts back, cruising like a porpoise. By then I have planted a popper squarely in the middle of the opening, and when he is within sight of it I twitch the line and the popper jumps forward. You can guess the rest.

It is astonishing how much heat a scene like that can generate.

For a moment last Thanksgiving Day I thought I had caught this fish. I went out early in the morning and fished straight through until dusk. It was a cold, blustery day. The wind piled up big waves and hurled them at the shore. Casting a heavy saltwater fly rod is hard work in itself, but casting it in the wind for seven or eight hours is pure torture. In the middle of the afternoon I found three small fish, two- and three-pounders, huddled up in a pocket of deep water, but catching them had rekindled no fires, and by evening I was numb and sore all over.

Even my fantasy had quit working. The tide had just about run itself out, and so had I. I switched to a spinning rod, a less taxing instrument than a fly rod, and waded out along a point of land for a few final casts. I tossed the lure, a weighted jig, into a trench the tide had dug between two sandbars. It was an ordinary sort of place, a place you fish because you know you should rather than because it appeals to you. I had fished the place many times before, ever since Brook Jones, a fine fisherman from Richmond, had pointed it out to me. Brook takes fish out of it all the time, but I had never had much luck with it. Today was different. The lure bounced down one wall of the trench, disappeared in deep water, then climbed up the other wall. It had just reached the top when a shadow rose off the bottom and pulled it back down. I knew it was a big fish by the size of the shadow. He lunged around in the depths for a while, then plowed off across the shallows with a second fish right behind him. Why the second fish, I don't know. Perhaps the two of them had been lying in the trench getting fat together. In any case, the follower soon veered off in the direction of the channel while my fish bore straight ahead. There is nothing spectacular about the way stripers behave after they are hooked. A heavy fish simply lays into a line and bulls his way along. He's a plodder. I could have let this striper run a mile before he reached anything to break off on, but it had been a long cold day and I was taking no chances. I could plod, too. So I set a hard drag and in time wore him down the way you break horses—with sheer force.

One thing he had done was thaw me out. I could feel again. He would go eight or nine pounds, I supposed. Holding him up against the horizon, I found there was more light left in him than was left in all the sky—no fantasy fish, but a good solid striper, all the same.

A Trout Stream Named Desire

By John Barsness

JOHN BARSNESS WRITES SUCH ENGAGING PROSE THAT YOU WOULD THINK entire shelves would be lined with his books, but the fact is that there are only two with which I am familiar, both published by Nick Lyons. Those are *Western Skies: Bird Hunting in the Rockies and on the Plains*, and *Montana Time: The Seasons of a Trout Fisherman*.

John writes frequently in *Field & Stream* and other top magazines in a style that captures the feel of the country in a way I find irresistible. Whether following a bird dog over land once roamed by buffalo, or casting to a cutthroat trout in backcounty waters few have ever seen, John Barsness makes the experience come to life on the printed page.

I can only hope that we'll be seeing another Barsness book or two before long.

Too much of a good thing can be wonderful.

—MAE WEST

Most western Native American tribes had a saying about grizzly tracks—about fishing or hunting someplace else when you found them. A few weeks ago I came around a bend on a mountain trail in the Bob Marshall Wilderness and found myself within sixty feet of a boar grizzly. I didn't recall any Indian sayings at the time, but the idea of fishing someplace else suddenly made a lot of sense.

This was a big bear. The fact that he was eating grass was not comforting, because I was close enough to hear the roots tearing. I whispered to my companion, close behind me, something like, "There's a goddamn grizzly." Perhaps the adjective was more vehement. The bear looked up and we backed around the bend, quickly and quite a ways. We weren't sure the bear knew what we were, so we decided to talk loudly, to let him know people were around. Bears are truly wild in the Bob—not like Glacier Park's bears, who sometimes charge tourists to make them drop their daypacks full of granola bars.

So we talked loudly and soon heard something large moving off through the alders above the trail. When we peeked around the bend again the bear was gone.

That encounter had three effects. The first was fright. After calming down, this seemed healthy, a sort of atavistic computer check of all my systems. If a large grizzly bear alarms me, I figure my nerves are still approximately as they evolved, not too warped by civilization.

After fright came a thrill. An innocent bystander might suggest that the same thrill could be had by climbing a vertical rock face. No. Unlike rock climbing, or whitewater rafting, or bungee jumping, or any of the dangerous pursuits some of us use to persuade ourselves that there is indeed life in the twentieth century, grizzlies do not thrill us when and where we choose. You do not choose to climb a grizzly—though he may choose to climb you. Living (if only for a few days) in grizzly country is like a tune-up after the computer check: It makes sure everything keeps turning over. Even in the moment before falling asleep, you are extremely sure you're alive.

But the third response was unexpected: a moment of recognition. Anyone who spends time around bears gains some of that; bears are sometimes too human. One reason people and bears have problems is that we like the same summer places: lakes, creek bottoms, berry patches, high cool mountains. Anyone who's had a black bear stand up a few yards away in a huckleberry meadow experiences a certain recognition, something like surprising Uncle Bill unbuttoning his overalls out in the weeds at the family picnic, if a trifle more startling.

But the face on that grizzly was unlike any black bear's. Black bears often look slightly unfocused, like Uncle Bill after his fifth beer, their long sloping faces seeming in need of a pair of reading glasses. But this grizzly was grizzly in the extreme: a chocolate bear with gray-blond trim, head as big as a beach ball, and when he lifted that head his wide-set eyes looked straight forward from a flat face, unmoving and totally focused. It was odd, but it was as if I saw a cautious knowledge there—a knowledge of being separate yet equal, the only two animals every other animal is afraid of. This didn't mean I wanted to hug the grizzly, like an old friend. But suddenly I recognized the terror that other animals feel for us, the terror they find in our flat faces and totally focused eyes—and even more than giving me empathy for a deer or trout, it gave me empathy for the bear. Being a grizzly must be a damn lonely profession, perhaps as lonely as being human.

Anyone who watches bears sees them looking for really good stuff to eat, scratching their backs, being startled by things as small as squirrels. But most of all you notice how they want to be alone. With the exceptions of lovers and immediate family, bears are strict individualists. Even when gathered on salmon streams, they observe codes of avoidance, small bears keeping out of the way of big bears, and especially not looking directly into larger bears' eyes. Up in the mountains, away from the enforced closeness of salmon, small black bears run when big black bears show up—and big black bears run like hell when grizzlies come round.

We are more like bears than we like to admit. Left to our natural devices in emptier country, we tend to spread out. We act like bears, good for occasional society but for the most part happier when alone or with one or two good friends.

Even when driving, the pattern is there. In the West there are always a few tailgaters, but all they want to do is pass, to get to the next town or next bar. But in much of this nation there are too many of us—we are the most numerous mammal on earth—and most of us live in crowds. We've become conditioned to crowding. Driving the back roads of Florida, I've run into retiree convoys, lines of maybe half a dozen cars with New York plates, zooming bumper to bumper along an empty highway between sand pines and palmettoes. Are these people related? Are they traveling together for protection, like a wagon train? No, they grew up driving bumper to bumper on the highways of Westchester County and Long Island and feel uncomfortable with any space between them and the next car.

Like bears, anglers tend to gather at the good fishing places, like the Henry's Fork and Madison and Big Horn. But as those places have grown more crowded I've noticed fewer local license plates. Perhaps it's the instinct of a bear who grew up unconditioned to crowds, but it always seemed that trout fishing should be a lonely occupation. Of course, the loneliest anglers I've ever seen were fishing a stream in Connecticut, not far from the New York line. We were taking the train from Danbury to meet a relative who'd drive us to Shea Stadium, where the Mets would play the Pirates, and for a while the tracks were parallel to a small creek. On the other side of the creek were a broad lawn and then some office buildings, and at each small pool of the creek was a fly fisherman (there were no women), plying his lonely craft on that pool and that pool only, looking as happy as a banker at a board meeting.

But the lonely I'm talking about is a different sort, a lonely freedom. Like grizzly bears, we should be able to fish where we want to, the reason the famous places have not really appealed to me. Lately there's been lots of press about how crowded even the Henry's Fork and Big Horn are getting. Well, they are, if not quite as crowded as the creeks between Danbury and Shea Stadium. But there are hundreds of trout streams out there—in the big Out There, the Rocky Mountain West—where a wader track is about as common as a grizzly's. After a time along such streams, the print of a felt-soled boot begins to look remarkably like the broad track of a bear, even without claw marks. Like any good hunter-gatherer, I have developed an aversion to each.

These are not mountain streams, either, but meadow streams, ranch streams, valley streams that flow between cottonwood groves and alfalfa fields and Hereford pastures. They are not strictly natural systems—for the most part they hold brown and rainbow and brook trout—but they are places where you can fish alone, for stream-bred trout. They do take time to find, something we seem to have a shortage of these days. Time is money, and trout are not money. You can buy them or earn them, but not spend them.

Like Ulysses and his oar, I earn these trout by wandering back into the hills and valleys until I find a place where, when I knock on a ranch-house door and ask permission to fish, the gentle folk within are startled, as if one of their Herefords just asked for a steak dinner. Where it is beyond anyone's comprehension why some fool would bother to ask to catch a trout. Like being a grizzly bear, it is a lonely life, but someone has to live it.

Streams usually cut a deep hole just below bridges. Abutments are spaced to accommodate normal water levels; during floods the widened current accelerates through the gap and carves away at the streambed. The hole on the downstream side of this one-lane wooden bridge, even in low August water, was "deep enough to float your hat," as an alcoholic ranch hand I worked with used to say. There was no railing and I leaned out the open window of the pickup and looked directly down into the deep water, thanking God it was not gin clear.

The pool was a translucent green, the color of a trillion phytoplankton yearning to breathe free. I reached into the ashtray for a new penny and dropped it into the pool, risking arrest for heavy-metals pollution. It disappeared a couple of feet below the surface. As it disappeared a fish tried for it, a green-silver curve deep in the water.

"How's it look?" Eileen asked, from the other side of the cab.

I turned and looked past her, upstream, where the shadows of cottonwood trees leaned across the water. The evening light between our bridge and the cottonwoods was filled with caddisflies, appearing white as they flew through the sun against the shadows, vibrating like a quick galaxy. "It looks good," I said. A blue heron took off, unfolding out of the shadows and heading upstream, made nervous by our stopping. Eileen pointed. "Too bad he left," I said. "I was going to ask how the fishing was."

The home place was a half-mile back, a two-story white frame house at the end of a gravel road bordered by more cottonwoods. The rancher had just sat down to eat, he said, otherwise he would have shown us where to fish, a half-mile downstream. "It's too thick by the bridge," he explained. "Lots of trees and willows. Not many folks fish there."

"That's okay," I said. "We'll take our chances." We thanked him, and he said if we were to come by again, just go ahead and fish, don't even ask. He'd know our outfit.

There was a place to pull off just on the other side of the bridge, a barbwire gate leading into a hay field. We sat on the tailgate and pulled on hip boots, then walked along the edge of the field to the cottonwoods, Eileen carrying the rod. Near the trees a whitetail buck jumped up from the tall grass, summer antlers full grown and thickened with velvet, as brick red as the rest of his body, and stood for one terrorized instant before running upstream through the trees, high tail visible like a firefly even after his body disappeared in shadow. We stood and watched, two clawless bears, then walked through low rose bushes under the trees to the edge of the stream. Both upstream and down from the cottonwoods we could see willows lining the bank, but the tall trees shaded out everything underneath them except the roses. Everywhere was the taste of late summer, heat and dust and the sweet-raw taste of willows and hay in our mouths.

A gravel bar angled across from the far shore, curving into the bank below us. On the far side the water looked deeper, and as we stood and looked I saw a trout rise in the bubbles below the bar.

"There's your trout," I said. That summer she had decided to learn to fly fish, as the water dropped and I started catching more trout on dry flies than she did on spinners. I pointed with my rod. "Over there, in the deep water."

She shaded her eyes and looked. "I can't see it."

"It looks like the bubbles, except slower." I watched and saw the same trout come up, and then another, farther downstream. "There's one below him now, in the slick water."

"I see that one. Are they eating those flies?" She pointed at the caddis in the air.

I shook my head. "They're rising too slow. Those are all in the air, anyway, not the water." I watched the trout rise again. "They probably eat anything that comes floating along." I squatted down and sat back on the edge of the bank, then eased my legs into the river, onto the firm gravel. Suddenly my feet felt pleasantly cool, and the shadows seemed cooler too, as if the riverbed held two rivers, one of water and one of cool air flowing just above the water. I turned and held her hand as she eased into the water, then started across, angling up the gravel bar, the water less than shin-deep. In the middle of the river I looked upstream. The water quickened again above the pool in front of us, but beyond I could see the current slowing into another pool.

We shuffled our feet slowly under the surface, moving within a short cast of where the lower trout rose. She whispered, as if we were stalking the whitetail buck, "Is the fly on my line okay?"

"You don't have to whisper," I said. "Just don't splash." She looked at me, frowning. She likes to get close to anything wild. She likes to fool all their senses, and was extremely disappointed to find wild turkeys can't smell. "Let me see it," I said. It was a small, sparse Elkhair Caddis that had been on the leader for a week now, since I'd last used the rod. I took a plastic container of line grease from my vest pocket and worked a little into the hair and hackle. It was an old fly, made before I started crushing every barb in the vise before I tied the fly, so I flattened the barb with the needle-nose pliers from my vest. "Okay," I said, letting the fly go. "Catch him."

She pulled some line from the reel and began false-casting, a little too fast.

"Wait on the backcast," I said. We'd gone through this all week, on the lawn.

She nodded, and did better. When she had enough line out she cast, the line landing in a snaking curve four feet below the fish. Her lips tightened and she breathed hard through her nose.

"That's okay," I said. "Its better if it isn't straight. Just let out a little more line and do the same thing again."

So she did, dropping two coils of line right on top of the trout's last rise.

"That's a little too much," I said. "He won't come up for a while now."

She shook her head, stripping in line. The coils caught one another and the line came up in a tangle. I held the rod while she picked at it. "You warned me," she said.

"About what?"

"About having to learn a whole new set of tangles."

"You remember. You always say there are too many things to remember."

"This is real—" She held up the tangled line. "None of that 'accelerate the cast' stuff." She smiled, looking up, the line finally untangled. "Now what?"

"The other's still rising, up in the bubbles."

She looked, bent forward like a heron. "Now I see him. When he comes up, it's like a longer, slower bubble."

I nodded. "Try to put it in the fast water at the edge of the rocks. Then let it float into the bubbles. He'll find it."

She nodded, very serious, and bent forward again when she let the line go. The fly landed perfectly at the base of the gravel bar. I lost it in the shadows but watched the yellow line. The trout curved up in the bubbles beyond the tip.

"He just took it."

She shook her head.

"Yes, he did. I saw him, right beyond your line."

"Then he didn't eat the fly. I never felt a thing."

"You don't feel them. You watch, then raise the rod."

"You never told me that part!"

"Well, it's obvious. Look at the slack in the line. You have to raise the rod to hook the fish."

"I never had to before."

"With lures you always have a tight line. With flies, you have to strike as soon as they take the fly. Otherwise they let it go."

"You mean they spit it out."

I winced. "You've seen a trout's mouth. They don't have spitting gear."

"That's not what Milo told me, that time we went fishing up Rock Creek. He said the trout spit my lure out."

"It's just something people say, Besides, you know Milo."

"Yes, and you know everything, but you don't tell me to raise the rod when the fish eats my fly."

I rolled my eyes. "Okay, okay. I thought you'd watched me enough to know."

She didn't say anything, just started casting again. She false-cast for a while, drying the fly, remembering that, and then let the line go. The sun had moved over the head of the pool, and I could see the fly floating between the bubbles, looking very phony. And then the trout took it, coming up in a curve so slow I could see his dorsal. "He—"I started to say, but the trout was already in the air.

"I got him!" she shouted. The trout jumped again, downstream, a rainbow bigger than I expected.

"Yes, you did."

She laughed. "What do I do?"

"The same thing you do with a lure. Let him go until he's tired. Let him have a little line if you think he's pulling too hard."

He jumped three more times, twice in the downstream shadows, then the last time upstream in the sunlight, so bright he almost hurt my eyes. After that he stayed underwater. She kept the rod up and when the trout began to tire I unhooked the net from the back of my vest and knelt down, feeling gravel and cool water under my knee, through the waders. "Back up and lead him over it," I said.

She held the rod up with both hands and waded backward, standing behind me, and the trout came up and slid over the black water and then over the aluminum rim. When I lifted the net he felt too heavy, like an aspirin bottle full of lead shot. I reached down and twisted the tiny fly out of his mouth, then held the net in the water, letting him breathe.

She squatted beside me, very elegant in jeans and hip boots, and looked at her trout. He had an olive back and a pale wash of pink over his gill covers and flanks, as if someone had painted a new chrome bumper with diluted nail polish. She shook her head. "Let me let him go," she said. I handed her the net. "He's heavy," she said, looking at me. I nodded. Then she tipped the net up and he went.

We straightened and looked upstream, at the bottom of the next pool. "Your turn," she said, and handed me the rod. I looked at her. "Thanks," she said. "Sorry I got mad."

I shrugged. "I've done it so long, I forget what I have to tell you."

She nodded. We walked up the gravel bar to the bottom of the next pool. The cottonwoods ended and there was a long stretch of undercut grassy bank above deep water. We stood and watched, but no trout came up.

"There has to be one in there," she said, whispering again.

I nodded. "Probably, if there are rainbows like you caught so close to the road." I took a small box from one of the bottom pockets of my vest and found a deer-hair grasshopper. I bit off the light tippet and tied the hopper onto the heavier leader, curling up the tippet and Elkhair Caddis and putting them in the box. Then I greased the hopper up like an English Channel swimmer.

The undercut was all in shadow and I first cast down at the tail, in six inches of water. At dusk you never know. Nothing happened, so I took a step upstream and cast again. By the time we'd reached the middle of the cut bank I had the range just right and was tossing the hopper into the loose overhanging grass about half the time, pulling it out to drop along the edge of the bank.

Then the water bulged up under the fly like the surface of a Florida pond when a sunken alligator decides to leave, and I jerked my rod hand slightly, involuntarily, and then stopped it voluntarily, because I could still see the fly. The slight jerk pulled the fly toward us, sinking it. Then it bobbed up again, and the trout hit it, head coming out of the water like a small gator. The rod was already halfway up from my involuntary jerk and the fish hooked itself when it turned back toward the cut bank, water flying. I leaned the rod sideways, trying to keep the fish out of the shadows, and the trout rolled on the surface.

"Brown," somebody said, and I realized it was me.

"Catch him," Eileen said. "Catch that sonofabitch." She gets like that, the city Irish kid who finally learned to fish. She would have been a good poacher, back in County Mayo, having that hard need to possess wild things, no matter what the cost.

The heavy tippet held and the trout held in the deeper water below the bank, bending the rod rhythmically in the slow cadence of a bass drum. I'd seen other big brown trout fighting the hook and could imagine his length bending, like a muscular hinge, as he tossed his head.

When that didn't do him any good he turned and headed downstream, through the shallow riffle, sucking the slack line through my fingers until it all disappeared and the reel whirred. I stuck my left hand inside the reel and touched the hardwound line to slow the spool. He made it over the lip of the bar and I followed, walking fast through the shallow water, not caring if I splashed now, feeling the trout tossing his head again as I wound line back onto the reel. I held the rod high, standing above him at the edge of the pool, feeling sweat on my forehead, suddenly cool in the evening. Then he stopped bending, holding steady in the stream. When I leaned back he came toward me, then ran across-stream, still strong but not uncontrollable, and I knew I had him.

Eileen knew it too. "Let me take the net," she said, standing behind me.

"I don't know if he'll fit." I pumped the rod now, dropping it as I reeled, then lifting again, and he came halfway across the pool, then ran again, not as strong.

She took the net anyway, unhooking it from my back, and by then I could see him, turning in the dark water. He was lean, not belly-heavy like the rainbow, lower jaw hooked like an osprey's. When I leaned back to try to move him toward the net he came and then turned again. Then I said the hell with it, I'd either break him off or land him, and brought him up and over the net, at the edge of the bar, and Eileen lifted.

His head hung just under the aluminum frame, but his tail stuck up above the other side. He was the color of the gravel under our feet, an old bronze, with red spots broken up by his scales. I breathed out and thought about killing him. He'd taste fine, cut into steaks and broiled with some butter and garlic and basil. Then I twisted the grasshopper out of the bone of his jaw and said, "Let's get him in the water."

We both knelt again, in the same place we'd knelt to release Eileen's trout. She dipped the net and I held the trout, both my hands under his lean belly, weightless in the current. His gill covers worked and he breathed among the bubbles.

"There's lots of air in that water," I said. Eileen nodded. "Sometimes I wonder," I said, holding the trout.

"Wonder about what?"

"Wonder about making trout swim up and down streams until they almost kill themselves."

She nodded again.

The trout moved in my hands. I took my upstream hand away, holding him gently by the wrist of his tail. Then he swam away, bending in a slow cadence, the same color as the new penny I dropped over the edge of the bridge.

"Next time, trout," I said. "Next time, I'll eat you."

A few years and three months later a high pressure system moved up from Utah. November fishing is like spring: better after two or three days of sun, in the afternoons when the chill is off the water. So we waited one day, worked the next morning, then headed for the bridge after lunch.

The leaves had been on the ground for three weeks now, all the grass and brush and trees along the river various shades of brown, from the bright tan crested wheatgrass to the rough gray-brown bark of cotton-woods to the smooth red-brown of peach-leaf willow. Even the wheat stubble had lost its metallic sheen. We didn't expect to jump a whitetail buck; by this time they'd be hiding back in the willow thickets, sensitive velvet stripped from their antlers.

But we did find tracks along the stubble edge, and fresh rubs on two alders when we entered the brush, the bark stripped away at high level. Looking closer, there were deep furrows in the green wood from a buck's antler tines. Farther on we found a piece of ground, as big around as a small coffee table, scraped bare under a hanging branch, with one clear hoofprint in the damp dark earth and a faint musk on the air. I pointed to the bare earth. Eileen nodded. The rut had begun, and a buck was baiting his rub-line like a trapper after mink.

Spring is thought of as the time of love, but that is mostly because of birds and bees, rather scatterbrained beings willing to make love in public. Many wild things replicate in fall, usually in secret places: whitetails in willow thickets, bighorn sheep in mountain cirques, and brown trout in the gravel of cold streams.

I used to write down dates of various wild matings I observed, but after a while learned that numbers don't make the best calendars. True, most temperature-zone animals mate at certain times of year, so their young (fawns, chicks, troutlings) will be born during a good period for survival. These deer, for instance, would mate over the next two to three weeks, across the middle of November, fawns gestating over about two hundred days to be born within the two or three weeks around June first, with the first summer burst of high-protein green. Similarly, brown trout would spawn now, eggs hatching in the first warming water of spring, insect life skittering over the creek-bottom gravel to gobble the first algae. Oh, how wise is Nature.

But how do they know? Most mating occurs when days are a certain length—what biologists call *photoperiod*. As the days shorten in fall, female brown trout grow orange eggs in their bellies, and male white-tailed deer rub the bark from alders with their antlers. Everything gets ready—and them boom, a year of lust gets packed into three weeks.

But the boom doesn't occur just because a certain day had nine hours and thirty-three minutes between sunrise and sunset. As a fisheries biologist friend put it, "Photoperiod is the dynamite, temperature is the blasting cap." The right temperature sets them off, trout and deer and birds and bees. No candlelight, no wine, no dancing. Just light and heat, or the lack thereof.

Eventually, I found my calendars nothing more than notes. It takes a few years to get the feel of light and heat, the peculiar combinations that bring the boom. Wild Merriam's turkeys usually begin gobbling in the hills beyond the river in mid-April, but if a late snowstorm comes down from Alberta they'll stop as if slapped. If the cold hangs around a few days, they'll huddle in the branches of ponderosa pines and say nothing, soaking up light and very little heat. But the first sunny day, with pasque flowers blooming along the edges of melting snow? Boom.

It becomes a combination of feel and observation, some of it direct: When whitetail bucks' necks swell, something is about to happen. But brown trout, I have found, don't begin spawning until the leaves fall from the cottonwoods. That could happen as early as mid-October in a cold year, or as late as the last week of the month in a warm one. (In the East there's the shadbush, a variety of the bush westerners call Juneberry or serviceberry, and Canadians call Saskatoons, that blooms when the shad run upstream to spawn. We once parked our pickup camper along the Delaware River around the first of May, and were eating our evening meal, after dark, when someone pounded hard on the door. "Are they here yet?" It was a young man who wanted to know if the shad were running. He'd seen a camper with a canoe on top and knew we had to be after shad; in the dark he couldn't see the Montana plates. In the morning I got up and stepped outside to see serviceberries—shadbushes—blooming on the hills above the river.)

It works in quirky ways. In early fall, the days shorter, male turkeys start to crank up their gobbles again, usually right after the equinox. The photoperiod isn't right—the day-length equivalent of late April would be late August—but it isn't until late September that the days are cool enough to delude them into thinking it's spring. About the same time a few male sharptailed grouse "dance" on flat-topped ridges, and ruffed grouse drum in the foothill aspens. They are all, of course, doomed to disappointment, because no matter what their light/heat clocks say, Nature won't let the females go along with off-season foolishness. (At least most of the time. Biologists have found newborn mule deer in every month of the year in Montana; Nature is not written in stone, and there has to be variation for evolution to work.)

I set my own inward clocks by signs both sensible and insensible: by the time of year, and the thickness of ice on the beaver ponds; by rubs on alders, and the feel of the air. And that day felt like brown trout spawning, and when they spawn, they attack anything that swims near them.

The sun was bright and warm, the air temperature around fifty degrees. That feels warm after a month of getting up before first light and walking through frost after grouse and deer. In early September we'd have worn wool jackets on days like this, but now I wore only a flannel shirt under my fly vest. The body adjusts.

One winter an arctic front came down and kept the temperature below minus-twenty for almost a week. Those were the daytime highs, with lows in the minus-forties, snow and wind mixed in. When the storm broke, the wind died and the sun came out. By nine o'clock, when everyone went to the post office, it was only fourteen below, and many were walking around in flannel shirts and down vests and beatific smiles, telling one another what a nice day it was.

So on this tropical November day I wore my flannel shirt, though Eileen wore a fleece-lined windbreaker. She also carried a spinning rod, since the wind blew in occasional whirling gusts, picking up cottonwood and alder leaves and spinning them onto the beaver ponds. (That is why she has never gotten really good at fly fishing; unless conditions are perfect she abandons it.) I stuck it out with a big rod, usually reserved for the Missouri.

We entered the river by the gravel bar where Eileen had caught her big rainbow years before. As we stood on the bank a big brown trout squirted up and over the bar, back out of the water. That would happen several times today. They live in three places in November: gravel so shallow nothing but a horny brown trout or a very flat frog would consider it habitable, the tails of pools, and the deep parts of the beaver ponds. They don't move into the ponds until October; before that the water is too warm.

I stepped down into the river itself and another, smaller trout zipped over the gravel bar. I shook my head, looking back at Eileen. She sat on the bank and eased into the water, then dusted the fragments of dry grass from the seat of her jeans.

"You want to try first?" I asked.

She nodded. We walked up along the gravel bar to the undercut bank where I'd caught the big brown. We hadn't caught him since that first time, perhaps because he really listened to my warning and headed some place safer. Very big trout sometimes do that.

But another not-quite-so-big trout had taken his place. He lived during most of the year under an overhanging alder at the head of the undercut. We caught him in spring by drifting a weighted Woolly Bugger, a fly that looks like a caterpillar with a peacock's tail, under the alders, then twitching it. We caught him in midsummer by waiting until dusk and swimming a fly imitating a tiny crayfish through the pool. We caught him in August by drifting a deer-hair grasshopper past the alders or along the undercut. We called him Harvey, because like Jimmy Stewart's rabbit, he was large and reliable.

We caught Harvey in November by standing far back from the undercut and slinging imitation minnows at him. I don't know when we found out that spawning brown trout go nuts over a floating minnow (either lure or deer-hair fly) twitched over their heads, but they do. They come up after it like a bass after a popping bug.

So Eileen stood back and cast carefully toward the deep water just downstream from the alders. The lure landed a little short, so she reeled in and cast again. This time it landed in the center of the pocket, and she turned the reel handle once to close the bail and take in slack line, then gently twitched the lure. It darted a few inches, wobbling once on its side, and the pale bronze side of a trout curved under it in the clear water, a small wave bumping the lure.

"There he is," she said, and twitched it again. And Harvey took it.

The water was too cold for him to jump, but he fought pretty hard. We netted him and the single hook at the rear of the lure fell out of his mouth. Eileen dipped the net into the stream and tilted it forward and Harvey went home.

We'd named him the fall before, after I'd taken a friend out fishing in mid-September and told him where to cast and what size trout he would catch. On his second cast he caught Harvey, right where I said he would. My friend turned to me and asked, "You know them all by name?"

There is some of that on any trout stream you really know. No stream, however, grows quite as predictable as the old story about the aging trout addict who dies and wakes up on the bank of a perfect English chalk stream, a ghillie standing over him, offering a beautiful cane rod.

"There's a good one rising on the far bank, sir," the ghillie says.

The dead angler rises to his feet, much spryer than before he died, and says, "But I can't cast that far."

"Try, sir," the ghillie says, lighting his pipe.

So the dead angler does, dropping the fly just above the rising trout, who takes it. It's a three-pound brown, which jumps once and then fights hard to the net. The ghillie releases it, then says, "There's another rising in the same place, sir."

The angler can't believe it, but casts perfectly again. The trout takes the fly, jumps once, and fights hard to the net, a three-pound brown just like the first one.

"This is amazing!" the angler says.

"Aye, sir," the ghillie says. "There's another one rising."

The angler casts again, catching another three-pound brown. After releasing it, another rises in the same place. The angler, by now sated with three-pound browns, asks if there are any bigger fish in the stream.

The ghillie shrugs. "There may be, sir, but the rules of the river state that you must cast to any rising fish. And there he is." A fish rises in the same place, looking to be another three-pounder.

So the angler casts again, and the fish turns out to be—surprise—another one-jump three-pounder. After a dozen fish, the angler turns to the ghillie and says, "This doesn't seem much like Heaven to me."

The ghillie lights his pipe again. "Nobody said it was, sir."

Our river never quite became that predictable, despite Harvey. A wild river changes. The beavers came the second year. They built five dams on the mile-long stretch we called our own, changing some holes, widening others, and after another year left. As the dams settled and rotted and washed out, and the bottoms of the pools silted in, the stream changed again each spring.

One year a hot drought persisted from June through early September. Yellowstone Park burned, and the next year all streams were reduced to a two-trout limit. None of the locals who very infrequently fished our stream bothered to show up. "Hell," they said, "It ain't worth buyin' a fishin' license for only two trout." They said this despite the fact that most of them never bought a license in the first place.

We never saw a wader track all summer. The drought hadn't affected the stream at all, and we caught more and bigger fish than we'd ever seen. Harvey seemed average.

Each year we learned a little more about the river, and it came to live on the edges of our minds, always there, like someone you live with and love, almost taken for granted but somehow surprising you every now and then, with reminders of why you love them. A river you live with every day and then, on occasions, want with all your being: a trout stream named desire.

November fishing always seemed like the last days with someone before going on a long trip. So on that day we fished slowly after Eileen caught Harvey, knowing that another good storm would send the fish into semi-hibernation, even if the season lasted until the end of the month. The next pool was a hole below one of the beaver dams, dug during high water when the current fell over the latticed willows. I worked my way upstream along the far bank, shook out some line and rollcast downstream, then flicked it upstream, the big Muddler Minnow settling onto the still water just below the dam, the leader draped over a willow branch sticking out from the dam. I let the current pull the fly slowly over the branch and it drifted free.

"Good going," Eileen said, standing in the shallow water below the pool.

"Thank you," I said, and twitched the fly. Two trout rolled at it, and when I twitched it again, one chased the other away, then darted back and slashed at the fly. I lifted, and the big Muddler came past my head with a sound like a malevolent insect.

"Good going," Eileen said again.

"I don't think he really had it," I said. I grinned, like a raccoon baring his teeth at headlights. "It warn't my fault, woman."

She smiled. "Never is."

But he hadn't felt the hook, so I cast again and got him, a hard-bodied foot-long trout that I whacked on the head and put in the creel. Then I whacked my hand on the thigh of my wader; holding him was like holding a chunk of ice.

We fished upstream, taking turns at each of the familiar pools. That river has a pool every hundred feet, most built like the pools in instructional trout books. There were hard-turn-under-the-alders pools, cut-bank pools, log pools, and gravel-bar pools. There were the beaver ponds and even some pools not found in texts, though they are common enough in the West: the leaning-barbwire-fence pool, the eroding-buffalo-bones pool, and the '37 Pontiac pool. They all had brown trout, and we caught or turned fish at each one, even catching a couple of rainbows from the beaver ponds.

Then we reached the last barbwire fence, beyond which was another ranch, where we had permission to hunt but not to fish, an odd situation you sometimes run into in eastern Montana. Deer eat haystacks, trout don't. A fox jumped from some rose bushes beside the stream and ran under the fence. The sun was an hour above the mountains.

"I'm cold," Eileen said. She had her jacket zipped up to her nose.

"Yeah, the trout are too." We hadn't turned a fish for twenty minutes. She shoved her hands in her pockets and sat in the sun on top of the bank while I cleaned the three fish we'd kept, two browns and a rainbow. One brown was a female that Eileen had hooked deep; I kept the eggs too, sliding them back into the trout after pulling out the gills and guts. The brown trout male oozed white milt, but the rainbow was sterile, autumnal photoperiod all wrong for his rhythms.

But the sudden cold touched something in us. Light and heat (or lack of it) make wild animals do other things besides reproduce. In squirrels and woodchucks and bears, they bring on a late fall lassitude, the slowing we call hibernation or estivation, according to our own definitions of rhythm.

Whatever. It touched us both. After cleaning the trout and placing them head to tail in the creel, I lifted my own head, like a bear's. It smelled like winter. To the southwest were hard gray clouds, tight above the mountains. Tomorrow they'd cover most of the sky. Tomorrow, like bears, we'd leave the stream alone. That is what winters are for.

A Moveable Feast

By Christopher Camuto

ONE OF MY FAVORITE READING DISCOVERIES OF THE EARLY 1990S WAS the first book by a young man Nick Lyons had recommended that I read as soon as possible.

The writer was Christopher Camuto, and the book was his wonderful *A Fly Fisherman's Blue Ridge*, published by Henry Holt in 1990.

Like Hemingway's young Nick in his short story "Big Two-Hearted River" Chris Camuto is willing to shoulder a pack and work as hard as necessary to find trout fishing in a wild and natural setting, someplace the crowds haven't yet found and spoiled. For Chris, as it is to many of us I'm sure, the camping is part of the total experience he seeks. Numbers of fish and sizes of fish don't necessarily figure into the equation. Being close to nature and peeking in on undisturbed wildness is what this kind of fishing is all about.

Unlike Hemingway's Nick, a short story invention, Chris' stories are about the real deal, accounts of his fishing experiences in the Great Blue Ridge Mountains, kingdom of remote tiny streams, rushing between deep-shadowed, rhododendron-lined banks beneath the folded hills. Camping and fishing in this area, Chris Camuto finds his own "Big Two-Hearted" experiences, but not without effort. Our heritage of pure rivers and wild trout in wilderness settings has been sold off, Chris bitterly reminds us. But what is left out there is still worth seeking, enjoying, and protecting.

As you enjoy "The Moveable Feast" Chris Camuto will share with you the possibilities that still await the enterprising trout angler.

Truth to tell, there is little romance left along the American road. In the east you are rarely treated to even the illusion of unruined space. The green breast of the New World has, for the most part, been franchised off to the beaming people who would have the rest of us make passionate distinctions between subspecies of cheeseburgers, or soft drinks, and for whom a trip to the mall is a solution to the angst that rears its head during nightly newscasts about toxic waste, world deforestation, and an Earth atmosphere that has begun to resemble Venus's.

Once a bucolic rite of spring, the gentle art of fly fishing has become more like an act of guerrilla warfare. I get on the road each year with some trepidation, and when I find the clear, cold, unpolluted water trout love, I fish with the pleasant if uneasy sensation that I have slipped behind enemy lines.

If the Blue Ridge suffers the indignity of a highway running along its crest for hundreds of miles, at least the CCC boys who built the Blue Ridge Parkway banked the curves and graded the dips and rises to fit the rhythm of the country music I prefer to listen to on the road. Get under way before the Winnebagos start to spawn during Memorial Day weekend and you can drive in time to the rockabilly that booms out of Winston-Salem and crackles up from Greenville. Or stash some tapes in the cab and let the perfect phrasing of Emmylou Harris's sweet voice lead you on.

The geography of the Blue Ridge helps sustain some useful illusions, and if you want the trout you catch to seem to be an enduring part of an untrammeled landscape, a modest illusion or two is worth packing along. If you follow the Blue Ridge's north–south axis and stay within its slender bounds, traveling as you would, say, in Chile, you can come away with a sense of endless mountains that give birth to an inexhaustible brood of rivers. Fly fishing is probably more a homage to the past than an act of faith in the future, but it is difficult to fish a region with expanding affection if you sense you are on the verge of using it up. It helps to be able to sense good water upstream and down, beyond the reach of a day's fishing, and rivers to fish beyond the rivers on this year's itinerary.

In short, there are enough miles of bright water in the Blue Ridge to support the fly fisherman's deep-seated need to believe in infinite possibilities. But only just. You can't get lost, physically or spiritually, in the Blue Ridge as you can in Montana or Alaska—for better or worse, you always know where you are. Some Blue Ridge trout streams flow within a hundred miles of Washington, D.C., and others within fifty miles of Atlanta. And although all the rivers eventually run unto the sea, most detour now through mall fountains from Fairfax to Spartanburg, jetting ignominiously for a few seconds into the greenish glow that keeps shoppers schooled at store counters like bream at the edge of a pond. The borders of the Blue Ridge are sharply drawn, and you know what to expect if you go too far.

By chance, my first trip to North Carolina was shrouded in minor visual illusions that gave the fishing a dreamlike cast, dampened as it was by a constant rain and enclosed in shifting mists. One May I drove two hundred miles south without escaping the nagging low front that pelted me with rain when I packed the truck at home. I had barely been able to glimpse the mountains as I drove, except for where the parkway descended into the wind gaps that dipped beneath the cloud cover. While concentrating on the soft white haze into which the yellow center lines curved back and forth, I could feel the dark bulk of the invisible mountains that surrounded the road and the bright empty spaces beyond the overlooks.

As I drove south into new country I couldn't quite see, I could feel the gradual rise in terrain and the broadening of the Blue Ridge as it gathered itself for its meeting with the Black Mountains just north of Asheville. I couldn't tell for sure, but I seemed to be getting somewhere. North Carolina was not New Zealand, but I had a week and two new rivers to fish.

After a night in an empty public campground, I backpacked off into the mist and rain within which I could feel dome-shape mountains and bowl-shape coves. Even half hidden, the horizon somehow projected the perfectly balanced succession of images and afterimages—mountain and cove, ridge and ravine, peak and saddle—that constitute the larger symmetry of Blue Ridge terrain. And although at first I couldn't see more than fifty feet down the trail or into the woods, I could feel the promising continuity of the mountains underfoot.

The constant rain and the steamy green warmth of the cove forest into which I descended seemed full of life, dense and various and growing at all points. The scale of growth was larger than I was used to. Hemlocks, pines, and the hardwoods I recognized grew much larger than they did in the hollows of Virginia. The woods were full of unfamiliar fern and wild-flowers. The rhododendron that were mere shrubs along streams familiar to me were trees here, and the sound of water dripping and smacking on their thick leaves was louder than the incessant shushing of the rain into the dense boughs of the evergreens or its staccato pattering into the tender, half-grown hardwood canopy.

The trail followed a ridgeline for a half mile before switchbacking down the steep head of a cove. Visibility improved a bit as I descended and left the clouds on the slope above me, but the rain kept on and a shifting mist hung in the air. When the mist brightened or gusted open, I got a clearer glimpse of the contour of the cove, a two-tiered amphitheater of unbroken green that opened toward the east. Runnels of muddy water braided gullies into the trail, but elsewhere the dense vegetation held all the moisture in place, suspending it in a kind of natural reservoir. The incessant rain was distributed drip by drip from canopy to glistening understory and then into a rich, deep mat of mossy soil.

I was listening for a hint of the river at the bottom of the switchbacks that dropped me into the head of the cove when I came on a spike buck browsing alongside the trail. The deer stopped and looked at me naively for a full ten seconds, tilting its head as if to resolve me into focus, before it decided I was really there. When it turned and bounded off, the watershed seemed less empty, and I heard a murmur of running water in the silence the deer's departure made.

I shucked the pack and stashed it beside the trail, grabbed the rod and vest, and then threaded myself through a game trail that bent distinctly into the rhododendrons. The muffled sound I heard through the rain wasn't so much a stream as a dark tangle of water and rhododendron roots, an arm-wide ribbon of water that burrowed a faint channel through the vegetation. There at the head of the cove, the terrain seemed to be holding the river back, hoarding it in the dense undergrowth. Balked every few feet by dams of dead rhododendron leaves and diverted by tiny deltas of clayey soil flecked with quartz, the miniature river was perfectly clear and colder, much colder, than the rain.

The upper cove sloped so gently the stream barely grew for the first half mile, emerging from the rhododendrons only to bog down in a sunken old field of grass tussocks cut up by innumerable deer tracks and guarded by a raucous jay that harassed me as I sloshed along. One slope of the cove eventually came nearer and then disappeared beneath the emerging riverbed where the terrain folded sharply. Beyond the fold the upper cove dropped abruptly into the larger amphitheater of the main watershed.

The ribbon of water pooled above the drop and then arced twenty feet before catching itself in a long cascade down the broken bedrock exposed along the fold. A river took shape in the air, and from where I stood at the top of the drop I could see a series of inviting, dun-colored pools leading downstream from the foot of the cascade.

I once briefly dated a woman who thought all trout streams looked alike. The first one I took her to was lovely, the second interesting, the third a pleasant reminder of the first two. The fourth apparently began a redundancy that quickly led to trouble. If nothing else, this served to remind me that fly fishing for wild trout is an acquired obsession. If the obsession deepens on home water, where a fly fisherman learns the knack of successful return, it broadens on new water, which offers a chance to begin again—a minor excuse to start over that certain simple souls crave.

If the way a river slides darkly along an undercut bank, or purls through pocket water, or holds its breath in the still water of a pool is always and everywhere the same, those similarities hardly count as defects in the eyes of a fisherman. Nature is not the avant garde. Beneath the picturesque similarities are differences worth getting into a river to pursue.

I lost the first fish I hooked in this promising new stream, a stout twelve-inch rainbow that took a wet fly I fished from the bank into the tail of that first plunge pool. I looped a ropy cast across the pool without stopping to shake off the dulling effect of the rain and the walking. Although I saw the trout come out of hiding to follow the fly as it swung through the current, my damp reflexes were slow to fire. The fish was upstream of me and in the air before my mind had closed around the take.

The rainbow was beautiful breaking the water each time, and with each twisting rise and fall my heart leapt and fell and I knew I would lose it. But with each charge into the dark-green recesses of the pool, when I could feel the trout's firm intentions telegraphing through the graphite, I thought, *Yes, you've got him, just stay tight to the fish.* I started anticipating the jumps and deliberately leaned a bit of slack toward the commotion when the trout was in the air. I thought I had caught up to its moves when it jumped for the fifth or sixth time, silver and rose against the cascading whitewater. I can still see it at the apogee of its last leap before it collapsed into the froth—wet fly hung in the corner of its mouth, game as a billfish.

The slack felt terrible. I cursed myself and milled around stupidly, trembling with a spike of adrenaline I no longer needed. The worst part of losing good fish is that you cannot release them. They tailwalk across the back of your mind for days.

I left the rod and vest where I now knew the river began and bush-whacked back to the main trail to retrieve my pack. I made camp about a mile downstream of where I had started fishing and then threaded my way back upstream through the witch hazel and rhododendron that picketed the river. The ledge and the cascade where the river began was obscured by foliage. When I approached the spot from downstream, the river seemed to come out of nowhere.

All the way to camp the river was full of wild rainbows that came recklessly to the fly and fought hard once hooked. They grabbed flies like trout that hadn't been fished over, coming confidently out of hiding for buggy wets and emergers and for big hairwing dry flies I drifted and twitched on the rain-pocked surface of the river. I had only to work my way slowly through the archway of shrubbery and flick a short length of line downstream toward obvious lies. I had a pleasant sense that my knowledge of the river was growing exactly as the river grew.

Even in the rain the river ran clear, and the sound and feel of it rushing downstream led me through the obscure afternoon. I waded the stream for passage, lowering myself from level to level where it stepped abruptly down the mountain. Except for the deer and the jay at the head of the river, the woods were silent and motionless. Except for the trout, life seemed hidden.

In front of a smoky fire that evening, I traced the day's fishing in my mind. I was sorry to have found no brook trout in the river, but the rainbows I landed and released were beautiful streambred fish, their silver, black-spotted flanks brush-stroked with iridescent rose along their center line and dabbed on their gill covers. The younger fish were marked with inky ovals that looked like fresh fingerprints. *Salmo irideus*. I liked the obsolete classification. The taxonomists might have taken the *rainbow* out of the name, but in hand the fish fairly glowed with the vermilion iridescence that leaves such a distinct trace in the mind. Rainbow. Whitewater trout full of western zest. You could sense a deep determination in them.

The rain never stopped on that trip. I fished for five days in the shifting mists and the foggy silence that was broken only by my own shuffling through the woods or the current and by the appearance of trout around the fly. To an observer I might have looked a bit forlorn wading and casting slowly in the rain, catching and releasing trout with such regularity that catching trout might have seemed not to be the point.

I was hardly in virgin territory, but for a few miles the river seemed untouched. I fished it down to its confluence with its sister stream and fished down the main stem until hatchery trout and the unmistakable signs of other fishermen began to undo the illusion. I flushed a pair of wood ducks from a pool at an old mill dam. The ducks rose low and fast off the water twenty feet in front of me and flew downstream, the male an unmistakable blur of color. I caught nothing but hatchery fish in the mill pool and killed three of these for dinner.

The next day I started back up the sister stream, a not-quite mirror image of the first, and for a day or two fished with the pleasant sensation that I had unbroken country before me, half a continent, say, of ridges and darkly forested coves and cold, clear-flowing streams full of wild trout.

There was, of course, no such expanse of unbroken country, but every May I have found good water to fish in the mountains of North Carolina between Blowing Rock and Brevard. The Blue Ridge reaches its greatest height and breadth there, and where those cove forests are left alone, pine and hemlocks and Appalachian hardwoods grow slowly toward their former grandeur, sheltering a world that has more variety of native plant and animal life in it than all of Europe. In the steepest, rockiest watersheds, irreplaceable fragments of trout streams drop over the rough terrain and flow quietly through forested river bottoms hidden in the quiet, cathedral depths of the coves.

The good trout water left in the mountains flows through what used to be called "the back of beyond," an Irishism, I believe, for mountaineer country. Bright creeks and runs thread their way around small mountain farms and hamlets and flow through dark river bottoms between hog-backed ridges. Forest Service roads, graded and graveled for the lumber trucks that keep the mills at Lenoir and Hickory busy, follow the rivers as best they can, but you will inevitably find yourself hiking down a steeply pitched trail to get to the good water. You are likely to pass the remains of an old still or the shotgunned carcass of an ancient Ford tucked away in the underbrush. You will see the remains of old cabins and homesteads as well as well-tended graves remembered with wildflowers or decorated with bits of pottery and quartz. The rivers are known locally more for the havoc they create when they flood, but in their headwaters they are fine trout streams. I know them mostly as late-spring streams, still flowing with a bite in their tumbling currents, but settled down from the high-water days of April.

I think of yellow birches, large *Ephemera* spinners, and rising brown trout when I think of Wilson Creek. There is a stretch of river I remember as much for a stand of yellow birches where I camp when I fish there as for the brown trout that inhabit the rocky pools bordered by the birches. I make a good trout camp there every year in the middle of May, and although the spot is three hundred miles from my house, when I get to that stand of birches and see the river sliding by I feel like I am home. In mid-May, when there are simultaneous spinner falls and hatches in the evening, the big browns, which are hard to catch during the day, come out of hiding to take the insect life coming and going.

I try to fish well on Wilson Creek because I know there are good trout in the river and because the river is so excellent it instantly commands a fisherman's respect. Certain rivers do that. You fish them as if someone were watching you. The Wilson Creek watershed has been logged and burned and flooded out during the last century in an almost biblical series of calamities, but nothing has ever broken the wild heart of the river or tainted its cold, crystalline flow. I have caught wild browns and rainbows in Wilson Creek, and I am told if you fish up far enough you will find a remnant brook trout population in the headwaters. I have fished pretty far up the river and not found the brook trout, but I believe they are there.

Perhaps there are no ideal rivers, but when I am watching a brown trout rise in the buttery water from the edge of my camp on Wilson Creek in the evening, I am not so sure. While dinner cooks itself and the trout rises in front of me, I can sit in the shadows, drink coffee, and wait for deer to appear in the half-light of the opposite bank. A belted kingfisher may chatter loudly over the river or a scarlet tanager flit silently through the understory. Pleasing colonies of wood fern grow profusely around camp, which, beyond the birches, is surrounded by Catawba rhododendron. The large purple flowers of the rhododendron put a subtle perfume in the warm evening air. The last long fingers of sunlight spotlight the painted trillium, fire pinks, and yellow lady's slipper that grow in open patches near fallen trees. As those last rays of daylight lift into the canopy, they briefly light the stately pink and white bloom of the tulip poplars that have flowered overhead.

A short walk would flush grouse, bring me to a bear-slashed tree, or bring to mind the stocky timber rattlers tucked away in the brushy slopes of the cove. Somewhere nearby wild turkey scratch for mast hidden in the leaf litter. As the woods lose light, raccoons slip from trees and make their way cautiously to the riverbank to fish while owls rouse themselves to hunt.

The brown trout rising in front of me is unaware of anything except the spent mayfly spinners drifting helplessly toward it. The spinners are plentiful, and so the trout's rises are timed as much to its hunger as to the availability of food. At no other time of the year does it have so much choice.

The trout's mouth breaks the surface of the river when it intercepts an insect. The white gape of the fish is odd to see. Sometimes it lifts itself high enough to bring its eye out of the water. When it slips back under the surface of the river it leaves a bubble in the spot. When the trout sinks beneath the opaque disturbance of its rise, the concentric waves of the riseform expand from that point, encouraging you to think of the trout's rise as a kind of center. If you keep watching that spot in the river, the rise will begin to seem like a pulse, as if the river were throbbing in the trout.

In the morning, before breakfast, I fish the stretch of river immediately below camp. The months collapse and fold in the coves, and there is an early April chill in the May morning. Sunlight comes late to the bottom of the cove. The river is dark, and its currents cold and confusing. Wading begins to wake me. I skirt the deep water, content to shuffle knee-deep through syrupy riffles. I don't like wading deep too early in the day—something about the river getting too much of a hold on me when the world is so quiet and I am only half conscious.

I move along slowly, casting myself awake. No insects are coming off the river. I cast too much at first, undoubtedly spooking trout I cannot yet see in the dark, wrinkled water. I strike slowly at takes and miss them, regretting without emotion each missed fish that tugs free. As I fish, I watch the line of sunlight advance slowly through the woods. I come out of the river when I see the line reach camp.

I cook breakfast and make a pot of fresh coffee on a backpacking stove perched on a mossy stump between the tent and the river. The tedium of camp chores complements the tedium of fly fishing nicely. There is always something simple to do—rebuild leaders, patch waders, chop wood. Routines underwrite the general pleasure of camp life. The line between work and rest vanishes.

I watch the river and the woods as I eat, thinking only that the clarity of morning light is humbling to thought. Along a river in the morning, the world meets you squarely. My impulse is to watch and listen, as if I might absorb the frankness that seems to hover in the air around me. The river slides by, patient and insistent, as generous and unforgiving as time.

A camp stakes a pleasant, temporary claim on a river. The pack and the tent, the makeshift kitchen and the small fire ring become a provincial capital from which you venture out each day with a larger stake in the river than the day fisherman. You've made a place on the river. You are always fishing either out from or back toward camp, and this gives a slightly more emphatic direction to the day's journey. When you come back to camp, you see familiar order in a strange place. Your time on the river runs a little deeper because you eat and sleep there.

The longer you stay camped on a river, the more you find yourself doing what any animal does: You sit still and watch the world around you very carefully in order to understand your place in it. You lean toward your first response to things: What is that? Looking and listening come to dominate your thinking. You see the order you have imposed does not extend far. You note how the short, faint trails of your knowledge give out when you look at the details of the world around you. You try to sharpen your thoughts against a growing awareness of the limitations of your senses, even while those senses expand their customary reach. You watch the river constantly.

The best water on the river is upstream of camp. I save that quarter mile of deep, well-wrought pools for evenings. Below the easy morning stretch of water, the river drops rocky and white and forms deep, green pools and narrow runs closely guarded by shelving of gray slickrock on one side and dense vegetation on the other. Below the rocky, mountainous stretch, the river flows more broadly and with a gentler gradient, like a quiet forest stream. The character of the river and the logic of its landscape has determined that a two-hour hike downstream will give me a full day's fishing back to camp.

A good stretch of river is never the shortest distance between two points. River time is slow and convoluted, and when I concentrate and fish deliberately hours disappear into pools, diffuse themselves in riffles, and contract in the eddies where I wait for good trout to show themselves. I don't think about it while I fish, but all day the river does what it will with my time. I know that all the studied, somewhat pretentious practices of fly fishing—the slow progress of wading, the metronomic beat of casting, the watching and waiting and fussing with flies and tackle—only serve to create the illusion that I am in control, making the moves and choices.

The practice of fly fishing is pitted against the resistance of rivers. The resistance you feel in a river all day is real, at times almost animate. Working upstream through rushing water and over jumbled, broken bedrock may just be an ordinary day's fishing back to camp, but some days the fishing becomes an odd travail only fishermen who wade rivers understand. No creature experiences a river the way a wading fisherman does. Some days you look up and see camp before you even thought about keeping an eye out for it. You notice the long, low angle of sunlight poking through the trees west of you, and you hear the changed sound in the late-afternoon woods brought on by the coolness that has crept back into the air. Perhaps a woodpecker starts knocking on a distant tree, or a wood thrush darts across the stream, its long, glossy tail catching the late light.

You didn't know the day was half over and all of a sudden you have an acute sense of how brief a day is. You are not thinking of yourself so much as the day and everything in it—the river, the life around you, even the sound and odor of things. Being in the river all day has put you inside of its sinuous, convoluted time, and suddenly you feel you have shared the day, and lost it, with everything around you. And even though the river worked against you and, in some sense, betrayed you, you miss the nagging force of its current when you wade to shore and suddenly feel alone, even though you have been alone all day.

If you get down in a cove forest in the back of beyond and spend a day wading up a mountain stream that hasn't lost its spring snappishness, quietly concentrating on your fishing, the river will make you feel time pass that way. But because the river is so beautiful and was so truthful when it whispered in your ear all day that time was going—that your time and all time was going—you do not begrudge whatever in you it has taken away and you do not take lightly whatever you have taken from it.

If there is, on certain rare occasions, a reason for killing a wild trout, perhaps it is to symbolize the way you feel time in the river. River fishermen do not talk about this among themselves because it is understood; they do not tell others about it, because it is something only rivers teach. But they teach others to wade and cast and do the menial things fly fishermen do so that some day they, in turn, might feel the insistent, mortal tug in a river and be educated to understand the beauty of being and time the way a heron, or a fox, or a trout might be thought to understand such things.

You do not feel time in the river every time you fish, but sooner or later you will feel it. Some day you will reel in and turn your back on a river to wade toward shore, and you will see, or hear, or smell something and a sharp sense of time passing will come on you like joy, or fatigue. It will send a little shiver up your spine, and you will feel grateful and afraid. Then you will busy yourself with some practical task, and the fear and the gratefulness will subside.

Once you have felt it, you will understand why it is important to fish a good river properly. The intensity of the feeling will recede, and its relevance will often seem obscure, but every time you hike through a forest to measure off a length of river for a day's fishing, you will take a deep, unconscious pleasure in every downstream stride. The day's way back is the river's way. It will take you longer, and you will be hard-pressed to say where, exactly, the time went. That is what the river is for.

So I mark off two hours downstream on Wilson Creek to give me a day's fishing coming back.

I skirt the river so as not to disturb it, following a vague network of trails around impenetrable rhododendron thickets. Moving quietly over soft mats of brown pine needles, I enjoy the cool quiet of morning in the cove. The forest floor is lit here and there by shafts of sunlight that highlight a seamless reach of growth and decay. I keep an eye out for wildflowers and timber rattlers. The terrain forces me back and forth across the river several times, and at each ford I'm tempted to start fishing.

By the time I wade into the shallow tail of a pool to start fishing, the morning coolness has dissipated and the world around the river has grown quiet and warm. There is a special kind of silence in the woods in May. Rivers have subsided from the boisterousness of April. The summer buzz of insects has not started. Fresh, intermittent breezes rustle the crowns of trees, but the air over the river is still.

Wilson Creek is wide enough so that the canopy does not close over it. The river seems to follow the blue strip of sky overhead, flowing olive in its shaded depths and amber through its sunlit riffles. I fish slowly all day through its cool, lively water, taking time.

Two separate cascades of water spill into the first pool, creating a double current. There is a vee of dark green water upstream of where the currents converge. An Elk Hair Caddis turns a pleasing length of brown trout in the notch of the vee. The fly rocks on the wake of the refusal.

I wait and eye the spot while changing flies. The trout is not rising, and nothing is coming off the river. I shoot a sidearm cast low over the pool. A small Adams appears on the water, drifting freely.

The amber arc turns up toward the surface again and comes back with the fly, taking it just before it washes out of the vee.

The trout feels like a part of the river broken free, a slice of current out on its own. The rod plays the fish, which has few options. One charge left, one charge right, then it holds deep. I bring it in green rather than let it sulk and strain at the bottom of the pool. When the brown stops swirling in the water around my knees, I see that the fish is unusually dark and stout—a little larger than I thought.

I hold the mahogany trout on its side in the water and slip it off the fly with the help of hemostats. I right the fish and gentle it back and forth until it shivers out of my loose grip and holds in the stillwater, balanced on flared pectorals. When I straighten up, it glides a few feet away and then holds at the edge of the current against which it seems to rub itself. When it noses into the main current, it is pushed back out until it finds the right angle of attack and shoots effortlessly forward to the head of the pool.

Unless you are a trophy hunter, a fourteen-inch brown trout represents a kind of perfection, the platonic form of what a wild brown should be. The color and markings of the fish complement its size perfectly, as if it had grown to just the right proportions. A fourteen-inch fish is large for a mountain stream, but not a gargantuan anomaly. You can't brag about it. The brown is old enough to be wily, but because it inhabits freestone water, it is not impossibly selective. The fish doesn't make you a hero for catching it. When you tell someone about it later, you will call it a "nice trout" with a precise degree of emphasis that another fly fisherman will recognize and appreciate. He or she will see it in the mind's eye with uncanny accuracy—a fourteen-inch brown. Yeah. Nice trout.

This brown trout turns out to be the best fish of the day. I fish Wilson slowly but steadily all day, taking the water on its own terms. I fish dry flies—Adams, sulfurs, caddis—on the flat, slow water, Zug Bugs and Tellicos—Carolina standbys—in the deep white slots. I drift black woods crickets into the stillwater around juicy cover, twitching them to entice sulking trout. Small rainbows charge almost anything I put on the water. They remind me of brook trout. The more numerous browns are more selective. They take a longer look and sip flies down a little fastidiously, sometimes forcing me to come back with a lighter tippet and a smaller fly.

I fish as well as I can, and the river doles out an unspectacular mix of success and failure. Camp slides into view before I think to watch for it. A breeze rises, and evening begins to close around the river.

Days on rivers end in pools. After supper I head upriver with a cup of coffee and a fly rod. I am tired of reading water and of wading against the river. I am tired of casting. I am even tired of paying attention to the world around the river. I want an easy fish to end the day, a decent trout from a still pool.

Stillwater. I rarely fish ponds or lakes, but a deep, still pool in a mountain stream is a different kind of stillness, like the stillness within a heartbeat. In the evening, a large pool in a trout stream represents pure possibility.

It is too early for the spinner fall, so there are no rising fish. I leave the coffee mug on a boulder and wade back into the river. The cup looks absurd sitting there. The sun is not a half hour set, but a murky twilight is already flowing out of the heavy timber of the bottom of the cove. I tie on a fly I can see, an Elk Hair Caddis or a light-colored hair wing.

No false casting. Quiet. I let the fly trace the imperceptible motions of the surface of the pool. A tuft of tan elk hair wanders around the dark water as if it were on its own. Wait. Tail. Wait. Near side. Now midpool. Wait. The dark water rumples.

The fish feels strong, but not large. When I try to force it to the back of the pool, it holds the fly rod trembling in a deep arc. I let it take line back into the pool. The reel makes a brief squawk. I hold the fly rod high and let the trout tire itself. The river feels like a stage. Perhaps it is the half-light, or my fatigue, or the urgent feel of the fish trying to get back into the river.

Back in camp, I shave dry heartwood from a split quarter of pine and nurse a handful of flame out of the curled shavings. I build a fire around the blackened coffee pot. Resinous smoke rises from the kindling. The pungent odor of the wet Carolina woods mingles with the woodsmoke.

Spinners come to lantern light while I tend gear, the large *Ephemeras* on which the trout feast at night. I find them crawling across the contours of the maps laid out under the lantern, deceived by their glossy surfaces. There are large reddish spinners, clear in the body and blackened in places, their tails and forelegs enlarged for mating. These have clear, diaphanous wings etched with fine black lines. And there are large yellow spinners with nearly opaque, sulfur-colored wings, which they hold slightly folded as they walk across the maps of the rivers I plan to fish. When I kill the lantern, the spinners fly to the dying fire.

When camp chores are done, I rebuild the fire. The pitch of river-sound changes randomly, as if the river was shifting around in the dark. A slosh of Jack Daniels in a Sierra cup takes the edge off the coffee and seems to set the day back in a frame. I can see the trout I released back to the olive water of Wilson Creek swim off behind the flames.

If you drew a circle with a radius that stretched from my campfire on Wilson Creek to the Linville Gorge, twelve miles away, you would capture some fine wild trout water within it. I can see those rivers in the fire: Harpers Creek below the falls, Gragg Prong above Lost Cove, Lost Cove Creek in the deep recesses of the darkest cove in the mountains, where outsize timber rattlers guard trout pools and send many a fisherman back up the trail. I can see the nameless tributary of a hard-fished river where the largest brown trout I have seen in the mountains swims like a lord in the small stream's one good pool. The pool is impossible to fish. There is no place from which to cast, no way to cast into it. The pool forces you to watch, as the good places on trout streams often do, and the large brown swims and feeds as if it knows it is beyond reach.

Farther south I can see Curtis Creek and Shining Rock and, beyond Asheville, the Davidson. Most years I end May on the Davidson. The river will be crowded, but I'll fish a late afternoon and evening through the riffles below Avery Creek, casting long for the pleasure of it. I like to work this stretch fishing downstream, covering the beautiful water systematically, reaching toward possibilities difficult to make out under the choppy surface. I swing nymphs and emergers through every inch of water. Every so often a good rainbow will grab the fly, and I will have a tight line to the river.

In the mornings I like to fish the Davidson above the hatchery, where it is a small mountain stream. I'll fish dry flies upstream until the ledgerock pools begin to look like the pools on the North Fork of the Moormans and I start to think about heading home.

On Wilson Creek I can see the fading coals from where I lie in the tent. Occasionally a breeze rekindles the fire and small flames dance silently in the ring of stones. When the fire rises, I watch the glow of firelight on birch bark and listen to the river flow slowly in the dark.

A new edition of *A Fly Fisherman's Blue Ridge*, from which "A Moveable Feast" was excerpted, was published by The University of Georgia Press in the spring of 2001.

Thread of the River

By Odell Shepard

THE CLASSIC BOOK *THY ROD AND THY CREEL* BY ODELL SHEPARD WAS
first published in 1930 and had long been out of print when Nick Lyons
republished it in 1984. With an introduction by Paul Schullery, the new
edition was immediately embraced by new generations of readers, eager to
enjoy Shepard's insightful and illuminating reflections. Legendary *Esquire*
Editor and Publisher Arnold Gingrich said, "I can think of nobody who
has written about angling more beautifully than Odell Shepard, at least
since Walton."

❧

What seems to me the primary and most enduring source of the angler's
happiness has already been mentioned. This, in a word, is wild nature—a
very ancient word which has been grossly sentimentalized of late, and
is soiled with all ignoble use, but which must still serve our turn. Every
good angler will have his notion of what I mean by it—a notion that will
certainly over-lap my own without being exactly coincident with it—and
I believe that if he could analyze all the many elements of his pleasure
in fishing he would find that this one predominates. As a rule, and quite
properly, he does not analyze them, being too much occupied with what
seem for the time more important considerations. His impressions come
to him, as William James says the first experiences of life come to an
infant, in a vast humming and buzzing confusion. Nevertheless, for nine
good anglers out of ten, although nearly the same number would probably
deny it, the sights and sounds and odors that surround the fisherman are
more than the fishing. Set one of them to angling in an indoor swimming

pool well stocked with three-pounders, and the most dubious will admit the truth of what I say.

Angling is of course by no means the only sport of which this may be said, let any grown American who enjoyed a normal boyhood think back far enough through the years and he will find that all his recollections of his early out-door games are entangled with faint or vivid memories of weather and of seasons. Peg-tops and top-spinning are associated with the end of winter, marbles with earliest spring, kite-flying with June and July, baseball with the blazing days of August, and the thought of football comes mingled with colors of flying leaves and smoke of autumnal bonfires. Skating, tobogganing, snowshoeing, skiing, bring other associations not less vivid, and the still earlier games of childhood such as prisoner's base, pull-away, and hide-and-go-seek are even more heavily charged with memories of nature. There must be a million Americans living today who can recall the time when nutting was a festival that took us every October into the enchanted woods. We did not come back from those excursions in farm-carts and buckboards quite the same boys and girls that we were when we set out. Certain things were decided for us once and for all by influences of which we were scarcely aware—by the odors of decaying foliage, by the patterns of gold against the blue, by the twirling fall of a leaf. We may think that we have forgotten all these things, but the sight of a single flaming maple or even some vaguely related strain of music brings them back, and it would require half of an eternity to wear away the gold of those high hickories from our thoughts. All day long we were climbing trees, throwing sticks, gathering fallen nuts, and the closest observation would not have discovered that we paid a moment's attention to the banners of autumn about us, and yet today we discover this fine deposit in the cells of memory—whisper of ferns, scents, blue of the asters that withered three decades ago, gold of the leaves that have gone back into sod and climbed again into trees and flowers.

What can all this mean, if not that some part, apparently a large one, of our enjoyment in those old games and excursions was derived, although we did not know it, from natural influences? We must have seen those immense cities of cloud, splendidly domed and turreted, that loomed above the baseball diamond, and seen them with strange intensity, while we thought we were wholly occupied with watching the ball, else they would not come so vividly back to us now. The chill of evening and approaching winter, cold airs and odors of burning leaves and of woodsmoke, that used to creep or flow across the field during the last minutes of a football game, must have been felt most keenly at the time in the midst of all our rough-and-tumble, or else they would not now lie waiting for us in the darkened rooms of memory whenever we turn the keys in those old wards. No doubt it was the "subliminal mind" that snatched up and stored these treasures while all the conscious attention was earnestly trained upon the game, but that does not lessen their potency or dim their present charm. The game itself, even the mighty effort to win or to excel in that game, occupied the center of attention, but quite other things, having no apparent relation to the game, were seen, so to speak, with the more sensitive outer fringes of the retina and recorded indelibly.

Now there is no reason to suppose that this faculty of gathering impressions from fields outside the focus of attention is peculiar to childhood. We know that it is not. Considered all together, these impressions are more important to feeling than sport itself; they compose the nimbus or aureole through which the sportsman sees his game, whatever it may be, and only by reference to them can we explain how it happens that thousands of intelligent men derive from sport somewhat the same satisfactions that others do from art and religion.

What is the difference in attitude toward the game of golf between an ignorant and unimaginative spectator and an expert player? To the former it consists entirely in knocking a little hard ball here and there over the grass until it rolls finally into a hole, after which it is extracted and knocked some more—a sufficiently dull and childish pastime. To the skillful player it is ten thousand other things, such as a delight and a despair, schooling in accuracy of mind and body and in self-control, opportunity for self-conquest. He sees it not baldly and barely but as a multiple thing; he thinks of it in connection with all its rich connotations and in terms of a million memories stored away in nerves and muscles and brain. The most useful of these memories for practical purposes are those that preserve successful stances and strokes, bodily motions and balances, but the most important to his pleasure in the game are those that seem secondary or even unrelated to the sport. Say the word "golf" to him and he is as likely as not to smell the dewy grass just warmed by the sun of early morning, to feel the firm soft sod of the green under foot, to see a spot of brightness edged by shadow lifting against a summer cloud, or to hear the drone of friendly voices chaffing in the locker-room. He cares no more for merely knocking a small white ball about than any other sensible man, but he loves the game of golf—loves it in its entirety, somewhat as one loves a woman, not solely or chiefly because she has blue eyes.

Something like this may be said of all out-door sports, but of none more emphatically than of angling. There are people in the world who see nothing in the angler's occupation but tedium, laziness, cruelty, and lies—or, as some wiseacre has phrased it, "a fly at one end of a line and a fool at the other." Peace be to all such, and a better way—if they can find it—of spending their leisure time, more human, more humane, more fit for an honest man. Say "fishing" to the angler, however, or mention any one of the tools of his sport, and you call up more memories than could be named in a year—memories of sunny days and foul, of virgin dawns and serene nightfalls, of bending rods, leaping gold and crimson, rippling green, of camp fires far and near, of talk and of silence and of friends. Into his mental pictures of angling he has painted the sky, the trees, the ferns and moss, most of all, the water, and the colors run. Probably there is no other sport that carries one so far toward the secret heart of nature as angling does. This is to say that the memories of nature laid away by the angler are richer, more vivid and more various, than those acquired in other sports.—If one were disposed to follow this line of argument a little further he might succeed in proving what every angler knows, that fishing is the finest sport in the world. But anglers are seldom argumentative. They prefer to make their assertions and have done. Furthermore, they are never eager for converts, at any rate in our time, feeling more than satisfied with the number of fishermen they find on the stream at dawn of opening day. Therefore they may sometimes say that angling is the best of sports, but they seldom attempt to prove it.

Wild nature, as I have said, is the most important, as it is also the most enduring source of the angler's pleasure, and the phase of nature with which he is most concerned is the most beautiful, mysterious, and fascinating of all—wild water. Any one who has once seen and felt the amazing loveliness of swiftly running water, whether in the meadow brook or the mountain torrent, whether lustrous under leaves or flashing to the open sky, can understand without elaborate explanation the charm that lures and holds the angler. He has fallen under a spell that has been known in all ages and has been symbolized in many a legend of Sirens, Loreleis, Undines, and other water-witches. He is bemused by the babble of water, by the fragrance and song of it, by its broken and reflected and piercing and shimmering lights, by its constant change on the surface of its deep changelessness, and most of all by its motion. To his ears the stream sings in a hundred voices low and high, intermittent or continuous, and he can separate these voices and hear what each is saying as a conductor unravels the total harmony of his orchestra and finds the throbbing of a single string. To his eyes the stream brings glitter, ever-changing hues, curves of inimitable and never-failing grace, and the magical effect of motion in the midst of a stable landscape—the leaping white jet of life. And this beauty, moreover, is always mysterious to him, meaning something beyond what it shows and says; and after he has studied it for a life time it is not less mysterious but more so, more strange and so more alluring. It is this mystery and challenging strangeness that the angler sets his will and wit to explore. Standing in one element, he invades another, striving to search it thoroughly. With a fifty-foot finger of bamboo and silk and gut he probes the deeps and the shallows, feels along the riffles, glides slowly out into bays of glitter, striving toward and almost attaining a sixth sense, trying to surprise the water's innermost secret law.—But this, of course, he will never do. In other arts and crafts, and even in a few sports, we can distinguish the three stages of apprentice, journeyman, and master; but in angling few ever pass beyond apprenticeship, and masters there are none.

Wild water—how it draws us back to itself from our boyhood to our oldest age, and lures us on and on, down and down, as though just beyond each bend lay the answers to all our questionings and the goal of all our hopes. It draws and lures us by an infinite variety. No two stretches of any living brook are the same or similar to a seeing eye, and no square foot of it is the same for two moments together. Depth, color, bottom, angle of light from above and from below, rapidity of current, speed and size of ripples, vagaries of breeze and calm, time of day, season of the year—all of these and a thousand other factors and influences playing together and into one another make any wayside brook more bewilderingly various than anything short of a lifelong study can teach one to realize. In streams well supplied with rocks and boulders standing up from the surface there is, in addition all the grade of water-curves never-ending, looping long and far, shaping streams within the stream, edged and flecked with foam. Where trees grow near there is added the dappling of light and shade, slumbrous when the breeze is still and dancing when the boughs are set aswing.

But the brook is not for the eye alone; it is the string of a mighty violin, stretched between the mountains and the sea. And it has a great gamut, from the broad rumbling bass of the main current rounding a granite boulder to the tiny trebles of little ripples sparkling pizzicato in the shallows. Where the stream flows wide over gravel beds there are numberless singers blending their tones like so many leaves in a tree, but where it narrows and bores between rocky walls the voices crowd together in one vague shout. Comes a fall, and the shout deepens to a roar, overlaid by faint screams and splashings and by tones that sound in desolate places like those of the human voice calling from far away. Below the fall there is heard, underneath the sound of steady onrush, a half-drowned subaqueous grumbling from the under-tow as of some giant tossing there, and a clamor of somersaulting currents that boil upward and break outward into the day. Every bubble of the thousands bursting here adds its particle to the tumult, and the long sigh of the current slipping past reeds at the stream's edge is added also. One hundred feet farther down the water quiets into a pool. All the uproar becomes an echo, then a memory. There is only the faint ruffling of the breeze on the backs of the ripples. But at the sill of the pool a stickle begins; this grows to a water-slide; then comes a fallen tree through whose branches the stream washes and gurgles in muted tones. After that, once more there is the broad deep rumbling of the main current and all the repertoire is played over again, though never in the same order or with exact repetition of any part. Usually, too, more than one variety of stream-song is heard at the same moment. The string is double-stopped.

Thomas Hardy somewhere says that an English peasant who has been brought up among trees can tell where he is in a familiar countryside on the darkest night, merely by the sound of the wind among the leaves, which varies widely from one species to another. However this may be, it is certain that an experienced trout-fisher can guide himself fairly well in night-fishing by the sound of the water alone; and in the daytime he has always some idea of the stretches ahead of him before he rounds a bend. Instinctively, he estimates the depth of a pool and the strength of a current almost as much by the ear as by the eye, and the sounds of the water suggest to him many devices, warn him that rocks will roll or that the trout are lying against the farther bank. He hears and analyzes a hundred signals in the hurl of the water of which he is never consciously aware.

What can a man desire more when standing knee-deep in a mountain river, rod in hand, with trout on the rise? Here he has earth and air and sky before him, strangely interfused and woven into one element. The brook runs over the bones of the planet and carries the sky on its back, so that it is a complete world, and one who gazes into this crystal long and steadily will find there not food and drink only but work and play, patience and excitement, knowledge and wisdom, fact and dream. Here indeed is one of the forms of nature that pass into our moods with tranquil restoration. Either the stream teaches or else it recalls to mind some of the deeper truths that are seldom thought of but are good to know. Consider, for example, the almost universal belief—universal, at any rate, in the western world—that every one desires to live forever, preserving his own individuality forever intact. What has the stream to say about that matter? Well, we see that it is moving steadily, as swiftly as possible and by the shortest possible course, toward the sea and the merging of its tiny self into a vastly greater. What sort of water is it that "lives forever" and preserves its identity intact? The stagnant pool, mantled with obscene scum and foul with all forms of death.—Deeper teachings than this the stream has for us—as, how to mingle freedom with restraint and law with liberty. It keeps pace with us, or rather it runs on before. In its slender source far up the mountain there was already a sure and glad foreknowledge of the end. One who could understand wild water—as no man ever will—would be far on the road to understanding all things, so full it is of symbols and correspondencies with our lives; and it may be a dim realization of this that brings us back to the stream's side whenever we can get there, that keeps us bending for hour after hour over bridges, that makes the heart leap when we see from a passing train the white feather of a brook on a distant hillside, and that holds us awake in the night listening to the voice of a river rushing through darkness. That river is the metaphor of time to us, and we are children of Time. It rushes toward the sea of oblivion, as we do. It would linger if it could in this pool, in that eddy, under such a bending elm, but a stronger need and wish draws it down, forever down, toward its swaying and softly breathing rest.

Down and down, forever down. Imagination faints in the effort to realize how long it has been falling. The angler comes to a gorge worn hundreds of feet deep in solid rock by nothing but the everlasting trample of tiny water-drops. He casts his flies over huge circular pools of granite scooped by the slow gyration of pebbles and sand during years hardly to be expressed by arithmetic. Numberless pools such as these are to be seen in the Rocky Mountains, fifty feet deep and as many in diameter, where the great trout swim in a liquid emerald. "Earth has not anything to show more fair." Neither is there anything to be seen on this side of the Pearly Gates more lovely than the grottoes and caverns carved by flowing water in a mountain's flank, banked with moss and overhung by ferns. The boulders strewn up and down such rivers have a more savage grandeur than boulders to be seen elsewhere, as though they had learned nobility from the song of the water round them. The fisherman comes to a huge fallen crag rising thirty feet or more above the stream and commanding a long vista of checkered shade and shine, leaping foam and trembling sun-dazzle, and the sun may go down upon him while he sits there, his tackle at his feet. Or he finds small crevices in the rocky bed where the water is a flowing topaz that checks the swing of his wrist almost in mid-cast by its beauty, and many a pool that must contain good trout he walks round without throwing a line, because it seems too perfect for him to profane even by the fluttering of a tuft of feathers. He need not be superstitious, or even much of a scholar, to feel that such places are sanctified by some tutelary spirit or local goddess such as Milton's youths invoked:

Sabrina fair,
Listen where thou art sitting
Under the glassy, cool, translucent wave,
In twisted braids of lilies knitting
The loose train of thine amber-dropping hair.

Wild water left to itself can never fail to be beautiful, and it will not endure the slightest ugliness about it. This is true not only of the mountain river but of the meadow brook as well, flowing almost mute among reeds and grasses and under willow trees. There are stretches of the upper Thames, where it winds among the level lands that William Morris loved and flows twenty miles to make five of headway, that are as beautiful in their July coloring as anything to be seen in high Switzerland. The little Musketaquid also, that steals through Concord with so slow a tread that Hawthorne was for three weeks in doubt which way it flows, has nothing to learn in the lore of rivers. Indeed, almost any nameless rivulet creeping from root to tussock in a New England pasture reveals all the range of loveliness to be seen in the Amazon from source to mouth, if only one has the patience and skill to find it.

A Creelful of Zern

By Ed Zern

SOME YEARS AGO IN INTRODUCING AN ED ZERN STORY, I CALLED HIM "the court jester of fishing and hunting literature." Today, I still rather like that description. Ed's "Exit Laughing" column in *Field & Stream* produced decades of fresh wit and wry humor of a devil-may-care style that will never be matched. There was only one Ed Zern, and when he died the magic of his prose went with him.

Ed never forgot that fishing and hunting were meant to be fun, and throughout his life the favorite target of his barbs and ego-deflating anecdotes were people who took themselves and their sport much too seriously in the wrong ways.

This section I have chosen to call "A Creelful of Zern" is but a sampling from the many delightful pieces presented in *Hunting and Fishing From "A" To Zern*, published by Nick Lyons in 1985. That anthology is a true treasure of many of the finest and funniest of Ed Zern's pieces, including the "Exit Laughing" columns, his advertisements for Nash cars, and selections from his many books and magazine articles.

It was my privilege to know Ed as a friend, and to have shared many memorable moments with him, both in the field and in front of the fire, in places ranging from New York to Nairobi. I remember his work and his companionship, and I remember his courage as an old man fighting against the ravages of Parkinson's Disease in a battle he could not win. I am deeply grateful to have "A Creelful of Zern" for the conclusion of this book. Thanks to Ed, we will all once again "Exit Laughing."

Ain't It the Truth? No

Fishermen are born honest, but they get over it.

When a fisherman is going to tell you about the big musky he caught, he knows you will subtract ten pounds to allow for his untruthfulness.

So he adds ten pounds to allow for your subtraction.

The other ten pounds he adds on account of being such a liar.

Then he adds five pounds for good measure because what is five pounds more or less on such a big fish?

As a matter of fact, he didn't even catch that musky. He found it floating belly-up.

It died laughing at a Hokum's DeLuxe Weedless Streamlined Hollow-ground Galvanized Non-skid Semi-automatic Husky-Musky Lure with Centerboard Optional, $1.50 at all sporting-goods stores.

Lizzie Greig, the Gal Fly-tier of the Angler's Roost, was born in Scotland on the River Tweed. It was too late at night to borrow the greengrocer's scales, so they used the one her father used for salmon.

She weighed 17 pounds, 5 ounces.

How to Catch Fish with Flies

Some wiseguy once defined a fishing line as a piece of string with a worm on one end and a damn fool on the other.

This is a silly definition, of course—for many fishermen use flies instead of worms. They think it is more hoity-toity. If worms cost two bits apiece, and you could dig Royal Coachmen and Parmacheene Belles out of the manure pile, they would think differently. This is called human nature.

Fly fishermen spend hours tying little clumps of fur and feathers on hooks, trying to make a trout fly that looks like a real fly. But nobody has ever seen a natural insect trying to mate with a Fanwing Ginger Quill.

Of course, every once in a while a fly fisherman catches a trout on a trout fly, and he thinks this proves something. It doesn't. Trout eat mayflies, burnt matches, small pieces of inner tube, each other, caddis worms, Dewey buttons, crickets, lima beans, Colorado spinners, and almost anything else they can get in their fool mouths. It is probable they think the

trout fly is some feathers tied to a hook. Hell, they're not blind. They just
want to see how it tastes.

Trout flies are either wet flies or dry flies, depending on whether they
are supposed to sink or float. If you ask a wet-fly fisherman why a natural
insect would be swimming around like crazy under water, he gets huffy
and walks away.

Many fishermen think trout are color-blind, but that is nothing to
what trout think of fishermen.

TRUEBLOOD IS THICKER THAN BUTTER

About fifteen years ago I started to gather up a few books on angling, and
by the time I had several hundred volumes collected I commenced to feel
pretty cocky about it, and occasionally I referred in a studiously casual
way to my "library" of fishing books. Then one evening at a dinner party
I met a man who, when I brought up the subject, admitted that he too
had a modest angling library. "You don't say?" I said politely. "How many
volumes?"

"I'm not sure," he said, "but it's somewhere between five and six
thousand."

Up to that moment I hadn't known there were six thousand books
on fishing, and I slunk off into a corner and hid behind a potted palm for
the rest of the evening. But although I gave up collecting at that time, I've
added a volume, now and then, to my shelves—and last March a professional book reviewer offered me a pile of current fishing books which
publishers had sent him for reviewing. He explained that he would as
soon review a brochure on tea-leaf reading as sully his syndicated column
with mention of a fishing book, but he thought I might find something
of interest in the stack, and I graciously agreed to take them off his hands.

One of the books was *The Angler's Handbook* by Ted Trueblood, which
I found to be highly readable, and remarkably free from the delusions of
omniscience which assail most fishing experts when they get within ten
feet of a typewriter. In fact, I found a lot of good, practical information
in the volume, and one paragraph (on page 30) made an especially strong
impression. It reads:

If your rod weighs six ounces, your reel nine, and your line another ounce or two, it means that you are holding a pound of weight in your casting hand—much of the time at arm's length—all the time you fish. Try carrying a pound of butter around that way for four or five hours.

The following Saturday, at noon sharp, I purchased a pound of butter at the A & P store and started holding it at arm's length. (My wife insisted that oleomargarine would do just as well, but I pointed out that if Trueblood had meant oleomargarine he would have *said* oleomargarine; whereas, in point of fact, he specifically said butter. "He probably owns a cow," my wife said, "and is prejudiced. For carrying purposes, I'm sure oleomargarine would do just as well. You could color it, and nobody would ever know the difference." And then people wonder why women seldom make good fishermen.)

The first fifteen minutes went well enough, except that when I got back to the house and tried to take off my topcoat I found that the pound of butter wouldn't go through the sleeve, so I kept the coat on. After a while I began to feel awfully warm, so I went outside again, and met one of my neighbors. "How's tricks, Ed?" he said.

"Not too bad, George," I said.

"Good," he said. "What's that in your hand?"

"A pound of butter," I said.

"What are you doing with it?" he said.

"Carrying it," I said.

"Why?" he said.

"On account of Trueblood," I said. "He said I should try carrying a pound of butter for four or five hours. I've only got three and a half hours to go."

When George tiptoed away and whispered something to another neighbor and they both kept staring at me and shaking their heads, I decided to go back in the house where I wouldn't have to answer a lot of damfool questions. It was still very warm in the house, and after the butter got soft I figured I could get it through the sleeve of my topcoat, so I made another try. It worked fine, except that when I was squeezing the carton to get it started through the sleeve about a quarter pound of melted butter squirted out onto the living-room rug. This disturbed me at first, until I recalled that actually I seldom use a rod heavier than four ounces or a reel heavier than six, so that the three or four ounces of butter on the rug really didn't matter. In fact, I figured that even the butter that dripped onto the topcoat and my suit didn't make too much difference, because most of my fishing is done with a three-ounce rod and a correspondingly light reel. My wife, however, thought differently, especially after she stepped on the butter on the rug and sat down in it rather suddenly, and while she was making some remarks I put the topcoat back on over the butter, went outside and dropped what was left of the carton into the garbage can. It's amazing how excitable women are.

Come to think of it, though, I'll bet Trueblood *does* own a cow.

How to Catch Trout on Dry Flies

Last year I ran into a friend who showed me a snapshot of a 25½-inch brown trout which he said he had taken on a Number 14 Quill Gordon dry fly.

"How was that again?" I said.

"Well," he said, "I was fishing at a very fancy club upstate, with a strict rule about fly-fishing only, and I hooked this five-inch chub on the Quill Gordon floater. Well, sir, that chub put up such a battle that it took me down through four of the best pools on the club water, and on the fourth pool this large brown trout came out from under a boulder and ate the chub. Naturally, I was terribly upset by this, and managed to play the brown into my net in short order, so it wouldn't go around molesting other people's chubs. But it just goes to show that the Quill Gordon is a grossly underrated dry fly.

"If I get invited back again," said the friend, "I'm going to try a different fly. Who knows what a Number *Twelve* Quill Gordon might produce?"

"Who knows?" I said, and hurried home to patch my minnow bucket.

How to Run a Tackle Shop

If I had to name my favorite sporting-goods store, it would probably be the Angler's Roost, even since it moved into the Chrysler Building and became mildly respectable. Because so far as I know it's the only shop in which the customers either wait on themselves or are waited on by other customers.

The state of affairs, which makes for a certain comradely chaos, exists because any salespeople present are invariably deep in violent discussion with one or more habitués of the place concerning the relative merits of dyed versus naturally blue hackle on a Quill Gordon or some equally controversial and friendship-shattering topic, and they can't be bothered with dropping it just because someone wants to buy a rod or a rifle. However, the chances are that one of the lay brothers will fall out of the discussion for a few minutes to let his larynx cool off, and if he notices someone standing around muttering about the lack of service he will slide behind the counter and wait on him.

I dropped in one time to pick up an HEH line and met Dorian St. George, who needed a new pair of felt-soled shoes. After Dorian got behind the counter and sold me the line, we switched places and I sold him the shoes, and after putting the money in the cash register we fought our way out through a group that was arguing whether or not the so-called coffin fly is actually the spinner of the green drake, and went about our business. I was surprised that Dorian could pass up the coffin-fly argument, and told him so, but he said hell, he had started it the day before and was bored with it.